Faith in The Lord

Rico Nguyen

Dedication

I dedicate this book to my beloved parents, whose strength and resilience carried our family through unimaginable hardships. To the countless refugees who risked everything for freedom—may your courage never be forgotten. And to the Lord, who guided me through every storm and gave purpose to my pain—this book is for You.

Acknowledgment

I would like to express my deepest gratitude to everyone who played a role in the creation of this book. To my family, for their enduring support and love. To the mentors, friends, and fellow believers who encouraged me to share my story. To the editors and publishing team who helped shape these words into a cohesive testimony. And most importantly, to God, for giving me the strength to survive and the clarity to speak the truth.

Contents

Preface

This book is more than a collection of memories—it is a spiritual testimony. Born in the midst of political chaos and personal tragedy, my journey began in Vietnam and took me through refugee camps, cultural dislocation, and spiritual awakening. I have seen death, encountered darkness, and yet, at every turn, I was met with the hand of God.

The stories in this book are drawn from my lived experience—visions, dreams, and miracles that are impossible to deny. I've included them not to boast, but to witness the power of faith and divine intervention. Many readers may find parts of this journey unbelievable, even unsettling. But I assure you, every word is true.

It is my hope that through these pages, you find encouragement in your own spiritual walk. Whether you are a seeker, a believer, or someone simply trying to make sense of life's trials, I offer this book as a companion in your search for truth, healing, and the unwavering presence of the Lord.

Chapter One
The Wake-Up Call

I have been a deep sleeper ever since I was a child; when I was a baby, my mom would have to wake me up to feed me, and my family frequently had to check on me to see if I was still breathing.

And when I slept, I had vivid dreams. I dreamed of fighting demons and the Dragons. Often, there were Shadows attacking me, and I would fight them, too.

Now that I understand what this means, everything else in the world, my entire living reality, has become a dream. In that dream I see a path forward that few people can, a path that I chose out of many different ones, following a long period of pain and suffering. And I chose it because of everything that has happened in my life before now.

Nowadays, I also have a lot of déjà vu, because I have lived another life before this one. But wherever I am in this life, I know that everything leads back to a wise man who said I had an important fate and a destiny with all of humanity. I ask you to remember his words as I tell you how I came to understand my life's meaning and purpose and how we will help save humanity's future together.

Every child is born with a sixth sense, but my wake-up call came later because I was not yet ready for it. I had to experience more of humanity's hardship so I could understand what was causing it and how to help them.

I understood this much later in life when I read The Buddhist prophecy of Maitreya: "As soon as he is born, he will walk seven steps forward, and where he puts down his feet, a jewel or a lotus will spring up." The best source of this is "The Prophecy Concerning Maitreya," translated by Edward Conze in his book, *Buddhist Scriptures* (238-242). A lot happened to me before I read this, but as I got older, my understanding of things continued to grow.

For one thing, I knew from a young age that my mom was gifted: she had an eye for business and a nose for good luck. She had an eye that could pinpoint good or bad people. In the future, I would discover that I had my own gifts.

I was still living in Vietnam when my dreams became dreams within dreams and it showed me there were more layers to reality than I thought there were. One of my layered dreams involved being lectured by an old monk facing a mountain, his back towards me; we were sitting beside a tree. I can't remember what he lectured me about, but I can remember asking him to hold off on his lecture so I could go to the washroom, which he did.

As I was going to the washroom in the dream, I felt my body getting wet; I woke up and was all soaked with urine. Then I went to what I thought was the real washroom, pulled down my underwear, and started to pee. All of a sudden, I felt my whole body get wet again, and then suddenly woke up, having had a dream within a dream. The urine was like the waters of the ocean, whose importance I would someday realize, just as I would also learn to listen to the words of wise men like that monk.

Sometimes, my dreams took me to terrifying places, and I couldn't wake up. My worst and most vivid nightmares were the ones where I fell and fell with no support; I would fall while yelling and screaming, with minutes feeling like hours, until I woke up sweating all over. Those were the worst nightmares ever, and they kept coming back night after night.

I had these falling dreams until Grade 6, but I also learned things from them. I learned how to problem-solve: how to be patient until I found a solution, which was to make myself fly in these dreams instead of fall. With this record of my journey, I hope to bring similar decisions and guidance to the world.

When I was very young, I sometimes wouldn't eat for days. I also would not cry for days; I was mute. But that didn't affect my memory, and I recall a lot of things from my early childhood very clearly. For example, I can still remember my first step: it was right onto a lit cigarette butt, and it gave me a black mark on the bottom of my foot.

Later I would understand this was like the Matrieya's steps bringing up jewels or lotuses, but this mark still had to be healed. My family needed the help of a local psychic/wise man to remove it, and we went to him after getting his approval for a visit.

When we came to him, he spoke the words I will always remember: he said that I had an important fate and a destiny with all of humanity, and his words eventually came true.

And I can still remember when I got a hold of a firecracker during Chinese New Year. I was fascinated by the idea of it blowing up when I lit it, and I also wanted to see what would happen if I put the firecracker in an ant hole; I hated ants because they were always biting me. But as I thought about doing it, I was also problem-solving, trying to slow down and analyze the potentially destructive impact of the firecracker and how the ants could survive.

So, one day, my younger brother and I went to an ant hole and placed the firecracker into one of its entrances. I was young and stupid: when I lit the firecracker, I just sat close to the ant hole, waiting to see how it would blow up. My face was like a foot away, and the next thing I knew, the firecracker blew sand into my eye. That was the first and last time I ever touched a firecracker.

Then, a few years after that, I began truly seeing humanity's hardship. The Vietnam War had ended, but things were still going bad for my family because my father and my grandfather were imprisoned in the communist re-education camps.

I think I was only 5 or 6 years of age at the time. My family consisted of four brothers and sisters, my mom and father, my grandmother and grandfather, my teen uncle and two teen aunts, and my cousin. My youngest brother, Kevin, was still inside my mom; he was born on June 16, 1976.

My family managed to bribe the guards to release my father and grandfather early, and eventually, we left Vietnam after my sister was born on March 28, 1979, in Saigon. We would become part of the group that would later be called the "boat people," but first, we had to reach the sea.

We carried all our family's gold with us, hiding it around our necks and other parts of our bodies because, at every checkpoint, the communist army's guards demanded gold in exchange for safe passage. They would take the gold from the adults first, so because I was the youngest who could walk, we hid most of the gold on my body. We also hid some on my young aunties and uncle and on the other kids, and we reached our boat without having given away all of it.

When we got to the boat, my father paid the captain with a gold bar, but the crew still searched the adults to see if they had any more gold left. Luckily, my family still had more gold hidden in the children, and we gave most of that to the crew.

As we expected, we had to fight off pirates while on the boat. When three pirate ships appeared, the captain called all the men to the deck and told them to pull up any loose wood from the ship or pick up any spare pieces of pipe. Waving these improvised weapons frightened the pirates, and they left.

Even though we managed to drive the pirates away, life on the boat was still hard. The boat was so crowded, just full of people. There also weren't enough supplies, and I can still remember how thirsty we all were.

During that time, I mostly slept, but one memory sticks out in my mind. It was when a can of pop was our only means of energy and food, and to make it last, my mom gave each of the kids and teens a teaspoon of Coke, but I was so thirsty that I couldn't handle the waiting any longer. When it was my younger brother's turn to drink, I pulled the spoon to me and drank it instead.

That was the first time I had ever told my mom that I wanted more and the first time I ever cried out to my mom that I was so thirsty. My parents never punished me for doing this, but I cried. I now felt how other refugees felt during wartime, and this would guide me later in life when I would have sympathy for all the pain and suffering in the world.

Then, one day in March of 1979, our boat sighted a refugee camp. We were so happy, but when we tried to enter the docking area, the guard at the refugee camp waved us back out: the camp was already overcrowded.

Our captain decided to make everyone jump off the boat instead of swimming for land while he burned the ship so they couldn't force us back to sea, and the camp would have to take us in. It worked, but doing it was difficult for me. I was so scared because I couldn't swim, and my body weighed a lot because of the remaining gold around my neck. My father threw me off the boat and into the arms of my uncle, but my uncle missed the catch, and for a few seconds, I was drowning until my uncle picked me up and swam away with me before the fire started on the boat.

We lived in the refugee camp for a while. We would get food, but it was never enough. Because of this, and because there were no schools in the camp, the kids spent most of their time scavenging for food. Our main source of protein was some kind of water beetle that lived under the sand, and the other kids would dig about a foot to two feet deep until we found one, and then we would take it back to camp, where my family would make soup out of it.

We would also scavenge from the beach near the camp. The camp's armed guards patrolled that beach and were there to keep people from wandering off, to keep newcomers from the already-crowded camp, or to keep people from going to the nearby town. If an adult entered the beach, they would be shot, but kids could go. So, every time a sea animal washed up on the shore, my brother, sister, and I would run onto the beach to get it and bring it back to the camp; we would also catch little crabs. By having to depend on the ocean for food, I began to understand how it was full of so many different things that could be eaten. Small things. Big things.

Our only available vegetables were bean sprouts, which were another source of vitamins and proteins. My grandfather would trade a gold necklace for a bag of bean spout seeds, and then my father and grandfather would dig a big hole, add the bean spout seed, and cover it with a cloth. Sometimes my family would also treat us with Mama noodles, which they got from trading more gold necklaces for a box.

All of this trading of food for gold showed me how much greed there was around us and how there wasn't any help from the government—we were left to help ourselves. I would carry this knowledge of greed and of the government failing to help us with me all my life.

There were other hard things about living in the camp. I had severe hemorrhoids and was always going to the med tent to get needles. I didn't like getting them, and they always needed to be held down; they had to get more than one person to do it. But the needles also showed me that the medical field offered hope for the future.

And for a washroom, the people at the camp just dug a big rectangle-shaped hole and built an outhouse on top of it. But that washroom was off-limits to all the younger kids. We had to go do our washroom thing in the field near the outhouse and throw it into the outhouse later.

But my worst day came when I woke up and wanted to go play with my younger brother. I found his bed all covered, and my family was crying. That was when I knew that I had lost my younger brother to malnutrition. I remember that I left them to sit on a dead log, looked up to the sky, and asked, Why? Why?

At the end of 1979, my family got a way out of the camp through sponsorship. We had the choice of going to Switzerland, the United States, or Canada, and my family chose Canada. We were sponsored by a church in Edmonton, and our sponsor's name was Mrs. Shep. The first day we were in Canada, it was cold, and it is snowing. The snow was the most beautiful thing I'd ever seen, and the sight was the true start of my spiritual journey.

Soon, I was in a Canadian school for the first time. I had never done well in school: my first day of preschool in Vietnam was the worst day I had ever had. Back then I had been so nervous, because I couldn't speak. As the teacher introduced herself and then asked each student to introduce themselves, I only stared because I just couldn't say my name. When it came to my turn to introduce myself, I just stood in my seat and smiled. I understood what the teacher wanted, but the words would not come out of my mouth.

The teacher got so angry that she told me to put out my hand and then whipped me with a ruler. I couldn't remember how many strikes it was, but I could not feel the pain; later, I would understand it was because an Angel had shielded me.

I blacked out after the smacking, and the next thing I remember was waiting on the school stairs for my dad to pick me up. I looked up in the sky and asked Why?, just like I would in the camp. I also couldn't tell my father what had happened, and my dad just laughed and drove me home. We stopped at a toy store, and he brought me a gun. I still couldn't talk, but I knew I didn't want a gun. I just wanted to be back in school, but I didn't get back to school before we had to leave Vietnam.

At school in Canada, I was still mute, and I had failing grades even in elementary school. I ended up being held back two grades because of my speech problems, and I got suspended from school instead of being kicked out.

I wasn't suspended because I couldn't talk but because I was fighting. It started when I was teased, and one particular kid kept on making fun of me, calling me names at every recess and laughing at me because the other kids took only a minute to read a paragraph, but for me, even saying one word took minutes. And it felt like it took a thousand seconds. It felt like it took a thousand minutes. It felt like it took a thousand breaths. It felt like it took a thousand energies. It felt like it took a thousand strengths. It took so much energy just to say one word.

His teasing got to the point that I couldn't take it any longer, so I threw a rock at his eye. When I was caught, I couldn't speak up to defend myself; the school even called the translator, but I stayed mute. So, I was temporarily suspended.

I was also so embarrassed about my speech issues that I decided to just talk less while learning how to better blend in. I knew I was an outsider, watching the world from a distance, and so I would only speak up if I had to.

My brother and sister would usually go to mass with our sponsor during this time. But I didn't like it, and I only went there if they gave us a toy. This was a sign that I hadn't awakened yet.

Then, our sponsoring church transferred me and all my siblings to Sacred Heart Catholic School (a school that would eventually close in June 2003). Mrs. Shep had referred us, and said it was because the kids were kinder there, and so it would be easier for me to go there.

But Sacred Heart put me into a resource program for beginning ESL students instead of a speech therapy program as I needed. So, when we moved schools, I lost some knowledge and had to start over, meaning I still hadn't learned how to talk or say the alphabet properly. I don't know why they picked the wrong program for me: maybe it was budget issues.

I was also put into Sacred Heart's special program for learning sign language and started learning how to say my ABCs by using the first Apple computer. But sometimes, I still couldn't communicate, and every time that happened, I was so frustrated and mad that I jumped up and down because I couldn't get my words out. I knew how to read and could understand the words, but I could not pronounce them when I tried. And every time it was my turn to do public speaking, I could not do it. When my mom took me to K-Mart, she'd always ask me what I wanted, but I still couldn't talk, and I didn't know what I wanted. I guess I just wanted to talk but didn't know how.

At the same time this was happening, I continued to avoid talking to other kids, because they still laughed at me. I even kicked another kid in the balls once because he was always making fun of me. I still didn't have many friends, only a few plus my family.

Around this time, we moved to downtown Edmonton, to the inner city/the hood. It was hard because my family was still new to Canada, and therefore, we didn't have much money: my mom was a mushroom picker, and my dad was a janitor.

The house that we lived in was infested with mice and cockroaches; every time we went to the washroom at night and turned on the lights, it was like a field of cockroaches were crawling all over the place, trying to hide from the light.

This period was also when I was diagnosed with having a tongue tie (also known as ankyloglossia). I had to have three operations to help with that. Despite all the problems we had, the operation was still free, thanks to Canadian healthcare.

And sometimes, good things happened to me, like the way me and my brother always found money. There was a place that always had it, like it was left there for us, always between $50-$500; sometimes, we just found money on the ground. We were always buying junk food and snacks at the Mac store, while in the summer, there were mini-festivals with rides, and we would spend all our money there.

And there were always fun things to do around the neighborhood. I would do crafts, cutting out my drawing of a soldier so that the cutout would become my toy soldier. For one Halloween, I also cut up old clothes and made a robe to become a karate/kung fu character.

I would also go to make wine with a friend of mine who lived a few blocks away. We made it out of grapes, and his dad would tell us to step on the grapes. It felt weird, but it was fun. And we usually snuck down into his basement to have a taste of the homemade wine. Though he later moved out of the neighborhood, we had a good time together.

Even with my problems in school, I was a very active kid, including being a team leader in Sacred Heart's year-end track and field. And because we were an inner-city school, all our sports activities were free, and I basically did everything when I was at Sacred Heart, including swimming lessons, ski lessons, snowshoeing lessons, rock climbing, and even horseback riding. I wasn't good at anything, but I tried and enjoyed everything. One time, when I was on a Grade 6 skiing trip, I couldn't stop, so I skied straight down the slope and into the side of the instructor's station.

Sacred Heart School was full of other support programs. We had free lunches from companies like Pizza Hut and McDonalds, and volunteers made us snacks in the morning snack program. We also learned maple syrup making and had pancake breakfasts.

There were also activities put on by community groups like the Boyle Street, the Bissell Centre, and the Boy and Girl Clubs. Through them, I played even more sports, like volleyball, dodgeball, lacrosse, ice hockey, floor hockey, soccer, tackle football, ice fishing, and badminton…there was always something to do after school.

I still hated school and still didn't have many close friends, but I loved the activities that the community had to offer. These clubs, my coaches, and a lot of family support all made my life better than it would have otherwise been. They kept me active and busy, and if it wasn't for them, I would have just gone home and slept after school. Everything they did helped me learn to support myself and how to support others later in life.

For example, when I was in Grade 4, a volunteer for our lacrosse team drove us to Elk Island National Park for our year-end party. As we drove to the park, our donated van died. The volunteer had had no money for antifreeze, so we all took turns pissing into the radiator while nobody stopped to help us. Finally, the van started, and we reached Elk Island Park, where there was a service charge. Once again, the volunteer had no money, but a ranger was nice enough to let us go through.

The goodness and support of the people in my life made me see the beauty of living. Like the saying, "What goes around comes around," I will always remember these kindnesses, and I will spend my life spreading them to others.

And then, I began to see the Shadow. Almost every night, the Shadow would appear at the door to my room and then move straight towards me, to press against my body so that I couldn't move. I would struggle with the Shadow, and the struggle always got to the point where I would scream for my mom. And my mom would come running into my room and hug me. After she did, I usually fell back into a deep sleep so that every morning, my mom would have to try hard to wake me up again.

When I would cry to my mom, she showed me how to pray. At first, I couldn't say those prayers out loud, and my mom told me to just say, "A paul, a paul, a paul." It didn't mean anything, but it was a prayer that a tongue-tied boy could say, so that was how I prayed when I was young. And my mother also taught me that praying wasn't about the words but about the heart, with the true meaning of prayer coming from within thyself.

Through this, I learned that prayers didn't have to be said out loud and that one could say the prayers in their head and their heart at any moment. All that mattered was that your prayers came from the heart and mind.

To pray correctly, the mind only had to be pure, objective in thought, and not corrupted by evil or deceiving thoughts. The heart would help the mind stay pure, and together, they would make a prayer as pure and innocent as thyself.

This was important to me because not only could I still not speak, but I was also dumb; I was so bad at school that I could not do basic addition or subtraction, and I let my brother do my homework. When I reached Grade 6, my marks were still so bad, and I still couldn't speak. The school wanted to keep holding me back, but I was too old.

I also kept on wetting my bed. Not because I had a physical problem but because I still had vivid dreams in my deep sleep. But I often dreamed about Heaven, where I was the Angel, fighting many demons. These dreams of Heaven made me cry because they were so relaxing and peaceful. I didn't want to wake up from my dreams, and I realized I was such a deep sleeper because sleeping was the way I saw Heaven.

But I prayed, "A paul and a paul" for days, for months, for years. With these words I dedicated my prayers to GOD. The words were still the only words that would come out of my mouth, but they showed that my heart and mind were pure and trustworthy of GOD.

By saying, "A paul and a paul," I was also asking GOD, "What am I going to be?" Eventually, I realized that He had already shown me the answer in my dreams. Not only my dream of being a Heavenly

Angel but my dreams of being royalty, of being a king or a prince.

In these dreams, I heard myself called "master" for the first time. The word master became implanted in my head so that for the rest of my life, I would refer to myself as Master Rico, after the name the voices called me.

During my entire childhood, I heard many spirit voices talking to me. Once, in the morning before school, I heard a female voice in my bedroom shouting, "Wake up! Wake up!" It woke me up even though my alarm couldn't. It woke me up even though I sometimes still needed a slap in the face to wake me up. But when I woke up, nobody was around. My bedroom was empty, with only silence, me, and the bed.

Another time, the same female spirit voice shouted at me, "Wake, Rico," and, "Wake up, Rico," or "Wake up, go to school," even though I hated school because of all my bad experiences there. I would keep hearing this same voice over and over again.

Even though I was still young, it was like I was putting myself together. But for a long time, I'll denied something that I had heard the voices say: An Angel's whisper that said, "You are Jesus." I denied it because of how I had interpreted the signs in my life: Jesus was my role model, but the Sacred Heart school was full of images of the Cross, and if I was Jesus, I could be crucified again. What made it worse was that crucifixion was already my worst childhood fear, and I had already dreamed of the Crucifixion before. Because I didn't want to be in a world where it could happen to me, I didn't tell anybody about this.

And then, one day in Grade 6, I started to become smart. I was finally able to memorize a chapter after spending all night studying. But it still took me longer to get to where the other students were because I had a lot of work to do outside of school.

I had been working in the family business since age ten, and whenever I wasn't playing sports or doing other afterschool activities, I was usually working after school and on weekends, too. My family, especially my grandfather, were very strict, and their rule was that if you weren't doing anything after school, then you had to be working. After I had to withdraw from lacrosse because it was too violent and extreme for me, I had even more time to work.

During the night, I would still see the Shadow hunting me, and when I was still in Grade 6, my mom started taking me to local psychics. Every one of them foretold that my life would be in danger in the future and that my guardian Angel was my little brother, who had passed away when I was in the refugee camp.

My little brother was close to me, and I always played with him when I was younger. When I prayed to GOD, I still asked Why? Why did my brother have to die? So, when I heard these words, I was overwhelmed with joy and happiness because I understood my little brother's purpose.

We didn't go to psychics for a while after that, but my mom was always worried that my life was in danger. So, when I was in high school, she met a friend who was a psychic, who she said could help with my fate and help me avoid the danger in my future.

This psychic was the mother of a local family, the Trans. For a while, I visited their house for readings, and then my mom decided to arrange a marriage between me and the daughter of the Trans. My mom took me to their house as usual but told me to bring a gift. I didn't know why at first; I thought it was just some random thing that my mom wanted me to do. The daughter was very pretty, but I wasn't interested and bailed out of the visits.

That was good because the mother of the Trans was just promising to save me in order to get money from my mom, and I mean a lot of money. So, she needed another alternative and took me to another psychic in Grade 12. But this time, he was the neighborhood's godfather of all spiritual magic and guidance.

His name was Bak Jou, and we had never visited him before; my mom kept the meeting with him a secret from my father. When I walked into his living room, Bak Jou saw my future. He said he needed to consult with the heavenly GOD to help me and then did a little spiritual ritual, calling upon the heavenly Angel to find a solution to my future trials.

Once he was back from his trance, he looked into me and said I was going to have an important fate and a destiny with all of humanity. It was as if Bak Jou was a medium for GOD, reassuring me of the power of my dreams, repeating the exact words that I had heard before, words that gave me a goal to live for.

He also told me the heavenly Angel wanted to give me a boy spirit and a girl spirit to help me with my life's journey. "This boy spirit and girl spirit will warn you of any danger you are in," he said.

Then Bak Jou performed a spiritual ceremony where he made me eat a blessed piece of yellow paper and said, "The boy and girl spirits are in you now. The boy's spirit will make your leg shake, and then you will know it is him. The girl spirit will give you vivid dreams, and then you will know it is her."

Bak Jou also warned me that if I was ever unsure of another psychic or spiritual person, I should ask them who my guardian Angel was, and my younger brother would be the only correct answer.

So, now I had a boy and a girl spirit to help me fight this unknown danger that I would be facing. I also knew what the local wise man and Bak Jou meant about my fate and destiny: because of my childhood dreams of fighting demons, I knew I was meant to fight evil.

Because I was very religious, I was overwhelmed with joy and happiness. Within the week, I also saw evidence that GOD was with me and protecting me: I got sick on a night when I was supposed to go out with my friends, and they got busted by the police. If He wasn't protecting me, I would have gotten busted, too.

Then, on July 31, 1987, Edmonton was hit by a tornado. The tornado was one of the biggest in Alberta's history, and there weren't any warning stations or signals at that time because nobody had expected it to come. Because of all this, the date would be known as "Black Friday."

When it happened, I was on a horseback riding field trip with the Bissell Centre at a stable outside of Edmonton. I was enjoying the ride until the horse suddenly became freaked out for no reason. It reared and kicked, then threw me to the ground and took off. The whole staff rushed up to me, and a staff member with first aid training started checking my head and body for signs of a concussion or major injuries. There were none, and everything proceeded as normal until we all went home at the designated time.

As we took our bus back to Edmonton, I noticed the funnel cloud starting to form. In my head, a voice surrounded me and kept saying, "It's a tornado, it's a tornado." I tried to say aloud that it was a tornado, but instead, I said, "Tocororo tooooo ttoooooo ttooooo totoooooo toooooo toooooootoooooonananananannanndi-o."

I yelled it so loudly that the energy and force of it exhausted me. I was also so embarrassed because of the way I spoke and the way the other kids laughed at me. But they stopped when the hail started to fall, just as we headed for the inner city.

Because the hail was so big, we soon had to stop the bus. They let us out to play in the rain, and we played tackle football. It was fun, and even with the tornado, I was still young and careless about life. Not knowing what all the voices really meant, not knowing what the signs of the apocalypse could be, I was just like any other kid.

The Tornado

Chapter Two
The Seed

In 1990, I started classes at Archbishop MacDonald High School, before finally ending up at Ross Sheppard High School. During this time, I got my first car and became the driver for my friend group, usually coming home late because I'd driven all of them home.

Some of my friends did have cars, though, and we'd race on Groat Road, because its track was curved back to front. I liked the challenge, the feeling of competition, and the excitement, which were the feelings that I'd have when I took up the Battle of Earth ten years later. We raced and raced until my friend Johnny crashed into the middle of the intersection during a run. Johnny didn't die, but it was the end of our racing.

When I started driving, my favorite game was trying to figure out why cars turned left or right, because I was fascinated by how people thought and behaved. It puzzled me for a whole year.

At that time, I was still having difficulties in school. I had gotten passing grades in junior high, but in high school, I couldn't pass English 10, and needed English to graduate. My other grades were at 60-70%, but my English grades were failing. Because of that, I took English 13, which students did when they were having trouble with regular English classes. I took English 13 courses in summer school and usually had to take English twice to get through each grade. I had the most trouble with Shakespeare, whose language was even harder to pronounce than English normally was.

Because of my issues with English, I knew that I would not make it into university or college, and I just wanted to get a high school diploma. I worked on just getting a pass, and while I was still in high school, I went into the International Baccalaureate (IB) program at Archbishop MacDonald High School; it was an academic course that let you skip courses in university or college.

I would still do my homework and study at night, but I still couldn't pronounce, talk, or spell correctly in English, and I totally lost interest in school. So, I started to skip classes, and would just go to the other high school and hang out with my other friends there.

But one day in art class, we had a project. We were supposed to draw something for the future, and this is what I drew:

The Buddha on the Cloud

The Buddha represented me, and the clouds were what I saw in my dreams. I saw clouds very often in my dreams, and sometimes I was inside those clouds. And when I was younger, my dreams of Heaven were also full of clouds. When I presented the art to Mr. David, the teacher, he asked me why I had painted it, and I couldn't explain why I had. When my friend Amanda asked me the same thing, I couldn't explain it, even though the school had hung my painting from the hallway ceiling with the others.

I would not be able to see its true importance until sixteen years later, when I had kids, and I was finding ways to combat the other Christ by using the tools of the information age. In the future I would also find out the painting represented the words of Revelation 14:14: "[14] Then I looked, and behold, a white cloud, and seated on the cloud one like a son of man, with a golden crown on his head, and a sharp sickle in his hand" (*English Standard Edition*).

Meanwhile, the voices in my mind got louder and louder. When I found out about the invasion of Kuwait in August 1990, I heard a female voice that intensified, saying, "This is the start of the bombardment of the Message of PEACE."

At that time, I was on the photography team at my school, and this voice was so loud that I messed up my first photo of a sports team, and then I quit. But now I understood: to spread the first Message of PEACE, I needed to figure out how to unite the world's religions. In my life, there would be three main missions. One was to spread that first Message of PEACE. One involved fighting the Battle of Earth. One was to spread the truth of the Revelation. Today, the Battle of Earth is dying down, and my next mission will be to prepare the world for the Revelation.

Yet though I had my first mission, I still didn't know what to do. I kept skipping school, only showing up to hand in my assignments and write exams. But I did most of my homework and finally turned to self-study to help me pass high school.

I started going to libraries, knowing I had to search for a book, but I also didn't know what kind of book it was. I usually went to the Rutherford Library at the University of Alberta to search, skimming through the large amount of information to find the unknown book I was looking for.

I was soon getting nowhere, not only because I couldn't find what I was looking for, but because I could still only speak one sentence or two, and it took so much energy just to talk: I only spoke if I had to. And the need for the Message of PEACE kept on bombarding me.

Though busy with my search, I would still hang out with my friends on certain days, being free and just chatting with other people. I had so many friends now, friends who came from all kinds of backgrounds, and religions from Christian to Buddhist, though I was only close to a few of them, and all of them knew me as the quiet one in whatever group I was in.

I had friends who were total goody-goodies in the chess club and the debate club; I had friends who broke into lockers and stole credit cards, or who stole cars or car stereos. Some of my most religious friends were committing these crimes, asking for forgiveness every time. Others I saw switching from one religion to another, because their religion was missing something for them.

During school time, my friend and I would stand up for another friend who was being bullied; the guy with me was somebody who would take on the whole football team to protect somebody if he needed to. My friends Mark and Tony would also fight, but whenever a fight got serious, I would usually just take off because I don't believe in fighting, because of my mom, who would always lecture me on what was right and what was wrong, even to the point of telling me that wasting food was a SIN. She was a strong Buddhist, and her faith informed my future.

But as I said, some of my friends were criminals. There was this other friend who helped teach me how to pronounce English words correctly as we did karaoke at the China Palace Restaurant. But that karaoke bar was also where a lot of criminal activities took place, and sometimes I was in the middle of them.

For example, another friend from junior high, Tu, introduced me to this other group that hung out at the China Palace. Every weekend, I was in the karaoke bar with them, still learning how to sound out the words so I could speak them. They all laughed at me, but we sang and sang together. This was also the first time I saw cocaine; they were drug dealers.

My friends were very protective of me. Because they all knew I was good, and my family also knew it, seeing the drug dealers at the karaoke bar was the first time I needed a lecture on drugs. My mom told me never to use cocaine, and it stuck in my head, so that I have never once used cocaine in my life.

When I spent time with my criminal friends, my girl spirit and my boy spirit both helped me avoid trouble. Every time something bad was going to happen, I got a spiritual warning and managed to get away before things started. For example, when my friends got arrested, the arrests would happen on the same date that I had decided to stay home. Sometimes I also had prophetic dreams that drove me to stay home, like the time my friend got stabbed at the karaoke bar.

Even though I managed to avoid incidents like that, by the middle of Grade 11, I had a bad reputation because I hung out with criminals. Because my mom was a cashier at our family business, she heard the word on the street about me, and would lecture me on what to do or what not to do, and lecture me on the way of the Buddha. She would wait for me to get home just to lecture me. But I was only having fun and hanging out with my friends, not really participating in crimes, but watching things happen, like I was Curious George.

Around this time, there were a lot of local gun thefts. It was because of a certain group of thieves in the area, not ones from our neighborhood, but from the rich neighborhood. It made me realize that all guns should be in a safe bolted to the ground, because most of the gun thefts happened when people got paid to tell this group where their family's guns were kept, and those guns were in safes that were easy to break into. At the time, it usually cost about $500 CAD to get the information, and guns sold for $1,000 CAD each; a lot of money. I didn't need the money because my mom always gave me money, so I didn't get into that kind of trouble either.

Meanwhile, it made me think about how, if I united the world's religions, it would fulfill all of an individual's needs, and solve most of the world's gun problems, because no one would have a reason to steal them, and gun crimes mostly involve stolen guns.

Meanwhile, I just hung out at the pool hall every day, because I didn't want to go back to work.

The rule still was that if I didn't have anything to do after school, I had to work at the store, but I had done that for most of junior high and didn't want to do it again.

Usually, I slept at the pool hall, too. I slept there because at that point, my clairaudience was so intense that I couldn't sleep at home. I knew my insomnia was because of hearing the Message of PEACE, and every night my mind was awake, trying to figure out why things happened, and how to solve problems. Being in the pool hall helped me get totally tired, which was what I needed to get some sleep.

The pool hall was also where I met a lot of new people. I watched and watched them, and observed and observed them. I saw that all my friends at the pool hall were criminals except for me, yet I understood them so well, and I loved them because they protected me in a way.

This still wasn't a good time in my life, and I saw that my criminal friends all lived in poverty. Most crime starts with poor street criminals, and if education and social programs were fully funded, people would be able to lift themselves out of poverty, and there would be less crime. I guess this helped me to understand the Islamic prophecy of endless wealth: that most crimes were caused by poverty, and eliminating poverty with endless money would eliminate crime.

One of my friends was Tran, who would become my best friend. He was somewhere between twelve and fourteen years old, and I first knew him through his brother, Kid, who often came to the pool hall. Tran and I became very close, and I treated him a lot, because he and his family were poor, and his mom and dad worked all the time. I supported Tran, giving him all the care a big brother would.

But Kid was kind of crazy, because every time he got mad, he used a gun to solve his problems. There was one time when I was out driving with Kid, and he stopped and told me to wait in the car while he got out. Then, Kid went up to another car and broke the windshield, trying to steal the car stereo. A bystander caught Kid in the act and tried to confront him, and Kid took out his gun and shot it into the air. That was the last time I hung out with him because he was just too extreme; I used all kinds of excuses not to hang out with Kid, and later on, he was deported back to Vietnam.

And Tran got in deep with drugs, because he'd been kicked out of school at a young age, couldn't speak or write English, and couldn't find a job because he was too young and didn't have the right language skills. He became a drug dealer because he had no other options, and when I couldn't convince Tran to stop dealing, I resolved to keep watching him.

I also knew a group of straight-A students who were dealing drugs; I guess they were the smart ones out of my karaoke friends. They were more organized than other groups and had connections through a father and an older brother. Using these, they became one of the biggest groups in the city while keeping a low profile.

Unlike a lot of other groups, they were greedy and wanted to make more money than they needed, even though they also started life with a lot more advantages than other people who turned to dealing, so I wanted to know why they'd decided to do this. I started to ask them about it, and, slowly, about how their actions related to the religions they followed.

Their replies were always that their religions, whether Christian, Buddhist, or something else, only condemned the crimes of old, so they wouldn't do any of those, but there was nothing in scripture condemning modern crimes like drug dealing. Through this, I learned again that every religion was missing something for the individual, and this prevented any one belief system from being truly fulfilling.

Later on, the Angel would tell me to choose between GOD, who is the LAW, or the life of a criminal.

When I was at Ross Sheppard, I saw for the first time how organized crime operated. It started with Joseph, one of my friends there. We were close, and I knew his dad was in the Triad, and in jail, and that the Triad now took care of his mom.

When she needed money, she had only to tell her Triad "little brother," and the money was handed to her. Once, I went out for a dim sum with Joseph's family, and his mother told the server that she needed money. Then, an hour after we finished eating, a server came back with a roll of $100 bills and passed her the money, and the meal was free.

Then Joseph moved to Vancouver, but he told me to give him a call if I was ever in Vancouver, but while I loved him, I didn't want to potentially get involved with the Triad: the stuff I heard about them was just too extreme for me, and I wanted to distance myself from that.

By the time I was in Grade 11, I had chosen to drop out of my IB program and now went to Victoria School in the inner city. I liked a girl who went to Ross Sheppard High School, and so I planned everything in my head: I would transfer to her school to get closer to her. It didn't work out with us, but it showed that once I was obsessed with something, I made plans to get what I wanted and followed them through. And even after going to Victoria School, I always visited my old school and its debate club and chess club, where some of my friends still were.

In Grade 12, my friends had a house party, and members of another Vietnamese gang showed up at the house uninvited. My friends asked them to leave, and eventually they did, but they started taking people's shoes on the way out.

Feeling brave, I confronted them, asking them to return the shoes and telling them I'd called the cops. I don't know why, but whenever I ran into trouble, I would bluff with the phrase, "I'll call the cops." And whenever I did it, it felt like déjà vu. I think my girl spirit was the reason I used the phrase.

The moment I felt it, I could see what could happen next, the dimensions of everything I could choose from, and the different results of these choices.

One of the big enforcers in the gang told me I'd be dead for bringing the police, and wanted to start a fight with me. I didn't want to fight, because none of my school friends wanted to fight them either, and anyway, I was still not a fighter, just a lover and a party animal.

So, the enforcer chased me around the block, wanting to beat me up, still shouting, "You're dead!"

But he didn't catch me before one of his friends said that the cops were actually coming and that they should go, which they did.

I knew that this wouldn't be the end of the fight, and that unless I did something about it, I would have to keep watching my back. So, I went to Chico, one of my other big-time friends, who was well-known and respected in the neighborhood. I told him what had happened that night, and he told the enforcer that I was his "little brother" and that nobody would touch me. "That's an order," he said.

I also told one of my other best friend's brothers, who loved me; he also told that enforcer not to touch me. And within a month, when I saw the enforcer again, he came up to me and apologized, asking to be my friend. Though there were rumors that the enforcer didn't like my school friends, I learned that if you respected your enemy and forgave them, they wouldn't go after you. And if I could go outside without watching my back, that was all that mattered to me. If an opportunity to do that was offered to me, I'd take it like I did back then.

Later, I stopped hanging out with my straight-A student friends; I just wasn't hanging out with the same friends I'd had at a young age, and so I was showing everyone that I wasn't a troublemaker. Instead, I started hanging out with some girls named Anna and Anh and their group. Anh's boyfriend would allow her to hang out with us until late at night, while we met up at the karaoke bar. We all became best friends and hung out almost every day.

I did not finish high school until age 21, and in that same year, because I was now an adult, I took my first drug: mushrooms. I never forgot what my mother and my high school friends said about drugs, but my other friends taught me about different drugs and how to use them responsibly. They made sure to protect me, telling me which drugs not to take. I only took one stem and had a blast going to watch Jurassic Park with my friends: everything was slow-motion 3D, like the dinosaurs were chasing us in real life.

It was the clear result of using one of Mother Earth's creations, and I would use similar things in my religious journey to enhance my sixth sense. Eventually, I would realize that medical injections, in contrast, would kill all of my six senses instead.

A friend of mine named Kevin got a girl pregnant; he was only sixteen at the time. In Vietnamese culture, if you get a woman pregnant outside of a marriage, the family usually makes you get married. So, Kevin had to have a wedding before the baby was born. Kevin and I were close, so for his bachelor party, me and his big brother Tony went to the Kingsway strip club to choose a stripper to do a lap dance with him. The stripper we asked was pretty hot and old, and she agreed to do it on two conditions: that she would have her bodyguard with her during the dance and that there would be no touching; Tony and I agreed.

We had to pick a location for the bachelor party, and because we wanted to make everything a surprise for Kevin, we decided we should do it at the karaoke bar. Tony and I went and made a deal with the owner: for extra money, we'd have a party there with the stripper. Tony was a drug dealer, so money was no object, and the bar owner got a good tip after agreeing.

We had a blast there, partying and singing, and when the stripper did a lap dance on Kevin, it was a surprise for the whole group, as Tony and I were still the only ones who knew it would happen. But once the secret was out, almost the whole group got lap dances; it was my first time getting one.

Both of her conditions were met: there was no touching, and her bodyguard had a blast with us, too. We paid and tipped the stripper well, and she even said that if we wanted to do anything like this again, we knew how to find her.

I very much enjoyed it, and so did everyone else. It helped me understand that all people had a story to tell about their lives and why they did the things they did. So, I would respect the people I encountered in my religious journey because everyone had their reasons for everything.

Still, the wedding reminded me not to get married young and to practice safe sex. That was important because I was dating a lot of girls during this time. When there were girls who wanted to tie me down, or girls who got too stuck-up, or girls whose names I forgot, I broke up with them. There were always more girls; I went on a lot of double dates and did a lot of tag teaming.

One time, my friend named Benson and I went on a double date. To make the girls like us, we pretended that we loved to jog, but actually, we'd never jogged in our lives. I was also totally out of shape, and so was Benson, but we still went on the date.

Another time, I was with my other friend Chris, who was half-native and half-Vietnamese. We only dated mixed-race girls, like half-black and half-white. There were always cute and pretty girls, and one time I was Chris' wingman, going with a girl so he could get with that girl's friend. He got what he wanted, but my date was such a hard drinker that I couldn't keep up with her, and was knocked out before I could remember anything.

I had a good time dating girls. As I didn't believe in cheating after marriage, I would have my fun now. It also proved I wasn't as much of an outsider as some people thought; it had just taken me a little longer to do things than it took other people to. It was my friends who showed me how to have a good time; I have had a good time in life because of them.

Right after high school, I started working full-time in my family's business, supervised by my grandfather. I worked there because my speech issues meant I couldn't get any other job. I even tried applying at Future Shop, but I had the same problem I always did: it was so hard for me to speak that they wouldn't accept me.

My family's business was expanding, and they bought an old IGA, planning to run their own Western grocery store. Therefore, my job was to refurbish its old shelves and shopping carts to make them look new again. I sanded down shelves, painted them, and hammered them into place; for the shopping carts, we changed the wheels and cleaned off the rust and dirt.

It was around this time that I first met a man named Joe, who was selling his stone carvings at Churchill Square. Later on, Joe would marry my sister, and also start to say wrong things about me, accusing me of partying all the time and causing trouble, and not helping out with the family business— but he couldn't see what I was doing behind the scenes, how I was helping get the carts and store ready. In the future, I would also hear that Joe was my enemy.

At age 22, I decided to go to Grant MacEwan to take three courses: Business Law, Behavior, and

Psychology. My sister recommended these courses, but I also chose them because they were all related to religion to some degree. Especially Law, because of Luke 16:31: "[31] He said to him, 'If they do not hear Moses and the Prophets, neither will they be convinced if someone should rise from the dead'. To have just laws was the golden rule of all religions: to treat others as you wanted to be treated, and remain liable for the consequences of your actions.

I got As and Bs in these courses, doing bad on the written exams, but excellent on those with multiple choice questions. I knew my stuff; I only had problems with spelling and grammar. I did use my legal knowledge to help other people who weren't criminals. Asians were still banned from most local nightclubs, and other ones would check our IDs more than other people's. Because I knew business law, I went to the Human Rights Commission to file a complaint against a nightclub that asked for 3-4 pieces of ID if you were Asian. I won the case and was awarded a lifetime membership to that club.

I started throwing parties there, though only my family and guy friends would get free admission; my female friends and my dates still had to pay. I would usually make $1,500 CAD to $3,000 CAD a night just from the tickets, and then the partygoers would buy liquor and the club would get the money.

I always found ways to make money. I had helped my criminal friends in one way or another, but I still wasn't a criminal. During my spiritual journey, I would continue to use my knowledge of law to defend the homeless and others. Because of my knowledge of behavior and psychology, I knew how to make and keep a good workplace environment and atmosphere, and how to motivate an individual to feel better. I had also learned why people behaved the way they did, as individuals and groups.

By then, I had a girlfriend I thought I wanted to settle down with, but we eventually broke up. We had met through another friend, and while we were still dating, she often drove me between Edmonton and Calgary.

One time when we were out dancing, a man kept on touching my girlfriend's ass. I asked him politely to not do that, but he kept on doing it, so I punched him in the head. He was taller than me, and started a fight. When one of my other friends saw that, she threw a punch at him. Then her friends jumped in and hit the guy with a bottle. I felt so bad; I didn't want anyone to get hurt.

And shortly after that, there was a shooting at the nightclub where I hosted my parties. I can't remember when it was, but it happened because of an unknown person. Even so, the manager of the nightclub got pissed off at me, and started swearing and telling us all off. Then he took out a shotgun and said, "You fucked with the wrong group. This is the mob you're dealing with. You fucked with the wrong group." It scared the shit out of me, and that was the last time I hosted a party there.

There were plenty of other places in the city to have fun; I always went wherever my friend went. Every time we had a party, I would treat him to a 10-course Chinese meal with liquor included, and we always had a blast.

A few years went by, and he became more involved in drug dealing. Then my friends started to fight each other for drug territory. Disliking fighting, I stayed the neutral one. On one day, I would hang out with one group of friends, and on other days, I would hang out with another group of friends. I did this constantly to stay out of their fights.

It was around this time that I smoked my first joint. It shut down my whole vocal system, and I had to shout to make my voice to come out. But it also made me feel good, like I could do anything, and that with my new understanding of law, behavior, and psychology, I could challenge the world.

Because I still had trouble talking, I decided to expand my speaking skills by getting out of my comfort zone and talking to new people. It was nerve-racking and scary because I didn't know how strangers would react to the way I spoke. My friends and family were all used to me by then, but speaking to people I didn't know was still very stressful for me.

First, I tried again to get a job outside of the family business, and this time I got one, working at the Klondike Days Festival, back before it was K-Days. I worked the graveyard shift as a security guard, and worked at my family business during the day.

That same year, I volunteered at the Edmonton International Fringe Theatre Festival and the Edmonton Heritage Festival to get further out of my comfort zone. As usual, I had to use so much energy to talk that I got tired by the end of the day. However, volunteering and working outside my family business made me braver and helped improve my speech.

I had already had many different friends from many different backgrounds, but it wasn't until the Heritage Festival that I witnessed the bringing together of so many different groups of people under one banner. This was when I got closer to discovering how to merge multiple religions into a unified faith for the purpose of the Message of PEACE.

I still hung out with some of my school friends, but as more and more of them got into dealing, I saw more and more of them kill each other over drug deals and territory. One by one, they hurt each other;

one of my friends got shot in the leg by my other friend, and I even had a friend who moved to a different province because he was being hunted by another group of my friends. I still had the same girlfriend from before, but my life was getting nowhere. I was still looking in the libraries, but I had no clue what to look for.

I needed to get a fresh start, in a new city and a new place, o I decided to move to Calgary. My brother already lived there, going to the DeVry Institute of Technology. His room and board were around $900 CAD a month, and I said I was not paying that kind of price, so I looked for a house.

I found a duplex that was only $50,000 CAD, and drove down there to look at it. It was perfect; it just needed some renovation. I took the money I had made from working for my mom and used it as a down payment on the house. Then I got a student loan, and because my mom was already paying for my brother's room and board, I asked my brother to move in with me, adding $500 CAD to the house's total income. He agreed, and then I asked my sister to put the house under her name because I was getting a student loan, and she helped me renovate the duplex for only about $2,000 CAD because that was all I could afford.

By the time the house was ready to move into, my brother's classmate was willing to pay another $500 CAD for rent if he stayed there. So, I had two roommates who paid $500 CAD each. That was $1,000 CAD a month. With all this, plus a cheap mortgage, I was set and rolling, though I was still going back and forth between Calgary and Edmonton to get my groceries and visiting my girlfriend until we broke up.

Moving to Calgary was a new step in my journey. I realized that my religious studies could not go any further in Edmonton, and in Calgary, I would talk to more and more people about religion; I was especially interested in learning more about Islam because I was the least familiar with it.

And every year, I would visit the Heritage Festival, still wondering how I could unite religion.

Chapter Three
9/11: The Cross Will Rise

By the time I moved to Calgary, I was getting good money from work, and sometimes my mom gave a bit here and there, so I was okay for money. Meanwhile, I was doing excellent at DeVry, being a solid A and B student in everything except for English, and my B+ average allowed me to become a faculty assistant, tutoring students while helping the teacher mark exams.

During school, I would always help out some friends whom I'll call Nam and Sitnam. I tutored Nam and even helped him cheat on the final. Because I was fast at designing and programming, it only took me fifteen minutes to complete that final, and I also did Sitnam's exam in thirty minutes.

In my third term, I kept up my B+ average while starting an apprenticeship in the oil industry, working the morning shift and going back to school in the afternoon. I worked on the assembly line for oil pump control panels while getting taught about the control and design parts of the operation.

I was on a tight schedule and always on the go, but whatever I did, I was totally focused. My brother, however, was a total party animal, and he made our house into a party house; I always had to go upstairs to yell at them to keep it down.

Then my brother's friend, our roommate, asked me to help him get an ounce of cocaine to sell, going to me because I knew so many drug dealers. I was still working my oil co-op job, but I went back to Edmonton and had one of my high school friends hook me up, getting me below an ounce of cocaine.

I was stupid: the price of that cocaine turned out to be on my head, because my brother and his friend spent more to buy the cocaine than they sold it for. Because of this, an enforcer called on me. They said I was responsible because I had been fronted by one of the big-time drug dealers that I knew. So, I went back to Edmonton again and got a different friend to hook me up with another ounce, but he hooked me up with five ounces.

My brother kept on being stupid and dealing drugs, but even so, I felt responsible for him, because I was supposed to watch over him, and I didn't want him to get busted. I prayed for him and his friend, who had no education and nowhere to go, but my brother finally became a dropout.

Before he did, two undercover detectives came to my house with a nationwide warrant. Detectives had never come to the house before, and they returned a few times, checking on my brother and his friend, reminding them to turn themselves in. I was never around when it happened, because every time they came by, I was in Edmonton.

My clairaudience got worse, and I began to hear the words "conspiracy theory". Because of this, I went back to gathering information from books and talking to people. I went to the libraries in Calgary, looking for the same thing I did before: how to unite the world's religions. I also wanted to be certain that everything was real, and that my understanding of the Message of PEACE was correct.

I felt like an important time was getting closer.

Then, I began to understand that an unknown group was following me, with the same members following me everywhere. I had started to trust my intuition more, and so I was scared. After I reviewed everything about my life in Edmonton, I realized the painting I'd made at Archbishop McDonald High School explained why I was being followed, and I regretted making it.

I still didn't know who this group was, but I saw the connection between Bak Jou's warnings and the true conspiracy that was happening in front of my eyes. I would wander in the Sunridge Mall and in other places around the city, trying to see exactly where they liked to follow me.

My clairaudience got worse and worse by the day. In my head, all I heard was "conspiracy", so I devised two plans: Plan A was to observe and understand; I would keep gathering information on religion and searching the library in my spare time, like I did in Edmonton. With Plan B, I knew that I needed a group to watch over me, and so I would attract the attention of the undercover detectives by becoming a drug dealer. Then they would keep an eye on me while I gathered information, and hopefully would intervene if I was threatened. If they busted me instead, it would not be that bad, because I'd be protected inside jail. My main mission was to bring PEACE, and keeping myself alive to bring PEACE was worth the highest price.

Then I was laid off at work because my boss demanded I work more hours than I could. I had only been hired as a part-time apprentice, and they knew I also had school and was a faculty assistant, but they kept on wanting us to work overtime and on weekends. I refused, not only because I had school but because I needed to keep going back to Edmonton to see my girlfriend.

I also started to neglect school because I knew it wasn't my future; my future was with all of humanity. If I continued with school, I would have become another honors student with great ideas and unimaginable research and design abilities. But then I would just be stuck in Silicon Valley, designing things for a tech company instead of helping the world. So once again, I started to skip classes.

Now that I wasn't working or studying, I met up with a lot of different people. I began going to a place in Calgary where everyone said there was an informant. Because this could lead to me being watched by the detectives, I went there to check out the place, and there I met a man named Ray. I asked Ray so many questions about cocaine: what it was and how it was used, and if it was very addictive; he said that cocaine was turned into crack cocaine for smoking or injecting into the veins. He introduced me to some addicts, and they also said yes, yes, it was very addictive.

Ray and I became close, as I would hang out with him and try to understand why people became addicted to cocaine. My feelings told me Ray was an undercover informant, but I told nobody.

I also investigated the underground of the city's addicts, to talk to them and find out how they became addicts. Some had gotten paid to swallow drugs and smuggle them into jail, or were commanded to do it by other drug dealers. Others had no education, so they turned to dealing drugs, and that lead to their own addictions. One time, I even went to a place where a woman asked me to go skinny-dipping. I refused, just wanting to watch how they smoked and how they injected drugs into their arm. And sometimes I just sat there and watched things happen, figuring things out.

There was one guy who kept going in and out of jail because of drugs. I saw how he suffered, and tried to help him, including bailing him out of jail a few times, but he needed professional help, and I was just an average Joe that no one would listen to; eventually, he was deported.

Once again, I saw that there were no programs or help for the poor and addicted, even though there was help everywhere for the working man. Because of this, I asked Ray what the difference was between a working man and a drug dealer. He just replied, "[Drug dealers] work even harder than a working man." I agreed with him that drug dealers worked harder than the people I knew who were on welfare.

Meanwhile, my clairaudience was getting louder and louder. Once again, the Message of PEACE bombarded me.

One incident that got me so pissed off was when my stupid brother called another group to meet up with us without telling me. I knew it wasn't going to be good because my boy spirit guide had warned me. By the time I got there, I wanted to tell the other group to leave, but first I had to go to the washroom.

When I came back out, I saw the other group of guys had surrounded my brother and his friend. There was a bang and then another bang: one of the other guys had hit my brother's friend on the head with a pipe, twice.

As that other guy swung the pipe again, I ran up and grabbed it and asked him, "Let's talk." Then all hell broke loose, but it also felt like everything was in slow motion, like the Matrix movies. I told my brother and his friend what to do. The other side pulled out knives, and we started to rumble. I knew the value of restraint over violence, but while I didn't hurt anybody, I was stabbed in the left shoulder. I didn't go to the hospital because if others knew about this, I would be considered a violent criminal. So, I just let it be.

But I told Ray what had happened, as I wanted those guys to be off the street, and I knew deep inside that he could help me. The next thing I knew, one of our attackers got busted with a weapon in his car.

Then my girlfriend's Calgary friend hooked me up with the group's leader from that night, and we communicated. By doing all this, I was able to get others to see the fight as a misunderstanding and neutralize any further conflict. You had to respect your neighbour, and they would respect you.

And as time went by, the leader of this other group started buying me drinks and VIP entrance to the Calgary club scene. We went drinking, dancing, and did karaoke. I was offered cocaine many times, because it was the thing to have at parties. But I still preferred my mushrooms and my weed. I had made so many friends in Calgary, and I was happy.

But then things started to get worse: my girlfriend left me, and I was still being followed. The local drug wars had also gotten bigger and bigger, and I decided that this time I was going to defuse the whole conflict. I set out to find the big boss of all the other groups, calling up my connections to do it.

I knew the right person at the right time and managed to defuse the fight. But before I could, Tran's younger brother, the one who was still in the country, got killed because of the drug war. Tran was sad and depressed, and I went to visit him at the cookhouse where he worked. We chatted and chatted, and he explained to me how his group worked, and also said that, because of seeing his friends kill each other, he wanted to move to Vancouver and start a new life, though he would wait until he finished the schooling he'd started. I was so happy that he was going to do that, and I supported him all the way.

I knew the police from the local anti-gang unit would be watching Tran's brother's funeral, and I knew these cops had ties to the people who were following me, but I didn't want anyone else involved in my mission, so I didn't tell Tran about this.

Instead, I pinpointed the locations of the police's surveillance: they were doing it from a nearby hotel and from a white van, and I pointed both out to Tran. I also offered to take funeral photographs for Tran's family. My mother had told me never to take photos at a funeral because it was bad luck; though I usually listened to her, I had to do this to send a signal to the people watching me.

Before Tran left for Vancouver, I went to my first rave with him. Smoking weed was a normal thing for me at a party, but if you smoked weed at a rave back then, you'd get kicked out by security, so I didn't do it.

And on a different night, we went to a safehouse, where we first tried MDMA, also called ecstasy, or molly. There was a group of us, and it was like we were guinea pigs for testing this drug.

We used a sample of MDMA to test how pure it was, and found out it wasn't a fake drug but real pure MDMA, so pure that even half a pill would fuck me up so much.

But when I first took that half-pill, I just wandered off to a spot in the building where nobody could see me. Once I was there, I started doing some weed on top of the molly, and then I began to dance. The dancing and the loud music let me reject the voices that told me I was Jesus. I was still scared of those words and of other things, but when I danced, I was brainstorming and then rejecting ideas all at the same time. My clairaudience was going insane, but as I kept dancing, I realized my dream was still getting nowhere. I went back to my friends in the other part of the safehouse, and for the rest of the night, we only did weed. It was still illegal back then, but nobody kicked us out.

It was around this time that I understood I had another small mission. My first mission was still to bring PEACE to the world, but I also wanted peace in my house. So, I finally kicked out my brother and his friend. I made them get a motel, so they would stop dealing drugs from my house. There was no more feeling sorry for them because they would have no home, no more feeling like they were poor drug dealers looking for a place to stay: my brother was just too much for me.

By the time they left, I also had three teenage girls living there, with the tradeoff that they would clean the house for us. One was a runaway, the other had been kicked out of her house, and the other was in hiding from another group of criminals.

One got mad and offended every time I talked to her, and I felt like she'd been in the sex trade before. She didn't like to talk about it much, and we usually left her alone. She also didn't like to go to Chinatown to eat, only to white restaurants. The teenage girl who was in hiding was cool, though. She just wanted somewhere to sleep, and even though the girls all had to leave my house, too, I asked a friend to take care of her.

I am someone who respects everyone, and she had nowhere to go. There were no support programs or any other support that she could get, and this is something I promise to change in the future.

Meanwhile, I started working under the table for my dad. He was a wholesaler of imported rice and other dry goods to clients in Calgary, and I was the one who went there to collect the checks for him. My dad's workers would sometimes come over to my house to do business, and we had hidden everything that was going on in the house from them.

I also started to get back in touch with my ex-girlfriend's Calgary friends. Most of them were criminals or ex-cons: murderers, enforcers, big-time drug dealers, and so forth, but there was one who became my new friend. We also came up with a nickname for this group of delinquent schoolkids: The Animal Farm, and gave everyone in that group animal nicknames. The Animal Farm didn't get busted or do drugs.

I started dating other girls, so many that I would be considered a womanizer, but I still didn't believe in sex after marriage, and so I was still trying to have my fun before I got married: in that way, I was traditional but modern.

My family never talked about sex. Certain religions never talk about sex. But I wanted, and I got, a real sex education from my friends over the years. They taught me about how to please a woman, what they like and dislike, and how to make her come back for more. I began to get set up as a drug dealer for my Plan B. Even though cocaine was back in Calgary, I dealt weed instead. It'd be worse for me if I were caught selling cocaine, and I had seen how cocaine destroyed lives. And all my friends were into weed, meaning I could make good money. But I was getting tired of setting up so many things in my life.

Then, out of nowhere, I got a phone call from a lady who said her name was Lilian. I had to ask her for her name a few times, and then we started talking. She would ask questions, and I would answer them. Soon, we were flirting over the phone. She liked me for me, and I liked her for her. Though I never met her in person, I treated her like my girlfriend, and it was pure love. I told her some of my innermost secrets, and when I talked to her, my clairaudience wasn't as loud as before.

We said that we would look for each other so that we could meet up. I asked Lilian if she believed in faith. All I had at the moment was my faith in GOD, but I just knew she would be one who would save me. I didn't know what she would save me from, but I knew she would be important to me, so important I finally told her that after I graduated from DeVry, I would be working in Edmonton at my family's business at 167 Ave and 97 Street, if she wanted to find me in the future. I promised her I would find her; I was not playing a game, and I waited for her call.

After I met Lilian, I stopped trying to accomplish my mission, even stopping my involvement in the drug trade. There were still people watching me, but because I was so afraid of them, all I wanted to do was find LOVE, instead of confronting them.

But I didn't just stop Plan B because of Lilian. I was also afraid of people knowing I was Jesus, and that if they did, my childhood Crucifixion nightmare would come true. That fear was so overwhelming that I often wanted to drop everything. And I was still too tired and didn't want anything more to do with my mission.

I was still at DeVry. I had wanted to drop out, but I continued on just to get the degree. I didn't go to classes, but I would do all the assignments at home, at the University of Calgary library, or the public library, while continuing my search for information. I was supposed to finish school within that year, but I just didn't feel like going to school; I guess I just wanted to wait for Lilian to call again. She didn't, while my clairaudience started getting stronger and stronger, louder and louder. I had thought Lilian was my girlfriend, but now it didn't seem like it because she had gone quiet.

Then, one time, we were having a friend's birthday at China Palace, and I brought him a big joint. When we smoked up, I heard a voice telling me that a woman was watching me from outside the restaurant. "Go in, go in," the voice said.

Then an unknown group of girls entered the restaurant; I knew they were from one of the groups that were following me. By this time, I knew there was one group, another group, and for sure a third group following me. I knew they wanted to see me, but I was so high that I couldn't speak. All I could do was track their movements with my clairaudience, step by step. One of my friends approached them, but nothing happened.

Afterwards, we went to another rave. We went to a lot of raves, and because we had money, and money talked, we would get treated like VIPs. At one rave, I was surrounded by female voices who were all talking about me. I heard them call me "Rico", a name that only a Lilian knew. This helped me realize that I have telepathic abilities and an Angelic guide, and that all the women I'd seen following me around were part of Lilian's group, a group that now included my ex-girlfriend. I could always see right through certain people, and that was how I knew these women belonged to Lilian's group. I didn't exactly know why I had this power, but it likely came from my spirit boy and spirit girl.

I kept on doing my thing at that rave, but then I saw my first-ever aura. I could see it around my hand, even though my eyes were closed. I also saw the aura of a woman who was moving towards me. The movement of my hand's aura was following the movement of the woman's aura. I can't fully explain it, but it was like in the 2003 Daredevil movie, when they showed how he could "see". I felt overwhelmed. Like, I couldn't believe it myself.

Another time, the same girls who had come into China Palace followed us to an afterparty. My friend didn't notice anything, but I did, because I was always observing my surroundings. They even sprayed water on me when I was dancing, but no one else had noticed, and I decided not to confront them.

I started buying time again, by restarting Plan B. So, I went back to Ray, that so-called informer or undercover cop. I gave him a lucky cat figurine, telling him it was a gift from me. I did it to send an indirect message to Ray, telling him that I was not like any other drug dealer. Other drug dealers did not give gifts, especially not a gift of HOPE like I did.

For it was also a gift of HOPE. I had had a vision of getting busted by the cops, and I hoped that giving a gift to Ray would buy me more time. I also wanted him to know I wasn't just doing this for the money. I couldn't tell him the truth, but I only wished I could buy more time. I couldn't really explain it, but it was like the movie, *The Hunt for Red October,* when Ramius gives away the sub to the USA.

I also took a term off school to go back to work in Edmonton. I needed a break, and I needed money to continue my studies. My cousin Steve was now our store manager, and I worked under him as head cashier. Because our store made so little money, it had to cut back on staff, and we worked long hours while trying to improve the store.

One of my other jobs was walking the floor in plainclothes and catching shoplifters, who were always a lot of. Because we were a small independent store, we could have easily gone under if there had been more theft than sales. Whenever I caught a shoplifter, I would ask him to return what he stole, or I would take him to the backroom. He usually refused, so I had to take him down with force and make him go into the backroom.

Once, I handcuffed a shoplifter to a backroom pole until my co-worker and I cashed out. When we finished cashing out, we went to the backrooms where the shoplifter was still handcuffed. He started to mouth off at us, shouting racist things. My co-worker started to hit him, and I had to stop my co-worker from doing it.

We also called the cops, but usually they took hours to come. This time, the cops took so long that we had to just let him go. In the next few days, a cop came by and told us that we couldn't handcuff a person by ourselves, and we needed to have police with us whenever we stopped a shoplifter from leaving the store. That was when I learned that what my co-worker and I had done was forced confinement, meaning the police were nicer about it than I thought they'd be. I saw that they were trying to stop us from becoming corrupt.

So, I kept worrying about the store's front end while my cousin Steve worried about the shelving and the store's backend. We worked hard, but at the same time, we partied hard, though I avoided doing anything related to drugs, except when I once helped out a friend in Edmonton.

When I went to visit this friend, I found out his house was haunted. Wanting to confront my childhood fear of the Shadow, I went to his house and had drinks. I pretended that I was drunk and that I needed to go to sleep, then entered a bedroom and lay down on the bed. Inside my head, I repeated, "I command you to appear. I command you to appear." Then, from the corner of my eye, a Shadow did appear. Then I commanded the spirit to "Leave me. Leave me." Then the spirit came straight at me and was on top of me. I struggled and struggled, trying to take control of the Shadow. "Lift from me. Lift from me," I commanded it. Then suddenly, I had a total out-of-body experience. I could see my friends drinking in the living room, and hear them talking and laughing even though I was in the bedroom.

I knew it meant I had driven the Shadow away. I felt invincible, because what GOD had put in me was so powerful that no more Shadows could ever harm or scare me. I also felt like I was invisible to any dark forces or any demons that came my way.

May 8, 1998

In May 1998, my friends and I went to watch the movie *Deep Impact*. I didn't know what the movie would be about, but my friends insisted we go as a group. The moment I watched *Deep Impact*, my body and mind were overwhelmed with fear. Once my friends and I left the theater, an Angel's voice from above said, "Did you know that would happen?!" Now I can explain it in this way: seeing the movie was just like when John experienced the visions of the Revelation. Later in my life, I would see that I was the modern-day John. Please read Thebookofrevelations.ca for more information.

Meanwhile, I finally graduated from DeVry in 1999. Before graduation, I was interviewed by a company. One of the interviewers asked me a question: if I had to do a project or design a project, what would I do? Sometimes I think I am too honest, because I told them the truth: that I would first have to take a nap to visualize the whole design in my head. I had always planned things this way, and it was also how I'd chosen the different paths in my life.

The interviewer said that taking naps was not how the workforce operated. This is funny to look back on, because today's hi-tech companies now have napping stations for their engineers. In the winter of 2009, "A Case for Naps in the Workplace*"* by Jitendra M. Mishra of Grand Valley State University was published in the *Seidman Business Review*, and that article explained how taking naps in the workplace increased productivity and creativity, but that didn't help me at the time.

It was still hard for me to speak in job interviews, and I still had general problems with communication. By now, I had gone to a social worker and told her about my troubles with speaking. I told her that every time I talked, it was so hard and I used up so much energy that it drained me. But the social worker just laughed and said, "You are talking right now. How can you have problems?"

Now, I knew I had a speech-related disability and I just needed to get a diagnosis, so that certain programs and jobs for disabled people would become open to me, and now there are great subsidies for hiring disabled workers. But back then, nobody believed me. I was on my own, and it showed me that we needed more social programs.

I wanted to see how far my education would take my career, while I kept watching and waiting for Lilian. I wasn't working for my family anymore, but I was still picking up checks from other local grocery stores and getting paid under the table by my parents. I looked for a new job month after month, and it was hard because in every interview I told them the truth: that I did my best visual design when I napped.

But I eventually got a job at the Electronic Test Centre (ETC). By the time I was working for ETC, I had sold my duplex and given the money to my parents. They had once paid my monthly living allowance, and I wanted to help them in return, especially because organized crime was affecting their business, and my dad also needed money to renovate the store. Meanwhile, I had moved in with a drug dealer friend because rent was too expensive and I didn't know anyone else who'd be my roommate; I was now paying $500 CAD a month in rent.

My new job dealt mostly with electromagnetic frequencies, electromagnetic compatibility (EMC), and electromotive force (EMF). It was more about theory than practice, and I tested new electronic technologies 5-10 years before they came onto the market, checking their immunity to EMI (electromagnetic interference). I even tested military technologies, zapping them with a high electromagnetic frequency to see how the military equipment would withstand EMI; for this, I had to go through high security clearance and sign a confidentiality agreement.

I worked the night shift, and for the first few weeks, I had no idea of what I was doing, but as the months went by, I had read most of the EMC theory book in the office. I also learned from my beautiful manager how to treat employees well. He was my friend, and I also got along with everyone at work; I wasn't paid much, but happy. And when I later learned how to use an aura camera, I knew how spirits could cause interference with it, based on my knowledge of electrical interference.

But I was having problems with my roommate. The friend I was living with was someone I had helped in the beginning, and we were supposed to split rent and utilities, as he dealt drugs while I worked. But I'd made a mistake by living with him. He let too many people into the house, and his friends would drink, smoke, and party there all the time. I would buy food and find it all eaten up, and he'd drive up the cost of utilities.

And I still hadn't found or seen Lilian, so, tired of waiting, I started dating again. It was only dating, with nothing sexual happening, but I needed to see other women, because I was kind of going crazy waiting for Lilian. These other women came and went, with nothing getting serious. Sometimes I picked them up at nightclubs, because by this time I really knew how to navigate that scene, getting VIP entrance to the clubs where my friends were, who bought me round after round of drinks; I just loved to dance.

During this time, I dated women from gangsters to students. One time, I was dating a university student, and when I picked her up from her house, I was high on mushrooms. As I rang the doorbell, her dad came out instead. "Shit," I said to myself. I didn't want him to know I was high, so I just nodded my head when he said things. At the end of that date, the drive back to my friend's house felt like driving back to Edmonton: a 15-minute drive seemed like an hour. I was quiet.

I also dated a university student from Edmonton. She came to Calgary with her friend to party, so my friend took them out to see the Calgary night scene, going clubbing and then to karaoke. At the karaoke, I introduced them to my Calgary friends. I don't know what happened, but my date left with the club with her friend, and right before they left, her friend said, "I know people that you don't want to mess around with." *Fuck those women, coming from Edmonton and thinking they're hotshots,* I thought. That just knowing people made them fierce and powerful.

The next thing I knew, my friend ran into the club and yelled that my date's friend was getting beaten up. I knew who was doing it; it was another group that was neutral towards me, but were the ones I actually didn't want to mess around with. I called my other friends over to help and then told the karaoke bar's owner to call the cops.

I ran outside where the fight was, and my date and her friend were getting their asses kicked badly. The first thing I said was, "I called the cops." That was a mistake, because I'd said that, the leader of the group went after me.

My friends from both Calgary and Edmonton intervened, though my Calgary friends knew this group was both insane and powerful. I told my friend to get the girls into their car, while my other friends and I tried to get between the guy beating them up.

I was getting punched left and right. But my Edmonton friend Viet was protective of me like always, and went after the leader; Viet ended up getting chased around the parking lot with a bat. My other friend was still trying to pull the girls into the car, while I was still getting punched in the face, and trying to calm the leader. Eventually, one of my friends was able to pull one of the girls out of the brawl and push her into her car; this was my date's friend, the one who had told off the other group and started the fight.

We yelled at her to drive off. As she was backing out, the other group started smashing her car, but she got away. My date was still getting beaten, and we jumped in between her and an insane guy from the gang. My friend got hold of her and threw her into my car, told me to drive off.

I did, while she was in shock and crying. I drove her to the hospital, but I was pissed off. It was supposed to be a fun night, but her friend had screwed it all up. I brought her into the ER and told her the name of the gang leader, to tell the police his name, and that I would check up on her later. But this was the last time I spoke to her; I would never call her back or hang out with her or her friend again, because I blamed them for endangering my other friends.

As I left the hospital, I was worried and wanted to check up on my other friends. But as I drove off, my phone rang, and it was one of my friends, telling me not to go home because the other group had gotten their guns and were waiting outside. Now I was more pissed than ever.

One of the groups watching me would use this event against me in the future. But, though they were following me, this group had just stood by and watched me and my friends getting chased and punched while trying to help the girls. They didn't even call the cops as the incident was happening. This was the group that would condemn me, while being made up of terrible people themselves.

Then a rumor went around that the group we'd fought with wanted Viet dead because he had touched their leader. And weeks later, I found out that the owner of that karaoke bar had been beaten up.

I hid from the nightclub and rave scenes for a while, because me and my friends had made one of the worst enemies to make, one of the most insane and powerful groups in Calgary. Luckily, I had once dated a gang member's sister, and she was the one who eventually neutralized those tensions.

I stayed very cautious; I started to rave again, because going to raves had helped me express myself during this time, but I only raved in Edmonton, and would only go with people that I knew would have my back.

Minutes become hours, and hours become days, days become months, as I gathered most of the information I needed. My clairaudience was intensified, the female voices stronger and stronger.

I knew the familiar group of women from China Palace would follow me to a rave. My friend and I went to the afterparty, and this time I knew which dance steps everyone would take before they took them. As I recall it, I focused on my friend Amanda's dancing, as I heard a female voice directing her on what to do. Then I took a chance and approached Amanda, to ask if she was Lilian. She said, "What? No!" and I was totally confused and backed off right away.

Then on September 11, 2001, all hell broke loose. The 9/11 attacks scared the shit out of me because of how I interpreted the event, and how it related to what the Angel had told me. I didn't know how to explain what I heard. I didn't know how I was going to bring the Message of PEACE when each nation was cursing each other, and all of them saw each other as the Devil. In North America, it was mostly Christians cursing Muslims, and Muslims cursing Christians. I was supposed to unite the world with religion, but I knew 9/11 would cause both the extreme right and extreme left to condemn Islam.

I called out to GOD, "How am I supposed to bring PEACE?"

I totally changed the way I danced. I was in a trance of accepting, then denying the voices: one minute I wanted to be Jesus, and the next minute I didn't want to because I had so much fear.

To my eye, the World Trade Center represented the trading of the entire world; it was a symbol of the whole world's monetary system, of the merchant trade, and how it made its money. When I understood this, I looked back on the way first-world countries had enslaved second and third-world countries. Money could be used for evil or it could be used for good, but the Beast was within the world's current monetary system.

This was my first impression of the Beast, and the Sept 11 attacks meant a stake through the heart of that Beast. Revelation talks about the merchants of the earth and talks about the Beast, and that was how I knew the connection; I will describe it in more detail later on.

I knew the richness of a country was determined by its Gross Domestic Product (GDP). But, I thought, what if in the future, no nation were the richest nation in the world? What if all the world's nations were equal in riches, and we had eliminated the GDP?

Signs from 9/11

I was so scared. I prayed and prayed for guidance. I asked, "Show me a sign." Then, a few days after 9/11, there was a miracle: they found a metal Cross still standing in the middle of the mess at Ground Zero. When I saw that, my clairaudience kicked in and it said, "The Cross will raise" and "The Cross is you." At the time, I still hadn't read much about other religions, and the Bible was my main source of knowledge; I only knew that I was supposed to bring the Message of PEACE.

I respected Jesus, and so I asked, "What do you mean by 'The Cross is me'?" That was when I started being bombarded by the words, "You are Jesus". It scared the shit out of me because it meant the message of 9/11 was that I would rise like the Cross. It meant I would be crucified, or put in a mental hospital, because no one believed me, just like in the movies.

I went back to searching in the libraries; I knew I had to look up more information on Islam. I had the sense that time was running out, and I still hadn't found anything. And within a week of restarting my search, I got laid off by the ETC. But I had worked a lot of overtime, meaning that I soon expected to have extra money in the bank. So, I took a road trip with my friends to Vancouver, with eight or nine guys in a minivan. We stopped at a hotel on the way, and because the hotel charged by the individual, we went inside one at a time to avoid paying for a bigger room.

Once we got to Vancouver, we met up with Tran and went to a fantasy strip club, and the girl did a lap dance on all of us. I had a good time, but when I came back to Alberta, I discovered that I still hadn't received my EI, and my overtime and severance pay were part of my EI payment, meaning I was totally broke. I was so mad; I had lost a month of EI. It showed me how the whole EI program had to change, and now it has changed for the betterment of most people on EI. Now you can work part-time as well as collect EI at the same time until you get back on your feet: it wasn't like that before.

Meanwhile, I had no money for rent, but luckily, a female dealer friend offered to give me free rent, and I agreed to move in with her until I started to get my EI payments, and then I moved into the basement of my friend Hoa for $500 CAD/month.

When the EI payments finally started, I told myself I would take nine months off to party. Living off $900 CAD a month on EI wasn't much, but I was happy. I started dating another woman and became a VIP in the club scene again, where I got free drinks from my friends treating me. I got an offer to return to my old part-time job, but I turned it down because even if I only worked part-time, they would still void my EI.

One time, my friend from Red Deer got bored, and I called up one of my big-time drug dealer friends. He asked us to come to a motel and have a drink, and once we got there, we found out there was like a whole gang there. One of them was even a guy who had forced me to return money at the start of my time at DeVry. The money had been lost by my brother and his friends, and I had paid it, but he was also an enforcer and Tran's enemy.

I was fucked, I thought. But since we'd been invited by a big-time dealer, he didn't bother us, and I just sat with my Red Deer friend and had a few drinks. Then the enforcer asked me if I felt like fucking a slut. Me and my friend said, "No thanks."

But he insisted we should do a threesome, and wouldn't be refused. So, my friend and I went into a room in the motel. The girl was already under the blanket, and we had our "magic" threesome. But afterwards, we lifted the blanket and noticed that the girl was tied up.

We both looked at each other and said, "SHIT, MAN!"

"Fuck, fuck," I said to myself. The woman asked us to untie her, and we did. I was looking at my friend and we knew this was so *fucked up*. We told the woman to jump out of the window. She was gone, but my friend was still worried; we knew this wasn't good.

I told him, "Let's just get the fuck out of here," but the moment we opened the door, one of the guys looked into the room and told the others that the woman had jumped out of the window. The whole gang surrounded us, and I was terrified. But luckily, the big-time dealer stopped them from attacking us. He said I was good, not to touch us, to let us go. Then me and my Red Deer friend just booked it.

Later, Joe would use this horrible incident as proof that I'd raped my ex-girlfriend, even though that wasn't true.

On a different day, the phone rang, and it was Tran. He had finished a goldsmith apprenticeship and was ready to come to Calgary and start a new life. I was so happy and delighted, I offered to be the first to pick him up and told him he could stay with me, and we'd hang out together.

I drove to Vancouver to pick Tran up; I didn't like driving at night because I didn't have a good car for it, but I had to do it. As I was driving to Vancouver, I encountered two avalanches, and both times I had to wait for the road to clear up. The waiting was long, and time was ticking by very slowly. By the time I passed the Rocky Mountains, I couldn't recall how long it had taken, but I was so exhausted and tired that I wanted to just pull over and sleep.

I was worried and prayed and prayed that I would make it to Vancouver. My prayer was answered by the boy spirit that Bak Jou had given me: The spirit took over my body, and the next thing I knew, I awakened in North Vancouver, looking at a street sign.

Tran was living at another family's house and, not wanting to wake them up but having no money for a motel, I drove off to a park and slept in my car until a police officer woke up and told me the park was closed, so I drove off again.

Finally, I met up with Tran. We loaded his luggage and his goldsmith table into my SUV, and then we headed back to Calgary. I was only able to live with him for a short time because I was running out of EI and had to go back to Edmonton. The time we spent together was still great and fun: this time we were both VIPs in the night scene and had drinks with our friends.

Moving back to Edmonton, I bought a condo downtown; my unit number was 411. I worked for my parents during the day, and during the night, I reviewed all the information I'd gathered and figured out how to unite the world's religions for the Message of PEACE.

Chapter Four
411: Seeing GOD

From 2002-2003 I worked for my family again, and also worked at a restaurant called Asia Grill. While I did, I got to know a local homeless man named Riel, who would always drop in at Asia Grill before it was open. He was a hand reader, and always read my palm and gave me advice. In exchange, I would give him some takeout food from the restaurant.

Sometimes, I would meet up with Riel at the end of my shift, at that marble lantern surrounded by the Chinese Zodiac figures next to the Gate of Happy Arrival in North Edmonton's Chinatown. Whenever I met him, Riel would always be painting or drawing something unique.

After getting to know him, I started to ask Riel questions about his life. I found out that he used to be a lawyer until he lost a member of his family. He was unable to cope with the grief, so he turned to drugs to escape it. His life started to go downhill after that, leading his family and society to abandon him. But though he was an addict, I treated him as a friend; we always said hi to each other.

I would usually hang out with Riel for half an hour to an hour each night. Sometimes, I didn't see him at our meeting place, and other times, I gave food to the other homeless people in the neighborhood. One time, I was disgusted at seeing one homeless man picking garbage out of a bin and eating the food, and I asked him not to do that and offered him some fresh food instead, telling him that any time he was hungry, he could just ask me for help.

I never told my family that I was doing this because they were traditional, meaning they didn't like giving handouts and once even got mad at me for giving food to certain people. But I did this out of generosity, and it made me feel good.

 Once, when I was out with some friends, some of them asked the rest of us if we wanted a foursome because they knew a woman who liked to fuck in foursomes. I was curious, so I said yes, and we took her to my friend's home. We were all high and taking turns, but the weird thing was it didn't turn me on. And when it was my turn I couldn't figure out why she kept on mourning, and I just pretended I was done. Then, within a week, I was asked to do this again with the same woman, so I said yes again. Once again, we were all high. Then the third time where I finally declined the invite.

Working at Asia Grill, I saw a lot of so-called evil. I watched people waste food when other parts of the world were starving; North Americans were just wasting food like nothing. And not only did Asia Grill waste food, but our waiters and waitress treated people so badly. One time, a family of six came into Asia Grill. While they waited to be seated, I overheard our servers trying to pass over the family for seating just because there was a rumor that the family didn't tip.

Our servers were all educated and in school, but they still fought not to have to serve this family. I was disgusted by the way they treated this family like shit. Just because of money, they refused to serve the family until I made one of them do it. I hadn't wanted to say anything and just observe, but I had to do something.

Yes, I was mad; I believed in the importance of family gatherings and in going out together for a meal. I also didn't believe in only serving people if they could give tips. But these so-called educated people could not see what they were doing. They could not see the truth, the reasons why some people couldn't afford to tip, like being on a budget. They had totally divided the rich from the poor and disrespected the poor.

"Money talks but bullshit walks," I usually said. And I would walk the talk and take action for what I believed in. Like I said in Chapter 3, money could be used for evil or money could be used for good. My friends and co-workers only used money for evil because they would only serve the people who were supposed to tip good.

Meanwhile, I had become like a walking zombie. I saw signs and symbols everywhere, but I was totally lost, and my mind and clairaudience built up my fear as I prayed and prayed for guidance. One night, while my fireplace was on, I was lying in the middle of the living room with my face on the floor, exhausted from praying, completely confused, and so afraid. I didn't know what to do. The fear of crucifixion was overwhelming, and I cried and begged for comfort.

I fell asleep there. Then, in the middle of the night, a soft female voice said to me, "You have set upon yourself, my child." My clairaudience kicked in right away, saying this was the voice of the Virgin Mary. That beautiful voice gave me the strength and courage to get back on the right track with my work.

Then, right after I'd heard her, I did something that I could not explain, and an aura briefly appeared in the palm of my hand. Seeing it was such an amazing feeling that I wanted to do it again, and this motivated me to act further. I started to go to the Edmonton Public Library again, searching for what I needed in Islamic books, including history books that explained the science behind Islam.

Everyone I'd talked to about religion had shown me that there were a lot of similarities and a lot of differences among their faiths. I searched and searched different books, not knowing what phrase to look for, but also that I would know it when I read it.

Then, I found that phrase: "Religion is science, science is religion." I had finally found what I was looking for, the last missing piece of the puzzle: religion is science, and science is religion. I can't remember which book it was, but it was at EPL, and I realized that these words were already inside me and that I had been mistaken in trying to find the phrase in a religious text.

People were still following me, and right when I found that phrase, a woman at the public library approached me and told me to wait up before she ran away. Nothing else happened that day.

I kept on studying religion and started seeing signs everywhere. 9/11 had told me I was running out of time, that there was something important coming, an emergency in the near future. And everywhere I drove, I saw the signs for 7-11 stores. I realized that seeing the numbers 7-11 meant I would soon take action as Jesus; Heaven was calling.

Every day I would see a different sign, and follow its guidance to a different study subject. Then I noticed that my condo's number was 411. This was another sign that it was time to put religions together. 9/11 + 7-11 + 411.

I smoked more weed, and it brought back more memories. It was like *Total Recall*, except I was using weed to find the lost memories. I began to imagine the perfect religion, trying to figure out the scenarios and phrases I needed, how to find the best solutions to the world's problems, and the best ways to bring PEACE to the world.

My experience has shown me that people converted to different religions because something was missing in their earlier faith, and something was also missing in their lives. So, my first planned scenario, aka Scenario One, involved uniting every religion, both the ones similar to each other and the ones different from each other. But soon I realized that would not work because there would be too much conflict between them, and everything would be too confusing for the average Joe.

Scenario Two involved using the largest religions that were the most similar to each other to create this new religion, though while planning Scenario Two, I stayed aware of the differences between the religions I'd picked.

But these religions also had a lot in common: they were about teaching love and compassion, helping the needy, and treating others as you wanted to be treated. That was good because everything also had to be perfectly connected from end to end, with no loopholes, and everything cross-referenced with each other. In Christianity, there were the Ten Commandments, the Seven Deadly Sins, and the forgiveness of SIN. In Native religions, there was reverence for Mother Earth and the thanking of the animals that you killed. In Islam, there was the offering of the animals in sacrifice, and religion was science. In Buddhism, there was healing of the self through meditation and finding the gateway to enlightenment through the crown charka. These differences were important because I was trying to bring PEACE to the world, and using things that had too much in common might not work.

If I used Scenario Two, I thought it might work, especially because I realized GOD had planted His seed in all these faiths. It was like how the citizens of Shinar were scattered after the Tower of Babel: GOD had scattered the seed of His knowledge among every culture, including the knowledge of the Bible.

Christianity would be the head of this unified religion, and Islam, Buddhism, and Native religions would make up the body. By combining these four religions, one can find the way toward enlightenment and a purified soul.

After I was done figuring out Scenario Two, I heard another voice saying, "Use Canada." It would take some time before I realized what it meant, and meanwhile, the bombardment of voices telling me, "You are Jesus Christ," also intensified to the point where I had no sleep.

But I soon accepted the voices that said I was Jesus. I can't remember the exact date that it happened, but I started accepting it because when I heard it, my self-confidence grew, and my fear disappeared. Accepting I was, Jesus gave me the strength and courage to continue my journey.

And, because I had always wanted to talk to GOD, I decided to start trying meditation to open my 7th chakra, the crown chakra, and when I succeeded, I would see into the unknown. While the others in the house slept, I was working, trying all kinds of meditation.

I tried one-second breathing, then two-second breathing, then five-second breathing, then ten-second breathing, and so on. Every night I would meditate in a different position, like upside down with my head on the sofa, or in a sitting position, or on my side. I even did my own version of the lotus rising position: I sat in a half-cross sitting position, then raised one arm while my other hand was in the praying position before lifting my whole body up until only my butthole and one toe were touching the ground. Then, I would spin around and eventually crack my spine to align it upwards.

Through all of it, I prayed and prayed that GOD would speak to me. Then, one night, while I was meditating on my loveseat (in a lying position and focused on breathing slowly while in a trance), I saw a pinpoint of light, and then all of a sudden, I was zoomed into a world full of bright light, which I understood was another dimension.

It was like a dream come true and so beautiful. Everything was white light, surrounding me like clouds and shining all over the place. I could not hear anything but knew I was in a brightly lit room. I knelt, and I bowed, and then I knew to look up. As I did, I saw before me huge feet made from the glowing light. I tilted my head farther up to see a bright, shining man with a beard and glowing eyes looking down at me.

My clairaudience kicked in again, saying to me, "That is GOD. That is GOD," over and over. Then, all of a sudden, I was zapped back into my reality; it was like I had just had an out-of-body experience and was returning. I was out of breath and also saw a human figure in my living room: a spirit speaking to me and telling me to wake up. I think that I had crossed over to the other side, and if the spirit had not woken me, then I might have stayed there in Heaven. But because I had crossed over and seen GOD, I would now become stronger and stronger.

GOD

After seeing GOD, I knew that I would get another message, this time on a mountain. With my intuition, I knew it would come in the Rocky Mountains, near the Cline River. It would be like Moses getting the Ten Commandments on Mount Sinai. But unlike him, I didn't climb the mountain but drove there.

First, I went shopping for camping gear. I bought a sleeping bag that could handle weather from -20 to -30 degrees Celsius. Then, I bought some incense, a compass, a flashlight, and a flare gun. I brought the last item in case I ran into wild animals, and if that happened, I would only use it for defense. But I also brought it as a backup in case I saw a UFO, which I believed in even before what happened next.

Then, I headed out to the mountain. I drove and drove, not knowing exactly where to stop, but I did get dinner. Then I reached this beautiful spot, where I first had to drive down a narrow road from the top of the hill to the bottom of the valley and park my SUV at the riverside. I knew this was where to stop; I had picked a perfect location for my camp, in the middle of the valley with mountains on all sides and a river in front of me.

The first thing I did was gather up small branches and sticks to make a fire because it was getting late and would soon be dark. It was a small fire, but it did the job of keeping me warm. Then I took out my compass and figured out where the cardinal directions were relative to where I was. I picked up my incense (the largest stick I could get, about 48 cm long) and placed it facing one of the four directions before picking it up again and placing it facing the next one: West, East, North, and South.

The sky was cloudy as I went into my personal meditation position that I'd already described and started to pray and pray and chant and chant. I bent an incense stick seven times to be able to speak to upper Heaven, just like Bak Jou had taught me.

The fire still kept me warm, and in the middle of the night, the clouds parted above me to show the night sky. And suddenly, a white cloud appeared above me, exactly in the middle of the sky.

The white cloud started to become larger and larger, forming into the shape of an Angel. My clairaudience kicked in, and I heard the Angel say, "I am the Angel. I was first." Then, a black cloud shaped like a Dragon suddenly appeared on the right-hand side of the sky. The Dragon started to move towards the Angel's white cloud, then penetrated into it. The two clouds mixed together and spun in a circular motion, the dark cloud and the white cloud.

My clairaudience kicked in again and said that just as there was a Battle of Heaven (told in Revelation 12:7-12), there would be a Battle of Earth. I said in my head, "I accept the Battle." Then the mixed dark and white clouds disappeared completely before the white cloud reappeared and again formed into the Angel. Because only the Angel had reappeared, I knew the Dancing Cloud had given me a message: "The Angel will win."

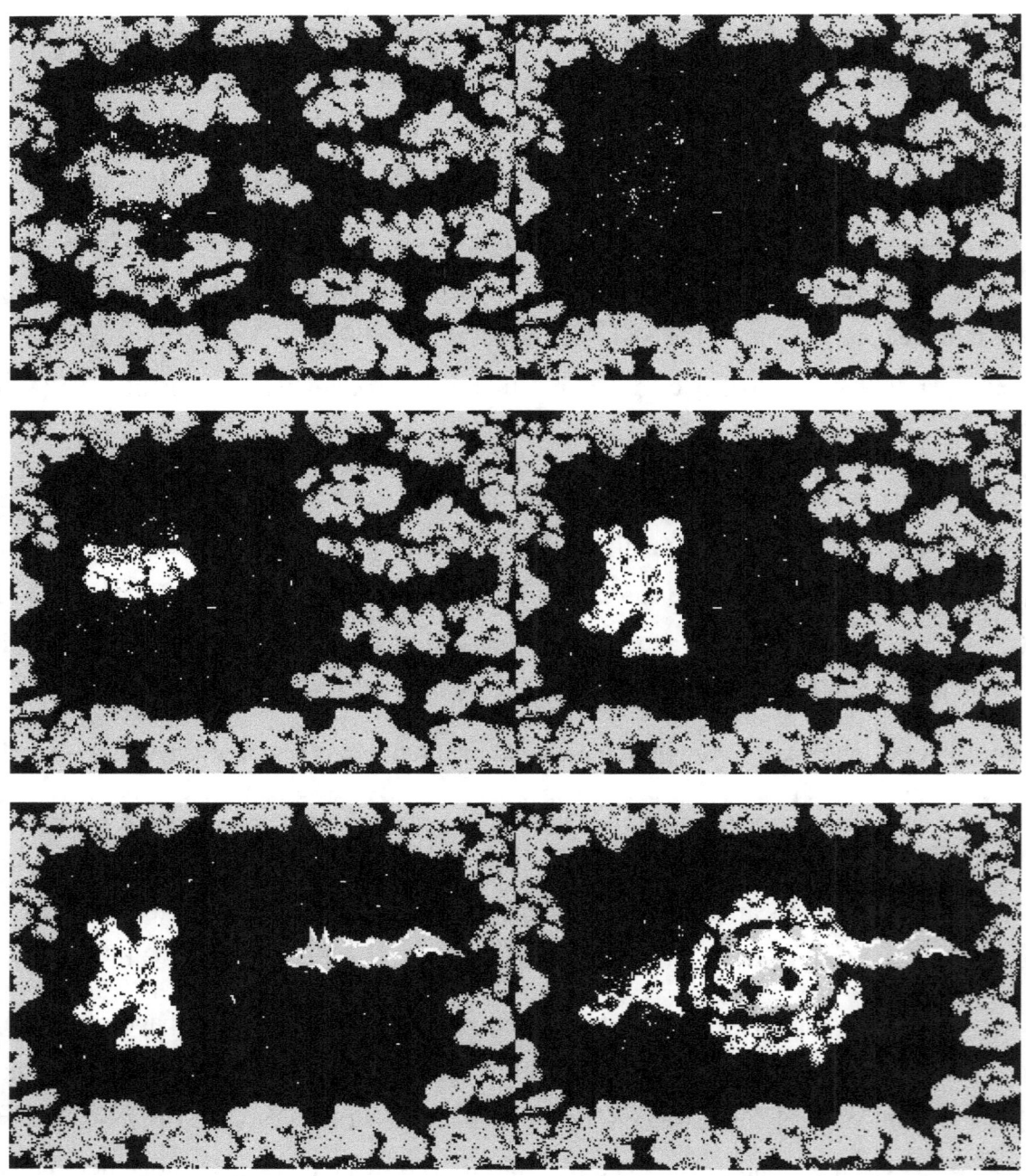

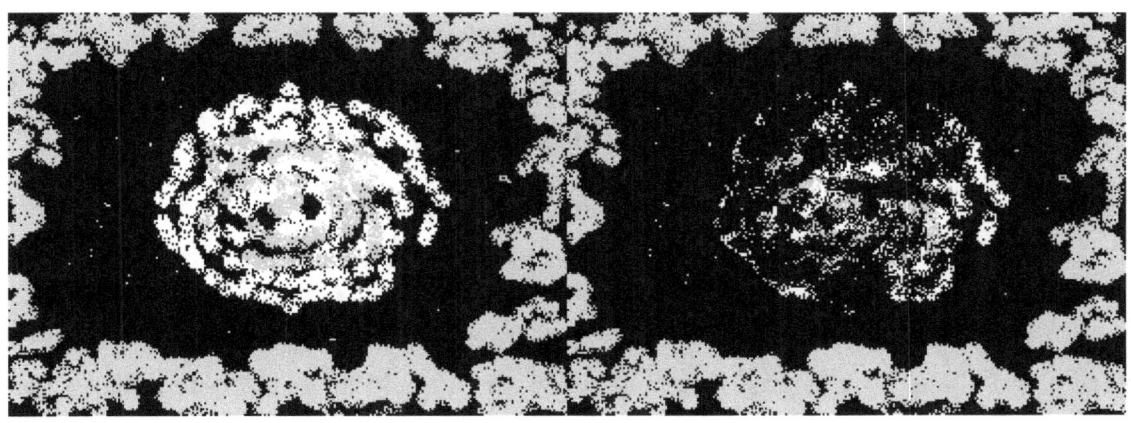

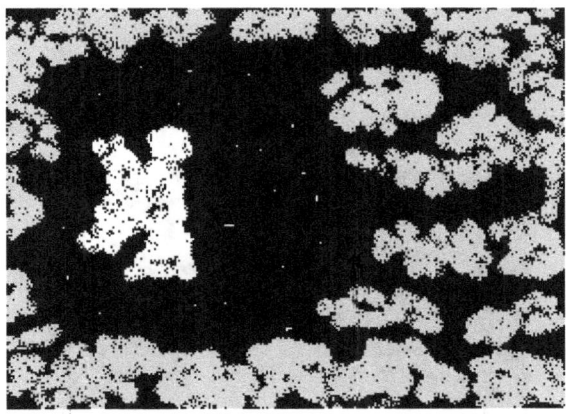

Message of the Dancing Cloud

But I still had questions. What was it that the Angel would win? Though I had accepted the challenge and that there would be a Battle, who was I actually dealing with? So, I prayed and prayed at my campsite, asking, "What does it mean?"

Then, when I looked back at my small campfire, it was burning high, and inside the flames, I saw a figure of the Devil burning. It was the Message of the Fire, and it told me of the Battle of Heaven between the Angel of Heaven and the Dragon. And there would be my battle, the Battle of Earth, and just like in that Battle, the Angel would win, and the Devil would burn.

I shouted to GOD, "What is this all about? What does the Dragon mean?" I had no clue because my mother was Buddhist, and in Buddhism, the Dragon was revered as a protector and a symbol of enlightenment. Therefore, I was confused as to why I would see a Dragon attacking the Angel. At the time, I didn't know that in the Bible, the Dragon meant the Devil. I didn't understand this until I studied the Bible later on in life.

But after I saw this vision at my camp, I said to myself, "The Battle of Earth will be easy." It was only about dealing with the Devil; no problem. With the power I had from seeing GOD and the message from the Dancing Cloud, I accepted the challenge, and I accepted the Battle. *I have GOD on my side*, I thought. I had so much confidence and thought I could see the future of PEACE.

Not only that but then I saw a moving star in the sky. I don't know what that meant, but it was the first time I had ever seen a moving star, and I used to stargaze a lot when I was younger.

But it was cold and late, so I settled into the sleeping bag and fell asleep, thinking of the message of the Dancing Cloud and how clouds were made of water. I would later understand that water was one of Mother Nature's elements that guided me, both the four western elements (air, earth, fire, and water) and the five elements of wuxing: air, earth, fire, water, wood, and metal.

But at that moment, I didn't know what I was getting into.

The Message of Fire, the Burning Devil

I had to look for the Devil, but I didn't know who or where he would be or how he would come. But I knew to use the guidance of the Dancing Cloud, which had shown me that the Angel would not move as the Dragon approached, which meant the Dragon would come to me first. The Dragon would also be related to the people that Bak Jou had warned me of, the same group that was still following me. So, I would just have to wait for them, too.

In the meantime, I would not let anyone except my current girlfriend and one of her friends into my condo because 411 was where I needed to focus on myself and my work. An easy task, I thought. I prayed and meditated, searching, and it was then that I understood why the voices had said, "Use Canada."

It was because I had to improve the world in ways beyond creating a unified religion, and Canada was the best model for a new world; Canada was the closest thing to a paradise on Earth. For one thing, Canada provided people with medical and social support programs, along with education. It wasn't like in second and third-world countries, where money talked, and if you didn't have money, then you couldn't get any of those things.

Everything I did and planned was related to the trees: the tree of life (good) represents GOD, and the tree of the Dragon (evil) represents the Devil. The Tree of the Knowledge of good and Evil gave humanity knowledge the knowledge of what is evil and what is good. I have seen all the trees in my journey and tried to do good and avoid evil. I hope human man will remember the difference, too, and then strive for the tree of life.

Canada was the best example of another tree, a tree of only the knowledge of good. But I still didn't know how to make this vision of a spiritual paradise become a reality for the rest of the world. One problem was that the world of spiritual life had no money or any other currency; there were just monks and nuns living simple lives and obeying GOD. But the rest of the world still depended on money, and the plan wasn't to get rid of money but to better distribute it.

So how was I going to make this paradise with no worries for anyone: a place with no war, no starvation, no poverty, and unlimited education and health care? And then how was I going to do it when there was always starvation, war, and poverty somewhere in the world and no education and healthcare for most people? Because of how complex it all was, I became deadlocked, trapped, and lost again.

One winter night, I was meditating in my condo when I sensed something was watching me. I went out to the balcony and looked up into the sky, and then felt an unknown entity over in the direction of a nearby church: The First Presbyterian Church near the Dockside Pub. I sensed darkness and thought I was dealing with an unknown evil spirit. I looked in its direction and telepathically commanded it to appear, thinking, *I command evil to appear. I command evil to appear.*

A big bang came from above me, the noise like a backfiring engine. It was so loud that I instantly looked back up at the sky. I saw a fucking UFO drop into the sky from out of nowhere. It had a circular shape with a light on the top, and within seconds, it reversed itself and flew upwards with a zooming sound, disappearing back into nowhere.

I freaked out and dropped to the ground. My clairaudience went insane, my mind went crazy, and my whole body was shaken. I was in total shock and went into panic mode, and it took me a while just to get back up again. When I finally did, I went back inside.

This was the start of my Prolonged Duress Stress Disorder (PDSD). It happened because my clairaudience was so messed up, and my experience had shaken me to the point of going insane myself. All I believed in was now out of the question; I had to refocus and analyze. I had to remind myself of what I was doing, and of the Dancing Cloud and that the Angel would win.

I prayed and prayed. Fear overwhelmed me. It was too big and too massive to contemplate.

I thought that this was the Battle of Earth that I had been told about, and I wasn't ready. I freaked out and prayed that this wasn't the Battle. I prayed to GOD that I would be the only one who suffered because the world was not really for this Battle.

And it was around this time that weirdly-dressed people started coming around to the family business. I had lived in the neighborhood for a long time and had never seen this crowd take so much interest in the hood. It meant the group of people following me was getting bigger. And that they would soon start something.

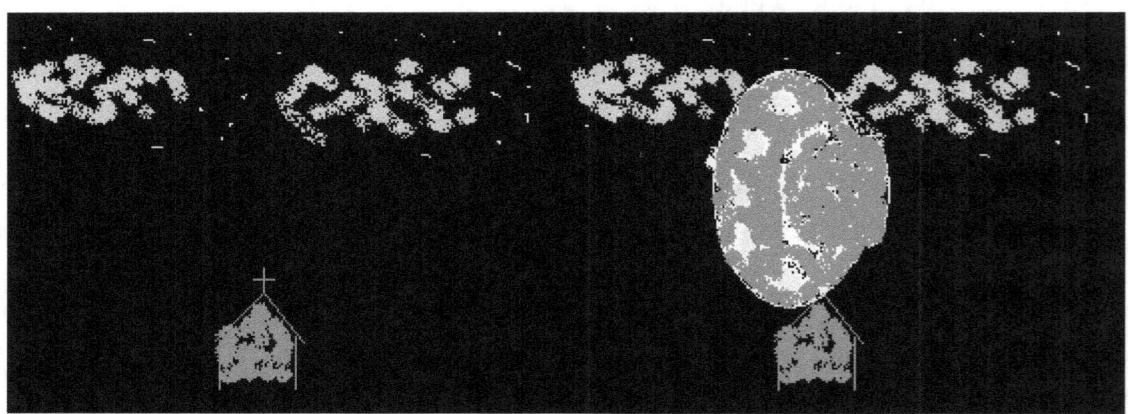

The UFO at 411

My clairaudience then kicked in, saying that "one" would be true and "another" would be false. Because I didn't yet know the Bible or the Book of Enoch in detail, I didn't yet know what this meant.

Meanwhile, I would go out to the R.J.W. (Dick) Mather Memorial Park every night. I watched objects in the sky, which always came in different numbers and always made different patterns. Sometimes, there were one, or two, or five, or even a cavalcade of objects.

One night when I was in the park, a group of objects flew so close to the ground that all I saw was a light, like it was pure energy. I can't explain what it looked like unless I use a movie: it was like one of the aliens, Drej, from the movie *Titan A.E.*, a being of pure and living energy. Or like the so-called Angels from Heaven. Seeing this was also like seeing the aura in the palm of my hand.

Shortly after this, something began telling me to commit suicide, bombarding me inside my head. I couldn't explain it back then, but it was a telepathic attack from the group following me. When they told me to commit suicide, their voices would first come to my ear because telepathy involves a force field wrapping around the head, going from around the ear to the third eye and back again.

The third eye is associated with the sixth charka of the human body, and after opening it, one can see both the inner and outer planes and can have spiritual visions and out-of-body experiences. But the third eye is limited in what it can see. In my mind, a third eye meant nothing compared to an Angel's guidance.

At the time, I already knew something about telepathy, but this attack was so extreme that it took me a while to recognize it and then to fight it off. But I was determined that no bombardment would stop me.

I kept seeing UFOs. At 411, I saw one object flying very fast toward my balcony, which broke up into five objects before flying up into the sky and disappearing. On another night, when I went back into the field at R.J.W. Park and looked up in the skyHawrelak Park, I could feel and see that someone was following me, as there were lights shining out of the bush that meant an infrared camera. I didn't go after them, but I knew it was the detectives that I wanted to follow me because of my Plan B. I still don't know what he looked like.

During all my photo tests, I could feel people watching me. Another time, I went to the field at R.J.W. Park, and two people showed up. One demanded to know if I had a smoke, getting aggressive until the other de-escalated the situation. They both seemed to be friends, and whether the second person was also watching me, I still thanked him for being there at the right time, in the right place.

But the weirdest thing that happened was seeing my Grade 6 homeroom teacher. She looked sad when I approached her, and I thought she was there to identify me, but nothing happened, and I was not sure why she had appeared.

By this time, my fear had overwhelmed me, leaving me in shock. I was living in fear, my face pale: I was afraid of UFOs, afraid of death, scared to go out in public, scared of the sky. I couldn't focus or think straight. But I still had my mission, so I had to keep checking for UFOs.

So, in the middle of the night, I went to different locations, like I had done when trying to take aura pictures. The fear was still inside of me, but I had to make sure that I was not dealing with UFOs. I went back to Hawrelak Park almost every night, parked my car on a hill, and walked down the slope to search for UFOs. On other nights, I would go out into the R.J.W. Park field around 2-3 a.m. and search. Because I also had to work long hours, I would take a nap during work so I could do all this at night.

I was totally confused, but I thought, *Yes, fuck this spirit*. Because I realized that when I had commanded evil to appear, it had come as a UFO. And every night, I prayed that I would be the only one to suffer. Because they were still not ready for the Battle.

Chapter Five
You Are the Messiah

In June of 2003, I got shipped to Calgary to work at my family's new store. We were expanding to another market because rent was so cheap, setting up a grocery store that sold both western and Asian food.

My sister was in full command of the operation, and because it was our first new store in a new market, my job was to both worry about product alignment and stock shelves; before our grand opening, I worked long hours seven days a week. New products would arrive every day, and I would have to realign everything all over again, but I always tried to put my dad's products in the best and most eye-catching position on the shelves.

During the preparation of the store, I sometimes went to my friend Hoa's workplace to chill, though I hid all my secrets from him. I prayed wherever I went, but one day, I wanted some real blessings, and I went to a nearby old church called Eastside Victory Outreach. I waited all day for the pastor to arrive, and then I approached him to ask if he could bless me.

He asked, "Why do you need to be blessed?"

I replied, "I am going through this difficult journey where I need to be blessed by a man of GOD."

The pastor told me to come in and kneel in front of him so he could bless me. It was dark because the pastor had not turned on the lights yet. As I knelt and prayed, the pastor blessed me. At that very same moment, I felt a warm light shining upon my forehead: the sun had shone through the window of the church onto me, and I instantly felt comfort and relief.

Around the time of our store's grand opening, my sister and I were crossing the street to get to one of the restaurants in Little Saigon when a car cut right in front of us. Even though the driver was Joe and in my old supervisor's car from the Electronic Test Centre, he didn't honk at us. My sister had been looking down when he had passed us, but still, why didn't he honk or wave?

I wanted to tell my sister about this, but my voice would not come out. I could only make a sound like, "Sisissiisissis didi dido didi…" before I gave up.

I didn't think anything of this at first, but I soon began to feel something was not right. After I started to talk with Joe again, I began to wonder if that car was a sign that Joe had set me up for something.

That became the first thing on my mind: was I being set up?

I wondered and wondered. I prayed and prayed. One day, when I was driving home from work, an Angel's voice said, "GOD is the LAW. Jesus is the LAW. You are the Law." Hearing this changed me to a certain degree: I had grown up in the hood, where most of my friends were criminals. I had stayed pure back then, but I still got deep into the criminal lifestyle and started to forget my destiny. Hearing Angel's voice brought me back to the beginning of my mission to spread the Message of PEACE.

I used to believe there were good criminals and bad criminals, just like there were good cops and bad cops. But all of those so-called good criminals always ended up becoming greedy, while they failed to see what they were doing wrong, because there was nothing good in the criminal lifestyle, only the bad.

I was Jesus, and I was on a mission to bring PEACE. Therefore, I would do a 180 degree turn from my past and choose GOD the LAW again. I would defend the LAW and foresee the best uses of the LAW to prevent harm to any individual or group. The LAW would prevail in first-world countries and then pervade other parts of second and third-world countries. An Angel has told me so, and it made sense.

Then, one day, Tran called me up, and I was so glad because I had been feeling lonely. I can't exactly remember it anymore, but I think he came to pick me up so we could go out. It was all good until he took me to his friend's house. We went in there, and all I saw showed me that Tran had gone back to his old ways.

He wasn't dealing drugs or committing any other crimes himself, but he was the bookkeeper for a loan shark. I saw him giving stacks of bills to his friend, who gave Tran other stacks of bills. They were also cooking and cutting drugs there.

Tran saw right through me and knew I was disappointed in him because we had had made an agreement a long time ago: he was supposed to let go of the criminal life. He said, "I'm sorry, Rico."

"It's okay," I replied, but inside I knew I would have to distance myself from him. It broke my heart and would leave me the loneliest I had ever been in my life. But I knew this had to happen because I had already chosen GOD and His LAW over my criminal past as I was now the LAW. Most of my current friends were criminals or associated with criminals, and that meant I had to put them all aside. I would pray and pray every day of my life as I tried to find new friends to hang out with.

Tran told me his story: when he was doing goldsmithing, he had a client who used a real bank draft to pay around $10,000. But this client later used a fake bank draft and ran off with $40,000 to $50,000 worth of diamonds while Tran had nothing. His business loans and his life savings were gone in the blink of an eye, with his investments gone down the drain. Tran had needed to turn to crime to make money, but as he became more powerful in the underworld, he got more greedy.

I didn't say much after hearing that, and then Tran drove me home.

In the days after that, I continued to pray, and one day, because I had chosen GOD the LAW, my eye was opened to the Kingdom of Heaven. I saw a Kingdom with no crime and no victims of crime, where God the LAW prevailed, where Good had overwhelmed Evil; I also understood that Yin and Yang would change. I traced the truth back to the tree of life and slowly understood the meaning of the Dragon tree, and that the Dragon was an evil and criminal being.

And then, one night, as I prayed in the garage, a strong wind blew, and a soft, gentle female voice said to me, "You are the MESSIAH."

Message of the Air, the Wind

Each element had sent me a message. The Message of Air was the Angel telling me I was the Messiah. The Message of Water was the Battle of Earth that I had just been told of. The Message of Fire was being told the Devil would burn. The Message of Metal was the Cross seen on 9/11. The Message of Water was the Dancing Cloud that I had just witnessed. Later on, when I was pointed towards the Revelation, I would find the Message of Wood through the paper of the BOOK, and then the elements would be complete.

When I wasn't praying or working, I spent most of my time hanging out with my friend Hao (who was still my landlord at the time) or with my current girlfriend when she came into the city. Meanwhile, my family kept telling me of a spiritual lady in Vietnam—I don't know her exact title—who wanted to talk to me and who could help me with what I was dealing with.

I told my girlfriend that I wanted to go to Vietnam for my personal journey, and she thought I was just going for personal pleasure. We broke up over it, and I was sad, but I knew I needed to take the trip. It was important to understand who and what I was dealing with, and right now, I was deadlocked and needed help.

I bought a plane ticket and went to a travel agent in Little Saigon to get a passport and visa. As I was picking them up, I saw the name (but not the photo) on another person's passport, and it was the same name as a woman I knew from DeVry. I wondered if she was the same woman who owned that passport

When I walked out of the travel agency, I also recognized a man following me; he had been following me around a long time ago. He was praying, but I don't know what he was saying, and I still don't know what group he was with. So, I just pretended nothing had happened, and I was out following a regular routine.

So, I flew to Vietnam, even though I was afraid to take the plane because of the UFO, a thing that was evil to my eyes. I had realized the UFO was after me, and it was the UFO that had sent me telepathic commands to commit suicide. Seeing the movie *Dreamcatcher* and other sci-fi and reading books on telepathy had prepared me for the possibility of a mental attack by a superior race.

And they had come because I called them at 411 when I commanded evil to appear, but I still don't know how to explain this UFO's evil to the world. I was fearful, paranoid, and anxious, wondering and wondering how it would try to stop me from accomplishing my mission. Because of that, I prayed and prayed as my plane flew over the Pacific Ocean.

Then suddenly, I saw an aura on the wing of the plane. It was the same aura that I had seen in my hand and in the sky above 411's balcony. By seeing it, I knew I was being watched over and was safe for now.

At the end of a 12-hour plane ride, I was ready to get out and have a smoke. But once I entered customs in Saigon, the border agent sent me to the waiting room. There was a rumor that if you didn't give the border agents money, then they'd make your life hell, and it was hell, sitting in that waiting room for hours. I was starving and tired, wanting to get out of customs. I kept going to the counter and asking if my passport was okay and if I could get released, but they always said no.

Then, a border agent called my name. I was so glad; I thought I would be able to go, but instead, she tapped on my passport. When they did that, they wanted you to pay up. I did not give her money because I had only brought $2,000 USD and one credit card, but more importantly, I didn't want anything to do with a corrupt official.

I had seen corruption before. It was so easy to bribe officials in second and third-world countries because the exchange rate was so high in favor of first-world countries' currency; $100 would be like half of their monthly paycheck.

But I had chosen GOD's LAW, and to obey His LAW, I would not pay bribes. So, I spent even more hours waiting. I cannot remember how long it took, but it was very long, and I was still starving and still tried. But eventually, I was released from customs; I was so happy and relieved.

And so, I reached Nha Trang, where my uncle picked me up. He asked me if I wanted to stay with my grandmother, but I told him I wanted to stay in a motel, and he drove me to a local one. He knew the locals and asked them to charge me the local price: it was only $100 USD for two weeks.

My other cousin came to visit me, and I often went out with him and his friend, who was a rookie police officer. I paid for most things on the trip by first giving the money to my cousin, who got the local price when he paid.

One time, my cousin's friend took me to a place with a small waterfall and a field of sugar apples. We paid to pick the fresh fruit off the trees, being allowed to take as much as we could carry in our hands. It was beautiful, though it was also full of trash because visitors did not clean up after themselves.

Most of the trash was plastic bags and bottles. They made the place look ugly, and I thought, *What if the Buddhists and the Christians knew that Mother Earth was also the Virgin Mary and the Bodhisattva Guan Yin? Would they still do this to her?*

I also loved seafood, so my cousin and his friend and girlfriend took me to a restaurant next to the beach where I tried the local lobster. Lobster always costs the most, but I tried it anyway. All the seafood I had was fresh and delicious, and also cheap because we paid the local prices. We ate like kings, and I saw a beautiful sunset with a beautiful breeze. I very much enjoyed everything.

But my true objective was to see the spiritual lady. One night, my cousin picked me up, and we headed out to meet her. On the way, everything became crazy bizarre. I saw spiritual signs all over the place, and a voice told me, "Turn back, turn back, it's a trap." My clairaudience became more intense, but I was like a zombie, moving forward with only a little fear in me. Here I was, acting like Curious George again: I wanted to dig into the source of what I was dealing with instead of avoiding it.

When we got to the spiritual lady's place, she seemed normal. Her place had incense burning and was decorated with Chinese art and statues; I thought she looked a bit like a Chinese goddess statue, too.

The first thing I asked her was, "Who is my guardian Angel?" She said it was my grandfather, and in my head I shouted, *FUCK!* My fear grew, but I still wanted to see who I was dealing with.

The spiritual lady then asked me to sit in the middle of the altar, so I did. And she asked me, in Vietnamese, "Do you believe in Christ?" I again said *FUCK!* in my head before my mind went crazy; my clairaudience went insane, and I just stood up and walked out.

As I did, it started thundering. Soon, it was pouring rain and coming down hard. But I told my cousin that I wanted to walk back to the motel, and I just walked and walked and walked in the pouring rain. I was soaking wet, but luckily, the sound of the rain made me refocus. Though visibility was low, I found my motel again, thanks to my boy spirit and girl spirit.

The next day, I went walking on the shoreline. My mind was still going crazy, spinning and spinning. My clairaudience was still going insane and out of control; I started to get triggered by hearing certain words. And after experiencing the rain the day before, I knew I needed the water to refocus. I decided that I needed to go underwater where it would be peaceful so that I could truly refocus and recharge; then, I would start to plan out my mission again.

I realized I needed a Plan B in case I was dealing with another Christ, not the Devil, but a Christ. I understood that if I was human and the MESSIAH, then the other Christ must be linked to the UFO.

Still, I took a driving course to find some peace again. I actually hated water, but I knew I needed to do it for the sake of my mission. And from the moment I was underwater, everything, and I mean everything, was silence. I was truly at peace and started to refocus. Weirdly, I even saw a vision of a woman I knew a long time ago in Calgary. It was like my mind was going back over all the people that I knew and trying to trace the ways the other Christ was using his power against me.

I still didn't know who was in that group, but I still noticed the same faces following me everywhere I went. I was still so afraid, and I wanted to talk to others to relieve my fear, but even though I was about to snap, I refocused and kept it to myself because I was on a mission.

But now I was even more afraid because I knew for certain that I was dealing with another Christ. I thought, *No fucking way am I going to be able to defeat this other Christ.* I said to myself, "I'm dead.

I'm just dead." I felt like I had nothing on my side except my faith. I knew I would have to change my plan and needed more resources and more information to fight this powerful other Christ.

Luckily, my cousin and his friend helped keep me occupied for the rest of my trip. And at the time of my departure, I bought my cousin and his friend cologne and they were very happy.

Before I left, I also visited my grandmother for the last time. She pulled me into a private room for a meeting and then fell to her knees, bursting into tears. She asked me to let everything else be, to just go back to Canada and get married and have children. She kept crying, begging me to do what she asked.

I hugged her, wanting to tell her the truth about my mission but knowing I had to keep it a secret. I had to wait for this other group to show itself, and I had to buy time. I cried myself: tears were falling from my eyes. I was dying inside and crying even harder inside. I asked GOD to help me and asked whether I should tell her the truth. With my head on her shoulder, I promised to get married and have kids once I got back to Canada.

I first flew back to Saigon, where I had to wait another day to get a flight home. I was bored, and my mind was still not right, so I wandered the city in the middle of the night.

I noticed a young boy in the middle of the sidewalk offering massages for cheap. I knew he was propositioning me, but I felt sorry for the young boy. I knew he did this only as a last resort; people were driven to the sex trade because they needed money, and maybe his family was sick or otherwise couldn't work. So, I let him massage me there in the middle of the sidewalk.

It was so uncomfortable because all he had to lie on was some cardboard, and he did an Asian cup massage. When he started asking to go to my hotel room, I very firmly told him no, but I paid him what he asked and tipped him the rest of my travel money.

And later, right when I had to go to the airport, the hotel staff said they had lost my passport. I was very angry: I yelled and screamed and pounded on the wall, demanding my passport. No fucking way had they lost my passport!

They finally found it just as some white customers came into the hotel. I thought it was lucky that those people had come in when they did, or I would have never found my passport and missed my plane.

Though I was finally on my way back to Canada, bad things kept happening on my return trip, and I knew there was a conspiracy occurring. First, I had to go through layovers in both Japan and Vancouver. During my Japanese layover, I found out that my credit card had been disabled without me knowing it, meaning I had no money for food or water after giving the rest to the boy.

The only food I'd had was the food on the plane. I was hungry, thirsty, and mad, walking around the terminal, asking for water or looking for it. I eventually had to drink water out of the washroom sink, and I was still starving to death.

It felt like the group who had been following me didn't want me to come back to Canada. The spiritual lady could also be punishing me because I had denied her request to accept Christ because I was Jesus Christ.

I finally got back on the plane and back to Alberta, but soon after I was home, an attack came. It came in the form of voices saying things to trigger me, including "Jesus is going to get you." Then came a second attack and a third; these left me angry, furious, and outraged.

I spent the night of Christmas Day 2004 by myself. I was so afraid, and once again, I prayed and prayed, still so lost and confused about having to deal with another Christ. I thought, *Fuck, this is insane.*

I needed a walk, and so I walked around my sister's neighborhood. I walked and walked, wanting to scream out loud. I checked the top of the street to see if anyone was around, and then I screamed, "WHO AM I!" and the voices said to me, "YOU ARE JESUS! YOU ARE JESUS!" This reassured me that I knew the truth, and I felt comforted and safe once again.

On the next day, December 26, 2004, the fourth-largest earthquake in a century erupted underwater off the west coast of northern Sumatra; the Indonesian province of Aceh was the closest point of land to the epicenter. The quake caused a tsunami, one that accelerated to speeds of more than 600 kilometers per hour and barreled one-fifth of the way around the Earth. Because of that, more than 228,000 people died in fourteen countries in Southeast Asia and South Asia and as far away as Africa.

After I found out about this, I went to my bank and pulled out $3,000 CAD to donate to the Canadian Red Cross. Wanting my donation to be anonymous, I sent the money in cash. I did this because I was paranoid again. I thought about all the disasters I had seen in my life. How could it all be a coincidence? Every important current event was based on something happening in my life, like the way 9/11 had spoken to me. What if I was the cause of this earthquake, too?

Then I was at my parents' house, sitting on the sofa. I was still afraid and still exhausted, and then I heard a powerful telepathic voice coming from above my ear, saying, "It's Joe." Fuck, the voice even sounded like his. It made me afraid that he was the other Christ and that he would be stronger than me.

By using logic and modern science in my journey, I also discovered that the Shadow from my childhood was the Shadow of Earth, but that it, and the other demons of the Earth, were not stronger than me. As a young child, I had been haunted by the Shadow of the Earth, and as a young adult, I had challenged the Shadow of Earth and took control of it by putting the light of GOD into me and banishing the Shadow. I told it and the other demons to leave, and they left like they had run back to the astral plane.

After telling the demons to go away, I thought I was ready for whatever came next. But now I was truly afraid of my enemies' telepathic powers. Having telepathic powers suggested my enemies had superior strength and were of a superior race to me. Fuck, was there fear growing in me. First, the telepathic attacks, and now, the setup in Vietnam.

But I had to find out more. I started with Joe; I was always like Curious George, so what else could I do but go there and test him slowly, cross-examine him? I went to Churchill Square and came up to him, saying, "Hi, Joe." I told him I was also an artist and asked him about the meaning of his stone carvings because every artist's work had a meaning behind it.

Then I asked Joe why he didn't ever give names to the stones he carved. In reply, Joe said some things that I sensed were about my future: "A change of heart of the lady of the lover" and "To change sides."

We talked and talked. I talked to him about the unfair division of the world into first, second, and third-world countries. He asked me why it was unfair. He said I already had everything, that my father was a businessman, and wondered why I would ever want to change things.

I realized that the luxury of my family's lifestyle used to tempt me into not wanting the world to change. But if I could not accept the burden of being the MESSIAH, I could not rule the world and would only live the luxurious lifestyle of a first-world country while abandoning the second and third-world countries. It was like Matthew 4:7-11 when Satan offers control of the world to Jesus if He agrees to worship him, but Jesus rejects him.

[7] Jesus said to him, "Again it is written, 'You shall not put the Lord your God to the test.'" [8] Again, the devil took him to a very high mountain and showed him all the kingdoms of the world and their glory. [9] And he said to him, "All these I will give you if you will fall down and worship me." [10] Then Jesus said to him, "Be gone, Satan! For it is written, 'You shall worship the Lord your God and him only shall you serve.'" [11] Then the devil left him, and behold, angels came and were ministering to him.

Then, I was asked to help out at my auntie's store in Vancouver. She and her family were going on vacation, so they needed someone there. My auntie's store was also where most of the local Vietnamese shopped, so I got to see all kinds of friends, even the ones I knew from Edmonton.

But most were criminals. They asked me to go out, or party with them, or go to their weddings, but I just wanted to be by myself. Day after day, I was asked to hang out with them, and day after day, I insisted that I was busy, but really, I was so lonely. Yet because of the guidance from GOD and the LAW, I had to keep distancing myself from any crimes or criminal friends.

Every night after work, I would pray and pray because the more I looked for signs, the more that I would see. I also prayed for my safety and that no one else would suffer in the future because the world was not ready for the UFOs.

And every morning, I drove to the wholesaler's market to pick up the fresh produce. One time, as I was driving through the street, I passed by some dogs behind a gate, and then something weird happened. It was like the dogs were talking to me through their barking. They told me to be patient and have hope. They reminded me that the Dragon would come to me, just as the Dancing Cloud had said.

Nothing else happened; when I got to the wholesaler's that day, everything was normal there. I checked the quality of the produce, made some bargains, and bought what I needed.

I used the time I spent by myself to analyze the situation I was in. I realized that the more I chose the path of GOD and the more I stayed on that path, the more of GOD's message I would see. I felt very good, certain that I had become better able to see the pattern of GOD's message.

But Joe was a problem. Soon, I would see him use religion as a weapon and he had the same ideas that I had. That scared me because until now, no one else had ever had those ideas.

I still told nobody, but I was so lonely inside; not telling anyone was killing me slowly. I hated it, but I had so much trust in GOD, in my dreams, and in the Message of PEACE, and these were the only things that kept me going.

Overall, I stayed in Vancouver for a little more than a month.

Chapter Six
The Message of the BOOK

I asked my girlfriend if she wanted to go to Jamaica with me; I chose Jamaica because it was cheap and all I could afford at the time. She said yes at first, so I bought an all-inclusive ticket for a resort in Jamaica because I had never gone on an all-inclusive trip before and wanted to try it.

Then she changed her mind at the last minute. I didn't want to go alone, but at the same time, I didn't want the ticket to go to waste, so I ended up going by myself anyway. I do not remember the exact date I arrived in Jamaica, but I brought my new credit card, and my debit card too.

When I arrived at the resort, I immediately hated it. While the servers at the bars and restaurants were nice, the rest of the people there were jackasses. One time, I was having a drink at the bar, and I accidentally spilled a drink. I ordered another one, but one of the patrons started shouting at me because I wouldn't wipe down the spill. I was pissed off at them, but I just walked away.

While I was there, I also noticed a woman at the resort who reminded me of Lilian. And I couldn't sleep, because I was hearing spirit voices. They said, "What are you doing here?" They repeated it all night long, and the next day, I asked the receptionist if I could transfer to a different room. The receptionist agreed, but later I would find out that all this shit was also a trap.

One morning, when walking around the resort, I found an old man's glasses in the washroom, and I gave them back to him. I was very observant of my surroundings, and I later saw him walking out to the pool and showing a friend/colleague his glasses.

Because I was an empath—someone who could feel other people's pain—I could also predict the sign and body language he used towards his friend: he passed the glasses to his friend with an open hand and smiled. When I saw this, I got suspicious, but I wasn't sure why I was or why he did those things. But seeing this was how I knew there was a church group involved with the resort.

Then, I met a local man while walking around and outside the resort. This Jamaican guy wouldn't leave me alone, so I offered to buy him a drink inside. He insisted he didn't want one and told me thank you. I gave him one of my smokes instead, and he understood that if I didn't know people I gave them presents instead of cash. He replied with something like, "This is how you roll," and he left me.

The following night came my first major attack at the resort. As I was sleeping in my new room, I heard a male voice, sounding like the Jamaican guy I'd just met. He was speaking in the Jamaican language and doing some weird Jamaican voodoo; I knew what it was because I had watched a movie about voodoo. I could also hear the sound of rattles being shaken, a reggae beat, and more Jamaican voices speaking in their language; the attack was so strong that I knew the people who had been watching me all this time must be called the Dragon group.

And then, the voice from my first room came back, saying again, "Jesus is going to get you, Jesus is going to get you." I was intimidated and scared, but now I knew it was a human who was saying that to me: it was the voice of the Jamaican man. I tried to use my power to command him to fuck off and leave me alone, but it went on for the whole night. All night long, I just heard, "Jesus is going to get you."

I got no sleep that night. Luckily, when I went out in the morning, I met a couple and talked with them. I asked them if they'd heard all the noise last night. They replied that they had heard loud noises, noises that were coming from nowhere.

We talked some more, and they said their orthodox church would welcome me, and that gave me a little bit of hope that I would find new reassurance because I was still scared, and now I was by myself in a foreign place.

I was out of it, totally lost and confused because of the voodoo attack on me, even though, while the voice said, "Jesus is going to get you," my inner voice still said I was Jesus. Once again, I prayed and prayed.

I couldn't wait to go home and kept myself busy while waiting for my trip to finish. I went on tours and visited local attractions; I hired my own taxis. Because I was afraid of the people at the resort, I drank at the local pubs instead. I didn't even care for the exclusive meals and just ate at the buffets. The food outside the resort tasted even better than the food inside, and the jerk chicken and jerk pork were delicious.

But even when something made me happy, I still felt this whole trip was a trap.

On the day when I was supposed to go home, I missed my plane because I was so alone, disillusioned, confused, and disoriented that I had lost track of time. All I wanted was to get another fight back home, but the airline worker said that I had to wait for another two weeks before I could get one.

So, I called a taxi and asked the driver to take me to the next closest hotel from the airport. Once I checked into my room, I began to refocus and meditate. I had to drink to get to sleep, but I kept meditating and prayed and prayed, and then my inner clairaudience told me that I had to go to Toronto to rest and recharge.

I bought the next plane ticket to Toronto. I can't remember exactly when I took the flight, but I remember wondering what the fuck was going on. Why were there two Christs? Why were there all these ATTACKS on me? Any answers I could think of just came from books and movies. I kept trying to analyze the meaning of all this and prayed for an answer.

When I got to Toronto, I rented a car. My Edmonton friend, Carol, was also in Toronto, and that night, I called him up and asked him if we could meet up later: he said okay. Then I got a motel room and prayed and prayed, asking to know what was going on, to know who and what I was dealing with, and what it all meant. Eventually, I slept, waiting for the next day.

The next morning, I met up with Carol. He offered to let me stay at his place as long as I wanted. Carol was roommates with another guy named Gerald and three other guys, all sharing the same one-bedroom suite, where you would get the bedroom when you had your girl over. They were so welcoming to me, and I even tried cooking them jerk pork, though it didn't come out like I expected.

They showed me around the city of Toronto. We went clubbing and drinking, and I even saw my friend Diep that I hadn't seen in a long time. I also went to Niagara Falls by myself; it was cold, so cold that it sunk through to my skin, even though I'd bought a new winter coat in Toronto, and the wet, moist air was unbearable. But the frozen Falls were beautiful.

The Message of the Wood/the BOOK

One day during my trip—I can't remember the date—I went for a walk around downtown Toronto. I just walked and walked until I passed by this one bookstore called The Light of Prophecy 1918. I instantly knew I was going to get another message in this store, so I went in.

When I got inside, I saw hundreds of books. Raising one hand, I began to walk through every row of shelves, moving my hand up and down each one. I didn't even know what I was looking for, didn't even know what subject to start with. As I was getting closer to the end of one row, my hand on the upper shelf, I saw a bright light. It was coming from a BOOK, and when I touched this glowing BOOK, I knew its title was *The Prophecy of the Light*. *Shit,* I thought. What did it mean?

I got the BOOK, paid for it, and left the store with the BOOK in my backpack. The moment I got out onto the street, I suddenly heard voices behind me cheering my name. They said, "Yes, Rico! Yes, Rico! Yes Rico! Yes, Rico!" I turned back, but no one was there. There was only the bookstore and me standing in the middle of the road.

I kept the BOOK a secret from my friends because I didn't know who to trust. I only took out the BOOK and began to read it after they had left for work. I flipped the pages as fast as I could or closed my eyes and felt the pages while praying. I prayed in thanks for finding the BOOK, and prayed for this BOOK to tell me what everything meant.

I went through the BOOK very fast, knowing I was still outnumbered and overpowered, still dealing with another Christ and the Dragon group. Then I flipped to a certain page, and the tip of my finger went to the word *Revelation*. At the time, I didn't know much about the Revelation or what it meant. I was in over my head, and I needed more than my unified world religion to help me.

I needed Lilian's help. I had meditated and knew the reason I had found Lilian was that I would need her in the future. I had faith that I would meet her.

But I was done in Toronto. It wasn't only that I had already spent several weeks there or that I had received the message of the BOOK that I'd been sent to find. I had also spent a lot of money and needed to start working again; I only made minimum wage. I was also completely recharged and refocused and had received the Message of Wood.

So, I spent all the time with my friends that I could before returning to Alberta. We went clubbing and even got a personal trainer for a few days, who was one of my friend's friends. We enjoyed ourselves, and I thanked my friends before flying back to Calgary after several weeks in Toronto.

When I got back, I didn't want to work because I was still recovering from the attacks in Jamaica. I was scared and mad, and all I wanted to do was fire people instead. I told my sister about the people attacking me in Jamaica and Calgary and even in Vietnam but did not tell her who and what I was. She told me I was crazy.

And now she was back with Joe.

At that time, I still kind of trusted Joe because he knew my sister. But besides that, I was beyond stressed and filled with so much fear. I went back to my Plan B of getting the detectives' attention and protection; I knew the detectives had indirectly tested me in the past, at some point in my life when I had no money and needed help, so they knew a little bit about me and would help me.

Plan B also needed Lilian as well as her entire group. I didn't know exactly how they could help me, but I had heard Lilian's voice in my head, speaking about me and saying she was watching me. I had told Lilian secrets that I had told nobody else, so I trusted her.

I was still outnumbered and overpowered, knowing I was dealing with another Christ and with the Dragon group. This was all out of my league: I had only just finished creating my united religion, and if I was dealing with another Christ, I needed to have more than that.

I went back to Edmonton for a visit, and when I got there, I remember that I told Lydian that I was will back in the city. I asked if she would meet me at 107 Ave and 97 St in the future if we lost contract. I had faith she was still watching me. Like I said, I knew I would one day need Lilian.

The research I'd done helped me find ways to buy time. But despite the things I knew, I still had nothing to show for that knowledge. The only thing I had was time on my hands, and because I'd had so many attacks, I decided to use some of that time and asked Joe to drive me to a medical clinic where I got my first diagnosis of schizophrenia.

I didn't care about getting the diagnosis. I believed that I was stable, and my "sickness" was actually my gift to use to my advantage, something I'll describe in greater detail later. I knew the attacks were not coming from my mind but from a race superior to me, whom I had summoned by calling on evil to appear.

But because of my diagnosis, I had to go to group meetings every week and was also on medication. This medication made me gain weight and turned me into a zombie: I no longer had any clairaudience left to guide me, and I still didn't want to work anymore. So, I moved back to Edmonton and became a potato head for a few months.

And on top of that, I was still exhausted and scared from all the attacks.

Then, while still in Edmonton, I tried getting my girlfriend back, the same one who hadn't wanted to go to Jamaica with me; eventually, we started dating again. She was dealing ecstasy, and one day, when I was helping her count it, I said to her, "Baby, if you could leave all this behind, I would take care of you."

I wanted her to stop working and stop dealing drugs, and she agreed. It was lucky that she quit because shortly after that, her big boss and his friend were involved in one of the biggest ecstasy busts in Edmonton's history.

Now that we were in a more stable place, we went camping all over Alberta and into BC, where it became a road trip with camping on the side. I did it even though I was paranoid about UFOs and scared to go camping or out into a field because of what I'd seen before and because of my PDSD. I had been given so much guidance, and there were so many things going through my mind that I had to refocus. I was also recharging for the next round.

There were no attacks during this trip. I was relieved, but because I was still on medication, there was no clairaudience coming to guide me, either. It was quiet inside my mind, and I was just not myself. And after the camping trip, I still wanted to sit at home and rest without going to work.

I started to have anger issues because there was no inner voice to remind me to hold back my anger. Every time I was in a situation that was tense and extreme, like catching a shoplifter who started to get violent, I had to remind myself that GOD was the LAW and so restrain myself from using deadly force.

I bought my girlfriend an average wedding ring. We were planning to go to Australia for a month, and I wanted to propose to her there, at a revolving restaurant in Sydney. She was still using her own money instead of us combining it, so we agreed to split the cost of the vacation, then packed up and took a 24-hour flight from Australia to Canada.

Our first stop was King's Canyon, in the middle of the Australian desert. As we were riding the bus to get there, I noticed that many of the other passengers were wearing nets over their faces. I didn't know why until we got off the bus.

The moment we did, it was like we entered a plague of flies. They were all over our faces, hands, and bodies, and it wasn't a pleasant sight or feeling. I turned to some of the other tourists and asked, "Excuse me [sir or madam], where can we buy those face nets?"

They told us, and we got one each, but wearing them was very uncomfortable. The worst time was when we were eating and had to deal with flies; the food we had on the tour was also just average.

But when the tour guide drove us into King's Canyon, it was a beautiful place, even though it was a hot, dry desert with flies everywhere. We camped outside, and I loved it; we also rode camels up the canyon wall. Overall, we stayed in the desert for a week before moving on to Sydney.

We went to the Sydney food markets and tried everything bit by bit. We tried a lot of Australian food, like kangaroo meat dishes and crocodile meat dishes. I also had to try the crayfish, which was like lobster. There was also crocodile and kangaroo jerky, and I bought a lot of it on the trip because I already loved beef jerky in Canada.

We went to all the tourist places in Sydney, and I proposed to my girlfriend at the revolving restaurant like I planned. She said yes, but only if we had a baby before the wedding. I was very nervous about the idea because it would break the traditional rule of being married before having a kid and would make me the black sheep of my family again. But out of love, I broke the tradition, and on the trip, we conceived my first-born son.

During our trip, we also rented a car and drove along the shoreline; it was beautiful, and the sights and smells were all pleasing to my senses. At first, nothing happened except for having to pass through a police checkpoint, where they checked my driver's license—I did most of the driving on our trip—and said I was good to go.

Then, one day, when we were driving along the edge of a hill next to the ocean, my right leg went numb. I couldn't feel it, and I couldn't feel the gas pedal. I freaked out; I yelled out to my fiancée, and she put the car in neutral while I turned the wheel back and forth. We got off the road and onto the shoulder, where the gravel helped to slow down my car, and stopped just a few feet away from the edge of a cliff. That was it for my driving, and my fiancée took over from then on.

Later, we drove all the way up to Cairns, a city in Far North Queensland, where we were supposed to go to one of the nearby islands for a romantic dinner and sailing tour. But the day after we arrived on our island, a call went out for the evacuation of the coastline because a Category 5 cyclone was heading our way. We spent all day trying to evacuate from the island, waiting for the ferry to pick us up and take us back to Cairns. Then, when we finally reached the mainland, they put us in a five-star Hilton.

We were supposed to stay in our own room, but my fiancée and I got bored and went wandering, leaving the hotel grounds and going into the streets of Cairns. All the windows we saw were boarded up, but we kept walking around until we found an open pub and decided to go in and have a drink.

When we got inside, I saw, out of the blue, my Edmonton friends Brian and May. Nothing special happened because of this, and we all drank and chatted for a few hours until we got kicked out because of the incoming cyclone, and my fiancée and I headed back to our hotel.

When the cyclone landed, it was my first time being in the middle of a Category 5. We were fine, and on the morning after, my fiancée and I went out to have a look around; we saw trees and cars knocked over.

We had missed all our romantic plans, but it was time to go home. The next day, we flew back to Sydney. We ate simple food in a local mall, and from there, we started the flight back home.

When we reached Alberta, I was still worried because I had broken the tradition of *marry first, then have a kid.* I was scared to tell my mother and only told her that we were getting married.

As the days passed, my fiancée started planning out the wedding and everything else about the whole marriage thing. I was still worried about how to tell my mother and father that she was pregnant, and besides that, I was still in zombie mode. I had no thoughts, and my medication kept my inner voices dead and silent. I was just a walking time bomb.

My son was born on January 6, 2007. At first, I was scared that when I held my boy, I might drop him and break his bones because my medication was still making me like a zombie or like a robot…like something with no inner thoughts or feelings.

We had our wedding on July 14, 2007. Once again, I was like the Walking Dead, totally exhausted and tired because of my medication. I stayed a good, noble person on the outside, but inside, I felt trapped within my mind. It was just like in the movie *A Beautiful Mind*, where John Nash was trapped within his mind because of too much medication and electroshock treatment.

I watched my kid, but I couldn't play with him. I wanted to play with him, but my medication made me a zombie, my body like a robot's. I kept shouting inside my head, "Go play with your kid, go play with your kid," but I was trapped within my own mind.

So, in 2007, I began to slowly stop my medication. I had to do it bit by bit, but I immediately started to get my feelings and mind back; I also felt better and more relaxed. I felt like myself again, and day by day, I started to play with my kid more.

I started to see the Virgin Mary as I was meditating. I felt like a MESSIAH again, and it was a beautiful feeling and it made me stronger, full of strength and courage to start again. Until then, I had been buying time, but now that was over, and I had to restart my search.

Time was always a factor in my life: I had gathered information for ten years, but it seemed like I had done it yesterday. The numbers from my past were also important: 9/11—411—7-11 told me that I was dealing with time, which was endless for me, but I knew the world needed more time to prepare. Everything I had seen was so important, but I still didn't know exactly what I was dealing with.

On April 2, 2008, my wife and I had twins, a boy and a girl; this time, I called my parents and told them on the very same day instead of waiting. When we had the twins, it was also the beginning of what I called "the assembly line." It started with feeding them, then giving them a bath, then dressing them up for going outside. Then there was dinner time, then clean up after dinner, then snack time, then more cleanup, and doing everything over and over again. It was the hardest at night, and to get them to sleep, I sometimes cheated by giving them some gripe water, which was a drink made of herbs, water, and baking soda. I didn't tell my wife because she wanted to burp the babies naturally.

And on the twins' first day home, something happened that I thought was creepy: when my oldest son saw the twins, he pointed at them and said, "An—aaa."

After that, strange things started happening. One time, when one of the twins was crying upstairs, my older son pulled at my hand and again said, "An—aaaa," while pointing up the stairs.

I never told my wife, but I also began to think one of my twins was telepathic. I had tried telling her about telepathy, but all she'd said was, "Sure, sure," like she didn't believe it. I had even tried to tell her who I was, but she just started fighting with me. She got mad at me, saying, "It's all about you. It's all about you," and called me selfish.

 But one day, when it was hot and sunny, I had put my twins down for a nap and went onto the deck with a beer, taking a break from watching them. Everyone in the house was asleep, but I heard a voice that sounded like the boy twin crying, and the baby monitor wasn't on. I dropped everything and ran upstairs to see if he was crying, but he wasn't. It was only when I started to go back downstairs that he actually started to cry, so I comforted him until he went back to sleep.

My twin boy had used telepathy to show me that telepathic voices came from an area going around the forehead, then above the eye, and then to the top of the ear. He showed me that I wasn't wrong when I'd thought that before. It was just like how Joe put telepathic messages in my head later on, which was the start of my keeping track of the telepathic attacks on me.

I already knew that my mother was gifted and that she'd passed her gift onto me. I believed that everyone had a gift, and because of this, it had always been important for me to find out whether my kids were gifted. Now that one kid had turned out to be gifted, I grew so calm and relaxed.

Then came our last kid, a boy who was born on July 7, 2010. As they all got older, the assembly line kept getting bigger, with more and more work. Four kids for dinner, four kids to clean up, four to prep snacks for, and four to clean up again. Getting them to school was also an assembly line: I dressed them one by one, then sent them out the door, and their coming home was the same thing, along with undressing them.

I found out that my other twin, the girl, had the ability to see ghosts and that she was like an empath, too. I discovered this because our current house—which we moved into in 2010—was haunted. We couldn't see these spirits but only hear them, and we wanted them gone because they would even haunt visitors when they slept over. We tried everything to do it: we tried the Taoist way, where we gave offerings to the spirits so we could live side by side with them. We tried the Native way, burning sage inside the house to cleanse it. But nothing worked.

My daughter saw the spirits and talked to them. She told us there were three of them, a family. Before leaving the house in 2011, we got a psychic named Glance Hughes to come and talk to the spirits. She told us that a long time ago, there was another house on our land with a family of four living in it: a mom and a dad with a teenage boy and a younger son, all dressed like they were from the 1800s.

The house had been burnt down by attackers, and all of the family was killed except for the teenager, who was kept alive to be sold into slavery. Because they were waiting for their son to come back, the other three had become lost souls, and the longer a lost soul stays on Earth, the more power it has.

Hughes then did her thing and asked the older son to come down from Heaven to bring the lost family back together so they could all return to Heaven together. I was amazed to see that the psychic had this Jesus-like ability.

In 2016, I found out that my youngest son also had the ability to see the auras of Angels. It was just like what I'd done when I'd seen the auras in the palm of my hand, on the wing of the plane, and flying above my condo at 411. I will talk more about this in Chapter 8, but it also helped me realize that he was a reincarnation of my deceased brother.

Meanwhile, I was still working at the liquor store. While I was at work, I kept seeing familiar faces, people that I recognized from my past. One time, a girl came into the liquor store with a few other people. She spoke with a strong accent, and wore sunglasses, and at first, I thought she might be Lilian, but then I realized that she was the same girl from DeVry whose passport I'd seen in the travel agency. I wondered if she was with Lilian's group, and I didn't find out, but now I knew that Lilian's group was still following me. I felt safe and relieved because it meant I wasn't alone and that I could continue my research.

Another time, my female driving instructor from Vietnam came into the store. This was a sign that I was still being outnumbered and outsmarted. I had so many enemies following me that it was beyond my ability to stand up to them.

I knew that both the people I hired and the customers who came into the liquor store were part of a group, but I wasn't sure which of the groups it was. In my eyes, there were now three groups following me: the Detective group (whose attention I now had, though I felt bad because my family business was always being checked in customs for drugs and other illegal stuff, and I knew that was my fault) Lilian's group, and the Dragon group.

So far, none of them knew that my other name was Jesus. That year's East Meets West Festival made me think more about Joe and what he was up to while I kept testing people and hunting for the true message of the Dancing Cloud or the Dragon. I pinpointed and tested everyone coming into my life and coming into the store to see what groups they were with, but they did not realize I was testing them and there was no harm done.

Then I met a homeless named Richard, and he became a good friend of mine. It was funny how the first time I met Richard, he was at my store asking for a shopping cart to take away from the store and use. I told him we didn't want him to do that because it scared the customers to have him there.

Richard wouldn't listen and kept coming back, and then one day, I saw him take a cart away and

I took it back from him. Richard got mad and took a swing at me, but I was small and fast, so I dodged him and then stood firm. I told him again we didn't want him to do that and gave him back the loonie he'd used to get the cart.

I offered to buy Richard a drink instead. Selling drinks for money was my job, but I told him that any time he needed a drink, he could just ask me; that was the start of our relationship. Sometimes, I would give Richard food from the nearby supermarket, and sometimes, when he would come into the liquor store with his hands shaking from a lack of alcohol, I bought him beer.

I did this because people could get seizures from not having alcohol, which I had already seen happen at the liquor store. They just shook when they didn't have the alcohol in time, and eventually, they would have a seizure.

Richard and I talked and talked and became friends. He was suffering from a personal loss and from the memories of residential school. He had lost hope and started to drink, going downhill from there and becoming homeless.

One day, I asked him why he didn't just go home to his family so he could see them and they could help him heal; I even offered to buy him a ticket back to his hometown. A few days later, he came to me and accepted the offer. I wasn't paying him much, only $5,400 USD.

As we went to the bus terminal to buy Richard a ticket, I told him he also needed to look good for his family. We went shopping for new clothing, and because the bus was leaving the next day and I didn't want Richard to wander off and miss his bus, I got him a motel next door to the terminal.

Once again, the moment Richard said he needed his medicine, I went down to the liquor store and bought him a mickey of rye (375 ml). I wished I could stay with him until the bus left, but I had a family to take care of, so I had to leave him.

On the same week that I helped Richard get his bus, my wife got the Visa bill with all the payments I'd made for Richard. We got into a big argument; she thought the charges meant I had cheated on her. She was so angry that she didn't let me talk and started to push me into the garage. When we were inside, she threatened me with a hammer. It was the first time my wife had ever scared me.

I told her the reason for the payments, but she didn't believe me. At this point, I knew my wife didn't understand me and that she'd never really known me. That all I'd ever done was work, go home, and take care of her body. It also hurt me that she'd never given me a chance to explain things before threatening me with a hammer.

At that moment, I wanted to leave my wife. But then I heard the voice of the Angel of the Wind, the same one who had told me I was the MESSIAH. The Angel blew breath into the garage and then said, in a crying, soft voice, "SAVE HER," and I knew that my wife was getting manipulated by the dark side and was almost lost to it. If I didn't save her, I would have damned everyone, and no one else would ever be forgiven for what they did. So, on that day, I learned how to forgive because I held the power of souls in the palm of my hand.

And it had felt good to help Richard. Besides Riel and Richard, I had become friends with a lot of other homeless people, and through them, I had seen the pattern of people wandering the streets because of tragedies in their families or abandonment by loved ones. They were constantly struggling and losing hope because their religions did not help them cope with the loss of someone in their lives or help them become empowered by that grief.

Meanwhile, I continued my research, and through YouTube and other online research, I found out about the four-race theory: that the main races of humanity were the yellow, red, white, and black/dark races. After reading this, I now understood that to create a unified religion, I had to use the ideas of the four races, combining the religions of the yellow-skinned (East Asia, the Buddha, the 7 chakras), the red-skinned (Native Canadians, and Mother Nature), the white-skinned (Christianity and the Biblical GOD), and the black (dark)-skinned (Islam). The four races represent the four directions of the world (North, East, South, and West) and the Hopi four corners (where Arizona, New Mexico, Colorado, and Utah meet in the United States; the area the Hopis call Tukunavi that is part of the heart of our Mother Earth), and also the four major religions left in the world; together, their knowledge can save mankind.

Seeing that GOD had planted His seed in every religion gave me peace of mind because it meant I was on the right track to uniting the world. I felt that GOD had caught me and saved me. It also meant I had to look into their prophecies in more detail to see what would happen in the future. I decided to study Revelation last because I had already been guided to Revelation by the BOOK in Toronto.

This wasn't like my first time reading about other religions: back then, I had only talked with people I knew, and I only looked at each religion one at a time, gathering information and knowledge. Now, I was looking for connections, looking for patterns in each religion's prophecies. I dug and dug on the internet. I read and read. Visualized the other prophecies. Looked for more answers and more questions. I prayed and I prayed.

I discovered that all of the major world religions each had a huge natural disaster, usually in their history or predicted as part of the end of the world. For example, Islam talked about Al-Zalzalaha, the earthquake at the end of the world, and The Three Landslides that would occur in the East, in the West, and in the Arabian Peninsula. They were a sign of the Yawm al-Qiyamah or the Day of Resurrection/Judgement.

These locations match up with the tectonic plates. Even science says that someday, the Big One will hit North America, and part of California will sink. There is also the Ring of Fire, a tectonic belt that surrounds several tectonic plates, including the vast Pacific Plate and the smaller Philippine, Juan de Fuca, Cocos, and Nazca plates. The African Plate and the Eurasian Plate meet together, and the earthquake can take place there. Finally, the landslide will be in the Arabian Sea.

The Buddha talked about a great flood in Samudda-vāṇija Jātaka.

(As I've mentioned, Buddhist prophecy also talked about the next Buddha, Bodhisattva Maitreya, who would achieve his enlightenment under the Dragon tree. A Dragon tree meant a tree of evil, or surrounded by evil, and that made me think back to life of helping out criminals. Luckily, I had received that message in Calgary that said, "GOD is the LAW," and I had chosen the LAW. So, everything was different between me and Maitreya, and that was a relief because I didn't want to become a Buddha.)

Different Native religions talked about different disasters involving floods and earthquakes. For example, there was a story of the world getting shaken with one hand and then with two hands by the Creator. I can't find the book but there was one. The Hopi talked about the great flood of the First World and about the end of time that would follow the Fourth World, which was the world we live in now: the Fourth World will end when the Pahana /Elder Brother / Lost White Brother returns from the east to destroy the wicked, ushering in the Fifth Age.

The Hopi also tell of a "dwelling place in the heavens" that would crash to earth, thereby producing a brilliant blue star (called Sakwa Sohu or Saquasohuh), which would be one form of the Blue Star Kachina (spirit). When the Blue Star Kachina came to Earth, he would remove his mask in the village plaza during a sacred kachina dance. After that, all Hopi ceremonies would cease entirely, and it would be the beginning of the end times from which the Fifth World would come.

I figured out that people's dreams can be other people's reality. There were different prophecies and different books written about different people's dreams, but they were all true for the people who wrote them.

After I was finished looking into all these prophecies, I returned to the Revelation, which had the most detailed predictions out of anyI had studied. I skimmed through it, and then I found this website: www.thebooksofrevelation.cc. It described things that I had already experienced, including the voice I had heard saying, "Did you know this would happen?" after seeing *Deep Impact*. Because of this, I again fell in love with the words of John of Patmos and the mini-miracle of being granted the vision of the Revelation.

After this, it was easier to visualize how everything would happen. First, Revelation talked about the land being changed in 6:14: "14 The sky vanished like a scroll that is being rolled up, and every mountain and island was removed from its place." Then, it talks of an earthquake so great that no man had ever felt it before. "18 And there were flashes of lightning, rumblings, peals of thunder, and a great earthquake such as there had never been since man was on the earth, so great was that earthquake" (Rev. 16.18).

This reminded me of a tremor I had felt from the LA earthquake when I was young. And in junior high, I learned about the equator, fault lines, and tectonic plates. If the whole world's plates shifted, then all of mankind would feel it. So, I had solved one puzzle: the earthquake in Revelation referred to a time when the whole world's plates would shift.

Until I started my current research, I had never known there were so many nuclear reactors on the Earth, and many were on the East Coast fault lines, like the Indian Point Nuclear Power Plant on the Ramapo fault. I realized that when the Revelation said, "8 The second angel blew his trumpet, and something like a great mountain, burning with fire, was thrown into the sea, and a third of the sea became blood" (Rev. 8.8), it meant that the earthquakes along the fault lines would cause nuclear explosions, and this would be the burning mountain from Revelations, which would cause all sea life to die. Not just in the oceans, but the lakes, ponds, and rivers, too.

The waters would be so contaminated that nothing could live inside it, making it completely depopulated. Just like in Revelation 16:3: "3 The second angel poured out his bowl into the sea, and it became like the blood of a corpse, and every living thing died that was in the sea."

It was only after seeing *Deep Impact* that I could begin to understand this truth. Without the guidance of *Deep Impact*, I would have never understood the connection between the Revelation and the nuclear explosions along the fault lines. John was the first chosen to foretell the Revelation, and I was the second. I was to preach the modern version of John's vision. That was why no one had ever seen the connection except John and me.

It all made so much sense to me: the reason for my search had always been to see this, the worst-case scenario for the world. And I discovered all of this within one day of gathering information.

A Map of World Nuclear Plants

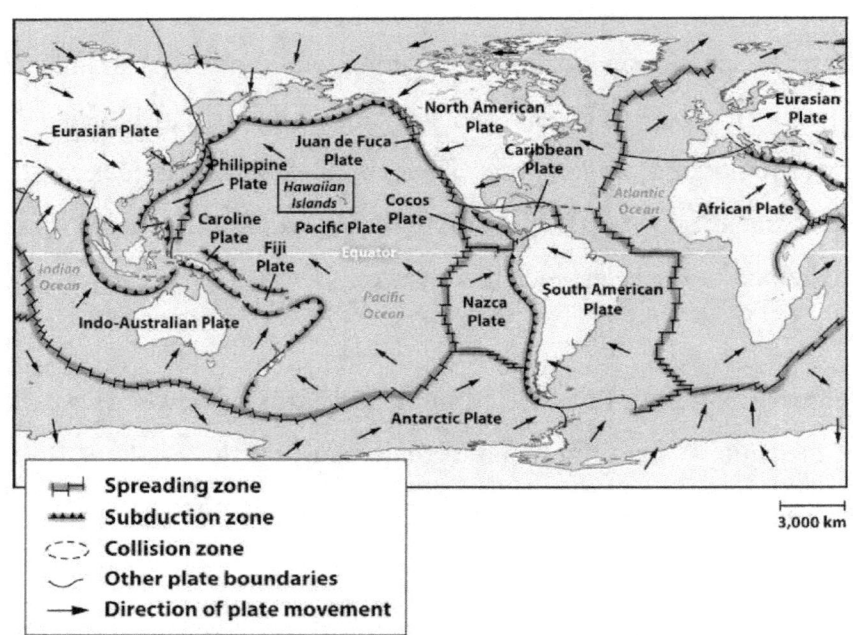

A Map of World Tectonic Plates

Because the Revelation tells us that all the animals in the sea will die, I wanted my kids to experience the ocean before it was gone. On every family vacation, I took them to the seaside or other places where they could see the ocean. They would be the last generation to know what it was like.

But then I began to think about building a new ark. One that would preserve ocean life and habitat during the Revelation so that the evolution of sea life would continue.

I continued my research while I kept working at my job. I cut down my meditation and research sessions to once every two to three months so I could better balance them with my fatherhood and married life.

There was a time when I said that I was a Buddha out loud in public. Though I didn't really want to be a Buddha, I said this to test the people of the Dragon group who were following me. The Dragon in Buddhism was meant as an enlightened force; the Dragon in Christianity was evil. So, I wondered what the Dragon group would say or do to me if I said something about a relationship with a Dragon.

And that was a mistake because everyone around me started to curse and condemn me. I was cursed from the left and the right, condemned from the front and from behind. My workplace became like a circuit of curses and condemnation, over and over. For example, a new worker I hired gave me the middle finger, and customers who were total strangers would attack me with words, saying, "Bring you back to Hell," "Damn you," and "You're not going to Heaven."

It went on for months that then became a year. I was so tired. The results were totally saddening and hurt so much. I understood why some people used religion as a weapon and that it was a powerful weapon.

Then, on a certain day, at a certain hour, I found a verse in Islam that said that the next Messiah would eliminate the pig tax. It was in Sahih al-Bukhari, the first Hadith (word of Mohammed) collection of Kutub al-Sittah / the Six Books of Islam. "Allah's Apostle said, 'The Hour will not be established until the son of Mary (i.e., Jesus) descends amongst you as a just ruler. He will break the cross, kill the pigs, and abolish the Jizya [pig] tax. Money will be in abundance so that nobody will accept it (as charitable gifts)'" (*Sunnah,* Sahih al-Bukhari 2476).

I thought about this verse while working the cash register. At first, I thought it was about how I didn't want to be Jesus, but there came an hour when I cracked the other meaning of this verse. It was like the seed of the knowledge was always in me, and I just needed to find the right clues to make it grow. It was like *The Da Vinci Code*: I kept finding clues in books and movies because they told my subconscious what things meant, and then my subconsciousness told my consciousness what these truths were.

The meaning of the seed was that anything was possible and that a paradise could be made on Earth. I called it "endless wealth". *Wow,* I thought. I was so excited that I started to write everything down while I was still at the register. For one hour I just brainstormed, writing and writing, and that night, I further visualized everything.

At the beginning of my journey I witnessed the ways that poverty caused crime in my friends' lives. With infinite money, we could end poverty. With infinite money, the government could offer free education, food, shelter, and medical supplies for everyone. With infinite money would come endless possibilities for the healthcare system, including funding cures for diseases and creating more and more social programs. What if healthcare was free for everyone in the world? And what if, then, all sickness could be cured? We'd have enough money to fund all the research we needed.

Infinite money would improve policing and also pour money into the economy, not just investing in big businesses but also in medium-sized businesses, small businesses, and individual people's projects. People would receive a monthly paycheck compared to a single day's paycheck.

Remember when I received the vision at 411 telling me to "Use Canada" as my model? Canada has some of the world's best health care, social programs, education, and policing, but they could be even better. What if we had billions of dollars worth of money to pump into these basic foundations of society? What if endless funding was given to the police, so that they could serve and protect the people and most crime would end? What if every social program in the world was free, and so were rec centers and public transportation?

What if everyone could retire into a comfortable life when they wanted to? Right now, not everyone in the world can retire comfortably: in other parts of the world, children have to take care of their elderly parents. Handicapped people all over the world must depend on their families. In Canada, the handicapped are taken care of with pensions, but the only way to get pensions is through the tax system, and right now Canada has high taxes, but infinite money could make it easier.

All of this would help prepare humankind for the Revelation and future disasters. We could end the world's suffering and reach salvation. I will discuss it in more detail in Chapter 10.

At the same time, I kept hunting for more information about the other Christ. I started to look deeper into Christianity, and until I started that search, I'd never known there were so many Christian groups and factions because I had grown up Catholic and only knew the Catholic faith. There was so much to take in, and I was overwhelmed by it, but I kept searching.

It was during this time that I started to write a rough record of my spiritual journey to explain the ways that I had reached my understanding. I recorded everything step by step.

I still wanted to see who exactly was following me and how they would react when I tested them. To do so, I asked people about their belief systems, then told them some of my stories, and used that information to test them further; I also asked them what their viewpoints were on certain important world events. I asked them their stances on certain social issues, like whether or not they liked the police.

I was very observant and had a good memory. I noticed when they said one thing but then did another thing, and it made me very suspicious of what anyone said. I responded to their answers with "Why? Why?" trying to see why they believed certain things. By doing this, I could figure out if they wanted to help me out or not.

Each time I tested a person, I would get different condemnations from them and from the world. For example, when I asked them about the police, I revealed that GOD was the LAW and that cops would be the army of GOD. They damned me, told me, "Go fuck your cops," and "You pig, you dog." Or they challenged me, saying that GOD was not the LAW.

Then I waited and waited until I knew it was the right time to test people by telling them that I was Jesus. Before I knew it, the condemnation was different. Now it was, "YOU FAKE," and "You're an imposter." But it was better than hearing, "Burn in Hell," "Die," "Suicide," or "Go to hell or die, demon."

Friends, workers, and customers all did that to me, but the Dragon group was behind it all. I knew the Dragon group would never accept me because of the kind of person I'd been and the things I'd done in the past. But they also didn't actually know what I'd done. And they couldn't see what I was doing now. All they could really see was me on the outside, in the present day, and make wrong guesses because of that.

While I was testing people, I also read more of the Quran. It told me that Jesus was the same as Adam. It was verse 3:59, which said, "Indeed, the example of Jesus in the sight of Allah is like that of Adam. He created him from dust, then said to him, 'Be!' And he was!" (*The Clear Quran*).

Wow, I thought. This opened my eyes to the connection between human evolution and religion. I realized that since Jesus was made the same way as Adam, then Adam must have been made the same way as Jesus. So, if Jesus came from the womb of the Virgin Mary, then Adam must have come from a female womb, too. Because I was also a man of science, I knew this referred to the evolution of mankind—which I had always believed in—as well as to Adam and Jesus.

Adam was the first man, so Adam was like the Neanderthals, the species that were the first closest to mankind. Adam was part of evolution, the same as the evolution of mammals, dinosaurs, and birds. Evolution was a miracle, the miracle of the womb of Mother Earth creating new species, thousands of new and all different kinds of birds, whales, dogs, fish, and so on. Adam was created through this same miracle, just like the Quran said.

The natural evolution of *Homo sapiens* could also be found in the Buddhist wheel of life. In Buddhism, humans can be reborn as animals, meaning animals could be our relatives from past lives, meaning that the human soul was always part of the animal kingdom. This was like evolution, where *Homo sapiens* came from animals. In short, science always went back to GOD.

More time went by. The condemnation I faced was getting worse by the day. The attacks came from all sides, nonstop, everywhere I went. I finally drew the line when I heard about a threat to Joe, the same Joe who was the other Christ. I heard a voice tell me, "He is dead," and then I heard the people I knew saying the same thing.

Because Joe was my street friend from the old neighborhood, I hadn't wanted to involve the police. I didn't want violence, didn't want to make the situation worse than before, and didn't want to end up in a war. But now that there was a threat to Joe, I decided to go to the police. I was so scared and so afraid. But, though I was full of fear, I was determined to go ahead.

I decided to accuse Joe of hate crimes for attacking me. Even though Joe was also being threatened, I wanted to end both his harassment of me and the condemnation for good. And by charging Joe first, I would stop any outbursts of violence that could have resulted if he had attacked me first.

So, I called the police to report a hate crime and had to go to the station; it was nerve-racking because it meant I had to explain myself to them. I had printed out my description of my journey and a record of the condemnation, and showed them to a detective named Bob, whom I'd never seen before. I told him everything that had happened while keeping my true self a secret.

I thought Bob would understand and accept my case, but he only lied to me, telling me he wanted us to leave the room and talk to another person who specialized in hate crimes. I was so excited, and I went with him to see this so-called specialist without thinking about it.

This other man got comfortable with me, and I started to explain everything to him. He kept listening, looking amazed. I told him about the attacks and harassment, about the voices that had attacked me from behind and in the front, from the left and from the right. I even told him how the middle finger was a sign of the Devil and that someone had cut me off in traffic while making it.

He read through my journey, telling me to describe each section as he went through it. I did so, explaining them to him one at a time over several meetings that lasted an hour each time. But when he asked me what I meant when I'd written the words "Going for the kill," my reply was the worst mistake

I'd made so far: I told him that "Going for the kill" meant I was supposed to take down the Dragon group, which was my mission in the Battle of Earth, and I had accepted this mission with honor.

But I guess saying this must have horrified him because I left the meeting, and the next thing I knew, a new officer and a psychologist—called Officer Stephan and Dr. Way—came to my mom's house looking for me because I was staying there after my wife had kicked me out. I finally understood that Detective Bob had just been playing along with me and had sent me to a mental health therapist instead of a hate crimes expert like he'd said.

I was scared and mad because I had never done anything and only told the truth. My mom started crying, asking what I had done. Once again, I wanted to tell my mom the truth about myself, but I couldn't, even though I was in so much pain. My dad said I should go volunteer at the temple on 97 St.

Not only was I being cursed and condemned, but now it was by my family. It was like the Crucifixion was happening again, but this time, the pain did not lead to the death of a body, but a psychological death that was more painful. It drove me to insanity, to the point of wanting to commit suicide, but I don't believe in suicide.

But I was mad at GOD and at the Revelation. I thought I had been shown the Message of PEACE and how to bring PEACE to the world, but now I might be bringing violence. How was I supposed to tell the world of the natural disasters that would wipe out one-third of the world when even my family cursed and condemned me? When I horrified people? Fuck and shit, was I mad. I was supposed to end war, not bring destruction to the world.

Maybe this was what made me so sick afterward, with no energy to get up and go into a world that still cursed and condemned me. I was tired of life, but my children kept me going. Every night, I prayed, and I prayed.

Chapter Seven
The Horseman

The attacks on me continued and became more and more severe. But after completely stopping my medication, I was more focused than before and could face the voices in my head and the attacks from outside. Yet I was still afraid of bringing destruction, and at 411, I continuously prayed to GOD that only I would suffer.

Around the same time that I met with the so-called Detective Bob, I was trying out praying and meditating, both with and without weed, to test what was better for gaining insight.

Sometimes, I meditated in the morning at work without using weed. During weedless meditation, I would go into a little trance and see into my soul. It started with seeing a small light and then pulling the light closer to me. As I did, the Virgin Mary appeared: she was a beautiful image that I cannot fully explain. At other times, I would see Buddha, the Cross, or a male figure, whom I eventually realized was the Archangel Michael, another of my guardians.

Other times, I would use weed while waxing the floor at the liquor store or meditating, sometimes while doing tai chi, sometimes while dancing, balancing my chi by dancing and enhancing the flow of energy.

Normally, I would preach and pray out loud while doing so, preaching something different every time, but always to remind myself of the Messages of the elements. At this point, I had been so manipulated by the condemnation that I believed I was evil and a devil, but I still trusted the guidance of Mother Earth's elements.

Waxing the floor on weed led to some off-the-chart prayer and meditation sessions. My clairaudience was far more intense, and the words "You are Jesus" were amplified, with the voice of them surrounding me.

Whether at home or at work, I moved my hand back and forth while praying and meditating on weed. I was watching its aura without opening my eyes; I could do this because using weed had intensified my pineal gland and let me see auras with my eyes closed. The pineal gland was the third eye and helped me see important things.

Everyone can unlock their third eye if they want. The third eye can take many forms: it can be clairaudience, clairvoyance, or the ability to see the future. Some have tried to say that the third eye is the only way to find the truth, but actually, the third eye cannot see everything, and sometimes it can't see through falsehoods. It's important to have intelligence, but it's also important to have wisdom, and only the wisdom of GOD can prevent you from believing falsehoods, like the so-called wonders and signs of the other so-called Christ and of the false ideas spread by others.

Their falsehoods were like the unclean spirits that fell out of the mouths of false prophets in Revelation 16:13: "And I saw, coming out of the mouth of the dragon and out of the mouth of the beast and out of the mouth of the false prophet, three unclean spirits like frogs."

I experimented further, taking weed and meditating or praying while listening to different types of music. I like all kinds of music, and with each one that I tried—trance music, frequencies from the Miracle Tones project, like 963Hz to open the third eye and 852Hz for returning to spiritual order, recordings of Buddhist chanting and so on—I entered a different kind of trance.

At the liquor store, I preached about the Message of Metal, the Message of Water, the Message of Wind, the Message of Wood, and the Message of Fire. But they did not know what I was talking about. They only knew that I was a Buddha and hated me because I was a Buddha. They cursed and condemned me because of my past history; there were so many attacks on me you cannot even imagine.

I felt I was missing something and kept looking for it; I was also searching for the true identity of the Dragon group. One day, I was on the Internet, and a New Age group called The Church of the Almighty God/Eastern Lightning found me and sent me a message.

I began to make contact with them because the Dancing Cloud had told me to let the Dragon come to me, and this CAG might be that Dragon group. I immediately saw that CAG was trying to convert me through their messages, but I was only studying them, trying to understand their belief system and their objectives; I ended up knowing far more about them than they knew about me.

For example, I started a conversation about the Bible with them and asked them if they believed the Revelation was real or just an illusion. I asked this question to find out if we believed in the same things.

A lady named Linda read my messages and then sent me a phrase from the Bible that I would never forget: Luke 17, 26-30:

26 Just as it was in the days of Noah, so will it be in the days of the Son of Man. 27 They were eating

and drinking and marrying and being given in marriage until the day when Noah entered the ark, and the flood came and destroyed them all. [28] Likewise, just as it was in the days of Lot—they were eating and drinking, buying and selling, planting and building, [29] but on the day when Lot went out from Sodom, fire and sulfur rained from heaven and destroyed them all—[30] so will it be on the day when the Son of Man is revealed.

Reading this quote from Luke 17 changed me completely. It made everything I had preached make sense and made me stronger and even more certain that the message inside me was not wrong because its words were from the Bible. I had already thought about Noah's Ark during my evolution as a Messiah, but after reading this verse, I was now completely sure that humanity needed a new ark.

In Noah's day, GOD flooded the world, and on the day of the Son of Man, He will send the Revelation. And unlike the Flood, everyone will be saved on the day of the Son of Man, not just one family. This time, the ark will be an aquarium to save all the ocean's animals that would have otherwise died when the oceans turned to blood; I will go into more details about this ark in later chapters.

Luke 17:26-30 also talked about the days of Lot, when the Angel told Lot's family to get out of the city to be safe. I saw the connection between the destruction of Sodom and Gomorrah and the dangers of the upcoming Revelation: the day of the Son of Man will be like the day of Lot, but on that day, Christians and other religions must obey me and trust me to get them out of the danger zone. The message of the Son of Man will not only be given to all Christians but also to everyone who will be saved; I imagine and hope that the other Christ will not speak false words and drown out this truth.

I continued to study the Church of the Almighty God very closely through both its website and its app. I kept chatting with them, trying to find out more about who or what this so-called Almighty God was, besides being the name of both a group and a false God.

But the Christian community is split because there are two Christs: me and the other Christ. The CAG is in favor of the other Christ and is attacking all the other Christians, mostly the Catholics, because of a phrase from the Bible. Revelation 17:9 says: "[9] This calls for a mind with wisdom: the seven heads are seven mountains on which the woman is seated;" And since the city of Rome is on seven hills, and the Vatican is in Rome, then the CAG thinks Catholics are the Whore of Babylon, and uses this to sow division, anger, and confusion among the Christians through hatred of the Catholic Church. The Christian community constantly points fingers at each other and blames each other. They do not see the CAG, the Dragon, or the Beast working against them.

At the time, I was still digging and digging into the Church of the Almighty God and its website, which had a lot of old and new information; it took me a long time to read everything. During my search, I stumbled across two things on the CAG's website. One was the hymn: "In His final work of concluding the age, God's disposition is on chastisement and judgement, in which He reveals all that is unrighteous, in order to publicly judge all people and to perfect those who love Him with a sincere heart" (The Church of the Almighty God). And number 28 of their 170 Principles of Practicing the Truth: "He condemns, curses, judges, and chastises so that you might know yourself so that your disposition might change, and moreover so that you might know your worth, and see that all of God's actions are righteous [...]."

These were the beliefs of the CAG that were the most opposite to mine. While I did judge people, I didn't do it publicly, and I never did it to try to make them perfect. I never condemned and cursed them to try to make them see that GOD's actions were righteous.

Reading that, I began to think and think. I brainstormed and brainstormed. I figured out that the Church of the Almighty God was attacking me publicly because of my past sexual SINs, and that they were trying to tempt me away from the correct path by putting so much anger in me. Everything they had said to attack me was related to my SINs. That was why the Church of the Almighty God had tried to convert me. Luckily, I took screenshots of some of the things they said to me, and they didn't know that I did.

So, I decided that I would change, but I still wouldn't become the person CAG wanted me to become. I would still go my own way.

It was like the CAG wanted total control of Humanity. They said that only their version of Christ held power. They often condemned people publicly because of what they saw as sexual immorality…and I believed something different. Their talk about sexual immorality scared me because I had been very sexually active when I was younger, and I knew they could use that knowledge against me if they wanted to make others hate me for committing SIN.

I realized my encounter with the Dancing Cloud had predicted this: the false God of the Church of the Almighty God was the Dragon, and the CAG were the group that had been watching me: the Dragon group.

Then, when I moved back to Edmonton, Joe began to accuse me of sexual immorality. I saw and felt Joe's fear. Maybe he had seen his downfall in me and now was using everything he knew about me to prove I wasn't a good person.

But it shocked me because Joe could not have known my past. In my eyes, it was like the movie *Minority Report*, where the psychics had the ability to predict the future but only saw limited flashes of events that had to be put together, leading to wrongful accusations. I was like John Anderton (Tom Cruise), fighting against the lies being told about me.

It is true that Jesus condemned sexual immorality in His teachings, but Christianity's final word on sexual immorality is told in Revelation 18:3, which says: "[3] For all nations have drunk[a] / the wine of the passion of her sexual immorality, / and the kings of the earth have committed immorality with her."

This was referring to Babylon, but it has an important meaning for today's world. The worst type of sexual immorality is the lust for money, an endless greed that mankind has to tame in order to be saved. First-world countries are full of that kind of lust: In first-world countries, the true "kings" are the merchants and businessmen. Money can be used for evil or it can be used for good, but the greed for it is only evil. That is the actual sexual immorality the Bible condemns.

Then something happened with my friend, Ernie: I was visiting him and his wife, Jorda (not her real name), and heard her provenly talking about the Church of the Almighty God, saying, like the CAG, things I could have said but were not my words, and then things that went against my beliefs. For example, she, just like the CAG, condemned the sexual immortality of the world but forgot about the other crimes in the world, ones that caused real suffering and pain. And then the CAG had no solutions to the world's problems, or any interest in warning the world about anything.

Jorda also said that when the Church of the Almighty God said it was time for battle if you hadn't converted or believed in the Bible (in the way they wanted you to), then it would be too late, and you would be damned. She said again that the Almighty God was her so-called God. This reminded me of Joe's words, too, which is how I began to figure out that Joe was also working with the Church of the Almighty God.

Ernie's wife also said that she would follow the Church of the Almighty God in everything they did and said. I told her that the CAG was not me and did not share my beliefs. She told me that the Church of the Almighty God was here to condemn SIN in this lifetime and make sure that history will not be repeated. But to my eyes, history had already repeated itself because Jesus was once crucified to death, and now I was being crucified psychologically, almost to death and almost into insanity, which was worse than death.

But I wasn't shocked at hearing her speak the words of the Church of the Almighty God because I already knew the Dragon group and the other Christs were everywhere, which was why I was hunting them. As I've said, the art of war is to know an enemy's strengths and weaknesses.

So, this so-called Church of the Almighty God are responsible for a shitshow. They are responsible for false accusations, and responsible for spreading false and hateful words. Everyone is afraid of them. They are users of the third eye, but theirs cannot outsmart the eyes of my Angel, the Angel of Heaven.

I knew this because in 2010, as I saw an aura flying through the sky at the liquor store, a message from the Angel of Heaven penetrated my third eye, and I heard the words through my third eye, "We are from Heaven. Heavenly Angel." My clairaudience even told me this was the real Angel of Heaven, who was on my side.

By this time, I also knew about Armageddon. While I was at my ex-wife's house, I went out for a smoke and heard a female voice shouting, "This is Armageddon!" I knew Armageddon was another name for the Battle of Earth. I prayed and prayed again that I would be the only one to suffer. And indeed, because of the attacks on me, I knew I was the only one who had suffered, and I thanked GOD for that.

Between 2009-2010, I decided to call on my allies and wrote to Lilian and the Detective group, telling them how to infiltrate the Church of the Almighty God. Today, I believe that Armageddon will include the release of my book and that it will be the downfall of the CAG and the Dragon group. Hopefully, it will open people's eyes.

In the summer of 2009, I learned about aura cameras. Someone I knew named Julie was the first person to introduce me to the idea; I think she wanted to check out my aura. I went with Julie to a workshop hosted by a local woman named Agnes Kraweck, who had done 20-plus years' worth of research into auras. She said auras had come from Hinduism and Buddhism and were only seen by people with certain abilities, like psychics, and she could determine a person's abilities by viewing their aura. Almost everything had an aura, including plants, but non-organic food didn't, while organic food did. And there were even people whose auras were so pure, they could transmit them into objects. For example, she showed us a cross necklace that contained an aura even though its owner (a priest) had passed away.

Agnes then used science and technology to crack barriers against seeing auras, leading to the invention of her aura camera, a thing that anyone could use. Agnes's aura camera was very interesting, and her research was so amazing that it opened my eyes to a new world, to new ways of using science to identify the auras of an object or a person, the level of a person's soul, the level of their chakra, or the level of their consciousness.

Agnes said that after the seminar was over, she'd take an aura picture of anyone who paid a fee. I was like, sure, I'd love to, so I went up to Agnes to say hi and paid for an aura picture. She told me to put my hand into a black box, took the first image of my aura, and then said, "Wait for a minute or two."

The aura picture turned out to be purple and blue. "You are very special," she said. "I want you to come to my next session." I agreed and got her contact information.

It was my first time seeing my aura through technology, and I started to research auras and aura cameras the moment I went home. I was so amazed that I said to myself, "I have to have one of those aura cameras like Agnes'."

But I was just an average Joe making above-average money, about $54,000 CAD a year. I also had four children to take care of, and an aura camera cost about $1,200 CAD; It was a big investment. But I gambled and bought the aura camera anyway.

I began to experiment with the aura camera. The first thing I did was test it on myself. I took medication (I can't remember which kind) for a few days, and then I stopped, taking pictures of my aura both times. It changed the color of my aura: when I took medication, the aura was blue, representing the fifth charka/the throat chakra. If I didn't take my medication, the aura color became more purple, representing enlightenment/the crown chakra.

Meanwhile, I had a dream of walking through a tunnel towards a light. The tunnel had so many doors, and I heard Buddhist chanting all around me. It was beautiful chanting, and I kept walking towards the last door in the tunnel. As I was about to open that door, my wife woke me up, zapping me back to reality.

The dream made me want to go to the 97 St. temple during a group meditation. The chanting of a group was more powerful than individual chanting, and I wanted to know how the experience would be similar to the trances I had had while listening to recorded Buddhist chanting. I also wondered what other things I might see there.

I asked Buddha Hao when the next session would be, and he gave me a date in December of 2009; I went without taking any weed. When I got there, I couldn't read the Vietnamese chants, but Buddha Hao told me to just say "Buddha" when I chanted. I waited for all the people to be seated before I sat down at the end of the row, though I didn't notice when more people came later and sat behind me. I went into the lotus position with both legs crossed and feet up to my body. I prayed and prayed even before the session began.

As Buddha Hao started his session, I closed my eyes and prayed to GOD, opening my prayer with, "Let me see what I have to see." I didn't chant; I only listened to the chanting of others. Because I was sitting in the lotus position, my lower body slowly started to go numb. Five minutes passed, then ten minutes, then twenty, and my lower body went completely numb, though I kept my hand in a praying position.

With the chanting all around me, I went into a trance and entered another dimension. It began with a distant light, and instead of walking or running toward the light as in my dream, I swam towards it in a circular motion, like a spiral going inward. The more I swam, the bigger the light got.

The closer I got to the light, the more it looked like a cross, and I saw a figure of a man upon this cross. It was an amazing sight, and I kept on swimming faster and faster to reach him. Because I was swimming in circles, it was like the cross was turning and turning in front of me. As I swam up to His face, I knew that the man upon the cross was Christ.

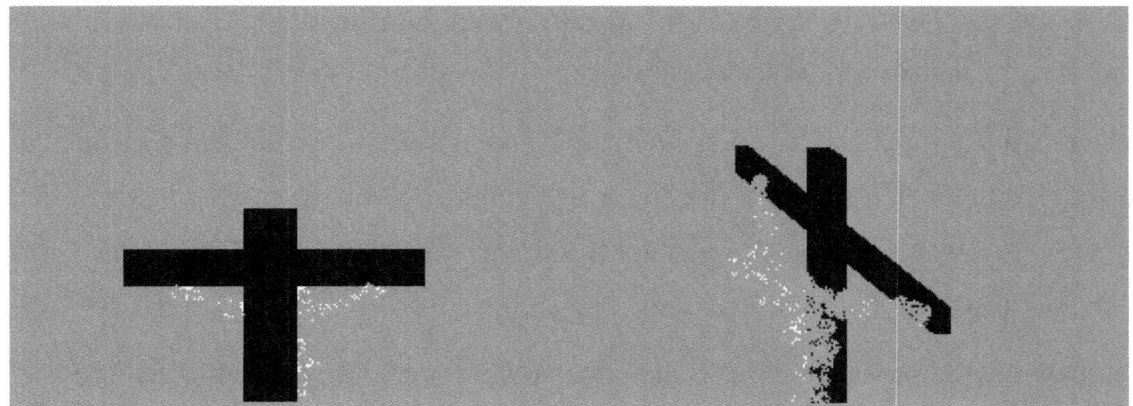

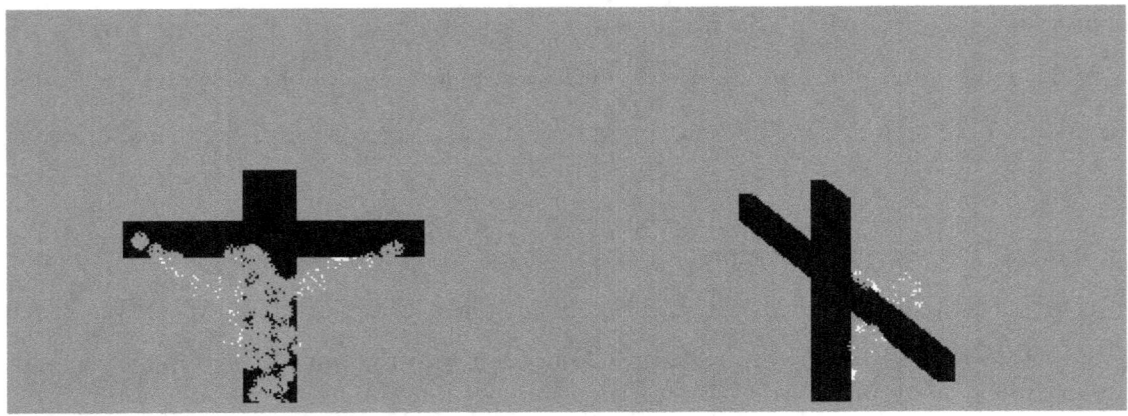

Jesus

His eyes were shut. He was suffering and in pain, the crown of thorns poking through His skin, and I could feel His hurt. But I was happy to see Him and wanted to ask Him a question about who I was dealing with because I was afraid of the other Christ. But suddenly, a loud attack came from behind me, saying, "Too late," and I was pulled out of that dimension and into reality again. *Fuck,* I thought to myself. *Who did that?*

My lower body was still numb, and I started moving my leg to get the circulation back.

While I was conducting my aura experiments, the attacks on me continued. The one that hit me the hardest was when I heard the voice of my little girl saying something like, "Father, you are not going to Heaven." Hearing that, I just blacked out in shock.

When I woke up, I prayed and prayed. I knew it wasn't really my little girl speaking because her voice had come from the upper level of our house, and at that moment, my little girl was with her nanny and not up there. The words were also false, but I still felt so sad and depressed because they had used the voices of my kid to attack me.

I still kept blacking out for minutes at a time until I got a hold of myself. I felt sad and defeated but also mad. That night, I parked by the temple on 97 St. and cried and prayed in my car. I stayed there all night long, and in the morning, I went to work.

But things had changed. Using my kid's voice was a no-no, and now I prepared to confront this other Christ; I wanted this nonsense to end. I kept on refocusing, reminding myself of the guidance I had received to save the world. I went back over the record of my journey, of my guidance, and figured out how to tell Joe the truth: that he was wrong about my past, and the stories he knew about me were all wrong. He had to be misguided.

I rehearsed what to say and how to say it and planned for many different scenarios and different results. Remember, I still had trouble forming words and sentences out loud and had to do a lot of rehearsing. I also printed out a copy of my journey to show him.

I found out that Joe was in town and staying at my mother's place, where I was no longer staying. I called him up and told him I wanted to meet up because I had something important to tell him.

On a day in 2010, I picked him up, and we drove to a Swiss Chalet, where he told the server we were dining for two. We sat down, and I told him that I was scared and didn't know what to do. I told him I didn't want any of what was happening to me. I hated it.

"Tell me, Rico," he asked.

I showed Joe the printout of my journey. However, I had taken out the last page where I wrote about "Going for the kill" because I still loved Joe and wanted to reason things out with him. Because of that, I also told Joe I wanted him to let things go so I could walk my path and he could walk his own path.

Joe took the pages and started to flip through them very fast. His eyes started to roam back and forth as if he were checking to see if other people were following us. Joe also kept looking up, seeming more and more nervous.

It didn't bother me that Joe might be the other Christ even though he was my friend because he was afraid now; I saw and felt his fear. I told him these papers were a record of the spiritual guidance I'd received in life. Joe said he wanted to leave the restaurant, but I asked him what I should do. And then, to test him and see if he was truly the other Christ, I asked him, "Are you Jesus?"

He said, "No, no, no."

And then I asked him again, "What should I do, Joe?"

"You should not tell this to anyone because they will not understand," he said.

I was getting nowhere with Joe and was so frustrated: if he was not the other Christ, then who was it?

So, I drove Joe back to my mom's, and then I just parked my jeep. I sat inside it and screamed and yelled. *What the hell am I doing?* I thought. I banged on the steering wheel, not knowing what to do.

Then suddenly, a rumbling came on my left, a sound like a thousand-horse cavalry pounding a field with their hooves. The sound got louder and louder, coming towards the house. To keep them away from the house, I pointed in their direction and said, "Back off." They started to retreat, the sound of them slowly reversing until there was silence.

Then the sound of a single horseman came up on my right-hand side, and once again, I pointed at them, and this time, I said, "Get back," and once again, it retreated.

Then there came an angry male voice coming from the stairs at the front of my mom's house, where there were two lion statues. It shouted, "HEHEHE isisisi in THERERERE!!" And then another angry male voice shouted from the same place, "HEHEHE is EVILLLLLLL!!"

It meant Joe because he was still staying there. My clairaudience kicked in, saying the horsemen were from Heaven, from the army of GOD, and that they wanted Joe because of the Battle of Earth because Joe really was the other Christ I that was hunting for.

But I was still so confused and disoriented that I couldn't accept it yet. I yelled and banged on the steering wheel again before other voices came right through the front windshield of my car saying, angrily, "YOU ARE JESSSSSSUS!!!" My clairaudience kicked in again, this time saying, "It's GOD, it's GOD," and this gave me new peace of mind.

I still loved Joe, but because the art of war involved testing your enemy and learning all his strengths and weaknesses, I decided to further test Joe with my new aura camera because it would tell me his power and strength.

A short time after the horsemen's visitation, Joe was still staying at my mother's house, and I went there to visit him. Because I was exhausted, I also decided to sleep over. I slept in the living room, where the household Buddhist altar was. While I was sleeping, I had a vision of three spirits standing beside the altar, who were my ancestors.

The next morning, I woke up and started taking aura pictures of my family, one by one. When it was Joe's turn, he insisted that he didn't want me to. "No, no, I don't like those things," he said and went up to his room.

I just waited and waited for the whole day until he came back down to the dining room. Luckily, my big brother started to talk to Joe, saying, "You should take it," and, "What are you afraid of?" before Joe finally agreed.

I was nervous and anxious as I took Joe through the process step by step. When I was finished taking his aura picture, it turned out all yellow. There was no aura, nothing except the color yellow. To help figure things out, I took another picture of my family, and it was a normal blue color, with my family still visible.

I worried the aura camera might be broken, and a few days later, I brought it back to Agnes. I told her it could be broken, and she performed a dowsing on the camera and said no, there was actually a dark energy around it.

"Fuck," I said, realizing that taking Joe's picture had fucked up my aura camera. I asked Agnes if the camera was still under warranty because I had just spent a shitload of money on it. She said the aura camera was too damaged, but she offered to give me another camera because I had just bought the first one. I said thank you so much and accepted.

Then, a few days later, Officer Stephan and Dr. Way came to my parent's house while I was there. They evaluated me on the spot and said I was going to be admitted to the hospital. I didn't know why they wanted to do that. I thought it might be because I looked pale, scared and confused—because of Joe. And now that this was happening, I was even more scared and frightened. I was even more lost and confused.

They said I could go peacefully, or they would have to handcuff me and forcefully take me to the hospital. So, I picked going peacefully, and they handcuffed me and took me to the Royal Alexandra Hospital on a day in 2010.

Once there, I was examined by another psychologist. He came in and yelled at me, "DO YOU KNOW THE DATE? DO YOU KNOW THE DATE?"

"No, no," I said; I really didn't know because I was scared of Joe and was in my own personal zone, where I lost track of time.

He left me in the exam room, and I just meditated there for a long time until they transferred me to unit 64, the mental health ward.

The male nurse assigned to me was a jackass. He'd somehow gotten his hands on the printout of my journey, even though it was supposed to be confidential. He waved it around and shouted, "LOOK AT THIS JOKE, LOOK AT THIS JOURNEY. IT'S A JOKE, A TOTAL JOKE," in front of me and the whole staff, laughing his head off. I was so embarrassed and mad.

The next day a female nurse came to give me an Invega injection in my butt. The doctor said it wouldn't hurt because of how thick the meat was in that area, but the moment she put the needle in, I felt like she had hit my bone, and the pain had burned back through to my buttock; I was in pain for hours and hours. I wanted to cry but focused instead on trying to relieve the pain, but nothing could get rid of it.

I was only in the hospital for two months, but I had to keep getting Invega injections after I left, once every month. The pain from the first was so unbearable that for the second, I was sent to an injection therapist named Gordon instead of the nurse. Because I never wanted to have it in my butt again, I got it in the arm instead. It didn't hurt as much as before, but it still hurt. There was a burning sensation the moment he injected the Invega, and then I was sore for weeks afterwards. I hated the injections. I hated the pain from each monthly injection, pain that wouldn't go away for weeks at a time. I told my wife about this, but she insisted it was better for me.

And I had no clairaudience to back me up; I also had no support because other people just saw me as crazy and insane.

But at least I got out of the hospital. To do that, I did the walk, and I did the talk. First, I was very observant and saw how the nurses were always writing things down when the other patients were walking, eating, or doing activities. So, I figured out that behaving well and doing all the assigned activities made the staff think you were a model patient, and they would let you out sooner. I started to do all the activities the mental health unit had to offer to show that I was doing okay, and it worked.

But even though I was free, I wondered how much ground I had lost in my Battle. And the attacks on me still didn't end.

Then, while reading more of the Revelation, I found the passage 7:4, which read, "4 And I heard the number of the sealed, 144,000, sealed from every tribe of the sons of Israel:" I had never known when I started my journey that I would have 144,000 supporters. Though I was lost and confused, these words comforted me with beautiful words of HOPE and were a sign that GOD had saved me. I prayed and prayed to the Virgin Mary, then heard her voice reassure me that I had already set up the 144,000 and because it was a long time ago, I had just forgotten. She told me, "You had set it up, My Child," I still haven't found them yet, but I know they are here.

I knew the majority of the 144,000 would be Christians, even though I didn't know which Christians were on my side. I also know that Armageddon will involve a final battle between the 144,000 and the dark forces.

Chapter Eight
The Power of Prayer

The days were going by so fast. I tried to buy time and slow it down, but minutes became hours. Hours became days. Days became months. Life moved on, and I couldn't stop it.

I was still so disoriented and sad, still feeling like an outcast. I had lost the Angel's voice and all my clairaudience because of the Invega; weed did not help. I had no support from family members and friends. It was like I was suicidal, and I was still being attacked and denied, even though I was minding my own business.

I didn't want to be Jesus because this meant the Revelation was coming. But I also didn't want to be denied GOD or denied my name, the name that was Jesus Christ. The attacks had made all these feelings worse; I even started to distance myself from my wife and friends because I was afraid for my safety and my children's safety. I was depressed and lonely.

I remember going to a party with my youngest son, who was still a newborn—it was in the winter of 2010. I was showing off my son to one of my wife's friends when all of a sudden, I heard a voice coming from her, sounding like her own, shouting, "DAMN YOU! DAMN YOU!"

I wanted to punch her in the head, but I reminded myself of the guidance of GOD, who was the LAW, and I didn't. But because of attacks like this and because I still had no one in my life to back me up, hearing that voice from my wife's friend demolished my motivation to work on my mission. I was also afraid the people who were after me might target my family, and I was so paranoid I couldn't sleep.

And so, I used even more weed to self-medicate and try to get my clairaudience back. This time, my spirit guides returned to comfort me and made me stronger again, giving me back a little breath of life.

I had dream after dream after dream, giving me a vision of tomorrow and giving me hope. I even asked another psychic if I should stop my Invega injections because they had closed me off from this support, but the psychic said that my Angel's voice would come through me even with the injections, and this gave me the determination to test Joe one more time.

Meanwhile, as the years went by, my father-in-law had gotten weaker. He had had bypass surgery on his heart and was dealing with alcoholism because of his residential school trauma. But whenever we met him, we still gave him beer every hour to stabilize his addiction. He finally passed away in 2012, after having been in and out of the hospital three times until he passed out outside the hospital and died right there.

My family was all in mourning and went to Flying Dust First Nation for his funeral. We held the wake there, and then a month later, we returned for a feast during a powwow.

During the feast, I went back to help build a sweat lodge from scratch; it took almost a whole day. My wife didn't want to go in because of how hot it would be, so I insisted on going instead out of respect for her dad. An hour before I entered the sweat lodge, I was changing my clothes so I would have something more comfortable to wear inside. A wind blew, and I heard a soft female voice say, "That is Evil." I knew it was talking about the sweat lodge, and I wondered how it could be evil. I decided I would test the sweat lodge and see. So, when I went in there, I sat in a lotus position; the medicine man was doing his stuff, and I was doing my stuff. It was hot, and I was sweating and had to bend over a lot. After three rounds of getting out to cool off and going back in, the sweat was done. *About time,* I thought. *That was intense heat.*

The moment I came out of the sweat lodge, I heard the medicine man saying, "Evil, he's evil, his thoughts are evil," and he kept on saying it. He was talking to other people in a mix of Cree and English, so I couldn't fully understand him, but I knew that "he" meant me. I went to him and asked why he thought I was evil and why the wind said the sweat was evil. I didn't get an answer I could understand, and everything was weird and unexplainable.

My brother-in-law was at the sweat lodge, too. He probably knew what the medicine man was saying but wouldn't tell me. I wondered again why the wind had said the sweat lodge was evil and why the medicine man had said I had evil thoughts.

Me and my wife were about to drive home when my wife's brother said he needed a ride back to Edmonton. Because he had hip issues, I offered to let him sit in the backseat of our SUV while I lay in the back.

We started to head home, and all of a sudden, my wife's brother pointed his middle finger at me and started waving his arm back and forth. I wanted to punch him in the head, but once again, I reminded myself that GOD was the LAW. So, I restrained myself, but I was very sad and disappointed by his actions and by everything I had experienced at the reserve.

I had gone to Flying Dust to mourn my father-in-law and support his spirit, but the people there must have gotten their hands on something of mine while I was inside the sweat lodge, like my hair or my belongings, and used them to scan me without my consent, then come to the wrong conclusions about me.

And my brother-in-law was so blinded by what he did not see: he hadn't known I was being scanned, but as brothers, we should have talked one-on-one, and he had kept silent.

A few years after the powwow, my wife wanted to do a memorial round dance at Flying Dust for my father-in-law and his brother. A Round Dance is a memorial to the dead and a celebration of their life, where family and friends both come together to dance and enjoy a feast. Photos of the deceased were on display, and everyone who attended was given gifts. The women were responsible for preparing the feast, and the men were responsible for passing it around while people chatted about the deceased's life.

But she needed extra money to fund a round dance. I loved my wife, and wanting to be helpful and supportive, I agreed to help with the fundraising. We set up lotteries and raffles, and I tried to help out any other way that I could.

We finally made enough money and went back to Flying Dust to set it up. My wife's whole family was involved, and the area was filled with so many cousins and uncles and people I didn't even know. I set up chairs and passed out food, and then later, I mostly helped out by gathering up the garbage, depositing the paper plates and bamboo forks, and picking up the recyclable cans and water bottles before helping clean up the whole area.

I was tired from helping out, but as soon as the round dance started in the gym, I heard the drummer say, "Joe has saved us," and I was afraid, especially because, at that moment, I was alone by myself. "What the fuck?" I asked. Why did they say that? I started to feel paranoid and needed to go out for a cigarette.

So, I went outside and prayed and prayed. I didn't know what to do. I didn't want to go back inside because it wasn't my place to be in there, and the people there weren't my people. But there were clouds outside, clouds so low that I could reach my hand up to them. A female voice came to me and said, "Stand up straight and walk back in there," so I did that, going back with pride.

After that, I helped out the most that I could so that I could get a ride home before everyone else did. Even though the voice had helped me, I was still scared and burned out, and I just wanted to go home and rest. I didn't want to get involved with anything else that night.

Because no one would listen to my truth, I felt alone and would sometimes think my guidance was all wrong before I realized that I had trapped myself with worry and had to go back to basics, back to retraining myself with meditation.

I took Jeffrey Allen's Duality course on Mind Valley to help, doing it on and off and ending up at level 10 out of 49. It showed me the basics of tapping into your knowledge and different breathing techniques for meditation. I did this because I wanted to experience for myself how to use music to enhance my abilities, like how I enhanced my chi by dancing to the rhythm of music.

At some point between 2012 to 2013, while I was still going back to basics, there was another incident at the liquor store. A woman entered the liquor store bleeding from a stab wound, and asked us to call the cops. So, as I called 911, an unknown man entered the liquor store and I saw in his face that he was the one who had hurt the woman. My clairaudience kicked in, just in time to see him taking a 750ml bottle of Crown Royale and going straight for the exit.

My mind was working fast. When my co-worker, Susan, was about to stop him, I yelled out to her, "Let him go."

He left the store but came back with another gentleman. This gentleman kept on saying, "It's my fault, it's my fault, it's my fault," over and over. He held the bottle of Crown Royal in his bloody hand.

At this point, the gentleman was calming down the thief, which reminded me of myself because I would always intervene to help, even when it put my life in danger.

Meanwhile, I was still on the line with the 911 operator, who asked me to describe the subject. I said I didn't know who they were and told them to just come fast.

"Do you see a knife?" the operator asked.

I said, "No, no, no."

Then the thief opened the stolen Crown Royal and drank some of it before pouring the liquor on the woman he had stabbed.

I was very relieved when the cops came 3-5 minutes later. One cop asked what the problem was, and I pointed to the thief. The cop asked him to put down the liquor bottle, and he refused. The cop called for backup to take him down while I went outside for fresh air; now that the cops were here, I knew it was okay to leave the scene. The gentleman with the bloody hand also tried to leave the store, and the cop outside, a woman, asked him to stay and file a report. But then she had to rush back into the store to be backup for the other cop, so the gentleman just took off.

I didn't tell the cops where he went because I thought the man might just be a bystander, just an innocent person who was helping. Or he might have been like another of my friends, who had a search warrant out for him. But whatever was true, if he'd wanted to talk to the cops, he would have stayed. So, to thank him for saving my life, I went back inside and helped to calm the thief down. If I hadn't, the thief might have stabbed all the customers and employees in that store.

Now that the thief was in custody, the cops asked to view our security cameras. We found out that the thief had stabbed the woman outside the store, and the gentleman had interfered to stop the thief from doing more harm. Because of this, I knew this gentleman was part of Lilian's group or the Detective group and had come to protect me.

Then, though it took me a long time, I finally busted a psychic attacker at the liquor store in the winter of 2015. I got video and audio of my manager pretending to be my guide, telling me, "Go, go, go!" It was disgusting manipulation as usual; fucking mind game shit. Just because I had schizophrenia didn't mean that people could do that to me.

I called the police about it around 6 p.m., and while waiting at the store and waiting at home, I waited more than twenty hours before an officer finally came to my house on the evening of the following day.

For all that time, I was full of anxiety, being so scared that my whole body was shaking non-stop and my heart was beating fast, I mean *fast*. I was having a breakdown, and at the same time, I was in a mini-shock. I couldn't believe that I had been right all along: ever since our expansion into Calgary, the attacks on me were not wholly spiritual attacks but attacks by other human beings.

I had nobody else I could talk to. But I also thought I had them. Now that I had evidence of the attacks on me, I thought, *This is going to end*. I didn't get any sleep, staying up all night until the officer came to my house.

I showed him the video and audio from the store and told him the incident was a hate crime against me, including the abuse of a person with schizophrenia. He watched the video and listened to the audio but determined that no crime was committed.

I was in shock again and mad. I had gone to the law two times for help, and both times they had failed me. I will admit that the first time I went to them for help, I had no proof, and they had put me in the mental health unit because of it, but this second time, I had proof when I filed a complaint, and the officer still didn't help me. I finally gave up on the system, gave up on the law.

The next few months were full of trouble, and it usually involved Tony. This was a different Tony than any I've previously mentioned, a Tony whose brother was my childhood friend. Tony had the ability to predict things: he had once predicted my uncle's "second mischief": an affair and a second kid. No one else had known about them until my uncle brought them over to Canada. Tony didn't tell me exactly when that had happened, but he kept on mentioning it to me.

People around me were always talking about Tony: Tony this and Tony that, like he was GOD Himself. He was more like the king of ravers, who always set them up for us. There was even one time, during a visit to K-Days (I can't remember which year it was) with Tony and my then-girlfriend, that Tony said he accepted a thousand years of damnation; it sounded like he was willing to accept a battle against me, even if it meant he'd die.

Tony also said he was homeless, just like the prophesied Maitreya Buddha: It is said that Maitreya will win his enlightenment on the very same day that he has gone forth into the homeless state. So, maybe Tony thought he was that second coming of Buddha, but I didn't find out exactly what he meant because every person that I asked about it tried to make me think that I was mentally ill.

For some reason, Tony also hated my father. Tony's mother even said my dad was talking to a cop in Vietnamese. Why? Why? Was the cop trying to get a statement from my dad?

But I got the most suspicious of Tony when his brother, my childhood friend, passed away on March 24, 2013. A Buddhist nun told us to come to his house for the funeral, which wasn't normal; a nun had never been involved with my grandfather and grandmother's funerals. And she told us that the funeral was at 11:00 am, but it actually started at 9:00 am. I had to speed to get there and missed the funeral of my childhood friend, though I made it to the burial.

It was the Dragon group who had stopped us from getting there on time; Tony was also working with them, and he didn't want his brother's criminal friends to see his brother for the last time and help send him to his final rest.

Tony often said he was connected and knew a lot of people. I began to understand that these people were responsible for the attack on the woman at my liquor store and the related theft. Tony might also have been the reason I kept hearing the Vietnamese workers in our meat department saying things in our language to scare me.

Overall, I felt I was being tricked by Tony. I didn't know why until I understood he was trying to defer my confrontation with Joe. My family and my wife's family were trying to do the same thing: one side supported Joe, and the other supported Tony. I heard other people say, "Ask Tony," and "Not Joe." I guess they were all trying to defer me from Joe. I had already heard voices at work saying, "It's not Joe," even though I knew that was wrong.

It happened because I knew the truth about Joe, even though I didn't accept it yet.

Around this time, I had a lot of arguments and disagreements with my wife. One time, we had an argument with my wife about the manager who'd attacked me. She said he'd done nothing wrong. Maybe he was trying to help, she said. It drove me crazy as I tried to explain to my wife that it was manipulation and harassment and that people were working together to intimidate me and misrepresent my guidance.

This arguing got to a point where my wife said to the cops that I was a danger to my kids. A police officer came to my workplace and asked me to come with him to the hospital, peacefully or in handcuffs. I was so mad—because I had done nothing wrong—that I asked him to handcuff me. So, he handcuffed me and brought me to the Royal Alexandra Hospital. The officer brought me inside and uncuffed me. Right when he did, I heard a voice coming from him saying, "Joe is God."

Nothing else happened, and this time, I only spent about two weeks in the hospital. I was prepared to fight their accusations with the recordings of my manager's attack, but then they let me out because my family had booked a vacation, and my wife wanted me out early.

But I wasn't done. I was going to fight the system with the proof I had, the proof of what people were doing to me, the proof that I wasn't just hearing things. Once I got out, I took my laptop and filed a new complaint on my own behalf. This time, I wanted to stop getting the Invega injections, and I even called a lawyer named Peter to represent me.

I did manage to get off Invega with the help of my wife: I told her it wasn't working, and she flipped out and demanded I get a new medication. The whole experience made me even more mad, so I wanted to test Joe even more. I prayed and prayed that God would hear my prayers. That my groups (Lilian and the detectives) existed and would keep protecting me. That one day, all these attacks would stop.

Joe had left town for a while, but when he was back in town, my mom and dad were away. Therefore, he stayed elsewhere. I'd spent all my spare time preparing for his return by rehearsing how I was going to test him. I was going to use my new aura camera to take his picture again because I wanted closure with him. I rehearsed the different ways to take his picture without him resisting: Scenario One, Scenario Two, Scenario Three, and so on. I trained myself with rehearsal after rehearsal, always thinking, "What if he did this? What should I do? What if he said this? What should I say?"

I started with Scenario One, which was to get Joe wasted so it would be easier to convince him to use the aura camera again. Because I didn't want to scare him or show that I knew others were following me, I just said, "Let's talk," and suggested that we drive up to a playground to hang out in the car, where we would chat and go through some weed and a case of Molson Canadian.

On the way to the park, I talked about my life, how I was partying and always out. How I loved Joe and we were like brothers. How I trusted him the most. I asked him, "Do you trust me?"

We stopped on the right side of the street from a park, and I offered him a beer while he offered me the weed. But I felt he was still afraid of something; he hadn't opened up to me enough yet. So, I shut down the engine, and we just started drinking and smoking to relax. One beer became two, and I guessed that Joe had already done some drinking that day.

We talked and we talked. About how I liked getting drunk and high. How I hated UFOs. How UFOs attacked me. How I thought I might get abducted by a UFO. I asked him, "Do you believe in UFOs?"

I asked him if he had ever been abducted by a UFO.

He rolled his head back onto the headrest of his seat and said, "Yes, I think I was abducted."

I got scared and worried, and then a voice came from nowhere, saying, "YOU KNOWWW." It scared the shit of me.

My clairaudience then told me, "He has no soul. He is a clone," meaning that Joe was one of the people who had attacked me after I had called down the UFO, something superior to me and also not human: a clone connected to the UFOs. By that time, I knew more about it, having seen one documentary that said that aliens were cloning humans and testing soul transfers with their technology.

I knew what the voice meant, but I also didn't want to know. Was afraid to know. But my clairaudience had been crying out the truth ever since the beginning, when I first tested Joe: the Joe I once knew, who I'll call JOE, had actually been lost a long time ago, and I had been in denial.

But the JOE, who was like my true brother, would not have attacked me. A true brother would have only sat and talked. The true JOE would not have let anyone hurt me. The Joe I knew now must be a clone, a Beast.

Now that I had seen this truth, it was like I got to tap into Joe's inner thoughts and found what was left of his mind; the old JOE was trying to reach out to me; his innermost mind was still JOE, and his love for me was still there.

I don't know how to explain it more clearly except by using movies. When I had picked movies to watch at 411, they were all movies made in 2003, and one was *Dreamcatcher*, which helped guide me to the truth. It gave me the Message of the Fossil: that normal people with normal dreams can still sense the future through the message from the fossils, even if they can't totally predict the future.

In *Dreamcatcher*, Jonesy was taken over by an alien and trapped inside his own head. It was the same with Joe: JOE was Jonesy, and Joe was the alien. But even though there was a little bit of JOE left, the JOE I knew like a brother was dead. I felt like everything was a dream, like my reality was my dream, and my dream was my reality.

Eventually, we drank all of the beer I'd brought, but Joe had had the most, while I'd only had two; I was also high. I asked him once again if he was Jesus, and once again, he said no. Then, I finally convinced him to let me take his picture with the aura camera. I had brought a portable power supply with a plug-in so I could use the camera in my car by attaching it to the starter. I let Joe see the camera and said I wanted to use it to see how gifted he was.

I took a picture of my aura first and then said, "It's your turn," and he accepted. I don't know why, but my aura came out bluish. When I took Joe's picture, I heard Joe speaking in a language I didn't know; it sounded like a chant you'd hear in a movie, but I knew it had to be some sort of spell. I wouldn't know the exact language until I met Cataline and another psychic, who gave me a ritual spell to perform for my healing journey.

But I knew Joe had cast it because he knew what the photo would show.

When I took Joe's picture, it was blank yellow again. I asked him to retake the photo, but the aura camera wasn't working anymore, and Joe asked if he could go. I agreed and drove him back to his hotel, where I helped him get into his room.

My sister was also staying at the hotel with Joe, and when I came in, she was there. I told her about the Horsemen, and I'm not sure how she reacted; all she did was nod her head.

I went back to my SUV and looked at Joe's picture one more time. The yellow color of his aura started to change back to a normal blue, but my aura camera had stopped working and began to fall apart. I tried to get a hold of Agnes to fix or replace the camera again, but her business had closed down. *No way is my aura camera broken*, I thought. But it had because Joe had cast a spell on it.

I knew I needed the help of another psychic because I needed a white spell to fight Joe's spell and a psychic to fight a psychic. I started a journey to look for them.

The attacks on me continued, but this time, I heard a new voice within me that shielded me from the evil, like a voice within a voice. When the attacks said I was damned or said something else bad about me, the voice said good things about me and reminded me of the good things I'd actually done. It made me stronger; the good voice shielded me until I could no longer hear the evil one. It was like an enemy had fired an arrow at me, and an Angel had used his shield to block the arrow; I can't explain it any more than that.

But I still wasn't completely at peace.

Around this time, I often went to a property I owned at Pigeon Lake, which I had bought a few years after my father-in-law's death. It was five minutes from the beach and was a place to get some peace and quiet by myself.

My kids also loved it there, and when my family took our RV to Pigeon Lake, we would walk the small trail nearby, pretending we were walking in the wilderness. They also loved the beach, where the water was shallow enough for even my youngest kid to go into the water. Before we went to the beach, I would always make them a lunch of BBQ hot dogs, and when we got to the beach, they would make sandcastles and play in the sand.

But my wife hated going to Pigeon Lake because she didn't like how much maintenance it took to keep the property in shape. So I paid someone to mow it weekly while I installed a water well, septic tank, and electricity on the lot because I was planning to build a cabin there. Pigeon Lake was a perfect area for going on a longer vacation because the property was even located close to a grocery store, which was good because whenever we came to Pigeon Lake, we always ran out of things or forgot something.

One day, when I was swimming at the beach with one of my kids, I started dipping in and out of the water because it was a hot day and diving under cooled me off. One time, when I came up, I heard a soft female voice saying, "This is going to be our ocean." This voice surrounded me; it was the voice of an Angel, and once again, it made me stronger, telling me I was not wrong and reassuring me I was right.

The number 411 became important to me a second time on the day of April 11, 2016, when I discovered my youngest son had the ability to see the auras of Angels, just like me. I was at my other sister's wedding in Cancun, and it was the night of the reception, which was held on the beach. It was a nice evening, and my children looked so beautiful. But, while everyone was dancing and drinking, I lost track of my youngest son.

I searched for him, finding him on one of the loveseats that had been put out on the beach. I said, "Hi; what you doing?"

"Nothing," he said. "Just hanging out."

I asked him, "Can I join you?" and me and my youngest son hung out on the loveseat. We talked and talked, and I asked him why he wasn't at the party and why was he there? I eventually asked him to come back to the party, and he said no, insisting on staying there because he was enjoying the scenery and the view, especially the beautiful sunset.

So, I asked him again, "Can I join you?" and together we watched the sky quietly and peacefully, and he said how beautiful it was.

Then I noticed something moving in the sky very fast. I wasn't sure what it was, but my son said, "I see an eagle, Daddy." Then, at the same time, I said, "I see an Angel." *Wow*, I thought. *He saw an eagle, and I saw an angel. What a coincidence.*

It meant the Angel and the Eagle were one. When Christianity started, it was guided by Angels, and across the sea, the natives of North America were once guided by a great Eagle. Both forms of guidance were right, and there was no wrong way, as all the ways came from the creator, who was GOD.

After that, we returned to the party. Joe was also in attendance, and I told him what I had just seen. He said it was something he was afraid of but never explained to me what that meant. Joe then said it was all manipulation; I wanted to confront Joe further, but then I got distracted by my brother-in-law.

But this wasn't the weirdest thing that happened on that night. That was later when I was walking out of the washroom and looked up to see not one, not two, but six to seven objects dancing in the sky. They looked like the auras I had seen in the palm of my hand, in the sky at my condo at 411, and on the wing of my plane; the auras that were like the Drej ships in *Titan A.E.*, but on my side.

They reminded me of the importance of 411, as it wasn't midnight yet, still the day of April 11th. It meant this was no hallucination, even though I had pinched myself to make sure and was still on my Invega.

I can't remember exactly when it happened, but one day, not long after Cancun, one of my kids was mad at me and my wife. He had had an argument with his mom, and she wanted to kick him out of the house. I went to his room to comfort him, and then a loud thunderclap shook the house before there came a female voice, the voice of the thunder, saying, "Your parents would be so proud of you."

Until then, I had always hated thunder and clouds because of my PDSD, but at that moment, I was comforted by the voice of the thunder. It reassured me that I was a good parent, even though I had been put in the hospital. Even though I had once been manipulated by other people's voices to the point where it was like brainwashing, brainwashing me into believing I was evil and not a good father.

This experience also taught me something about thunder: that the power of thunder was the power of GOD. Because of this experience, my fear of thunder was weakened, though sometimes, when the thunder was really loud, it would still rock my mind and body, and I would go into a trance.

Another time, my wife and I were watching a show about the best and worst places in the world to live. When they discussed volcanoes, I heard a voice that sounded different from my wife's, saying, "We have warned them, but they did not listen."

It scared me because all the messages I was receiving were connected with each other and connected to the Revelation: in this case, the voice was talking about how Mother Earth and GOD were warning people of the apocalypse through small eruptions and small earthquakes; GOD was doing it slowly, and they were still not listening. Even though science had also predicted the Big One, the megathrust earthquake in Western North America.

But with the power of prayer, I was now able to put GOD in me and go through life with new ease and comfort. Every time I was stressed, the Angel would comfort me. Every time I was attacked, the Angel would shield me. Every time I would lose, the Angel would reassure me. The Angel of GOD was always there for me and would always be there from the start to the end. With the Angel, I was stronger and more determined, with more strength and courage than before. I think that without that angel, I would not have been done. It was all because of the power of prayer.

Chapter Nine
The Angel in My Room

Through my dreams and through the voices of Angels, I have heard and understood the reality of the world. Almost everything that has happened to me is something that I've dreamt of before it happened. That is why I continued to feel like I was living in an illusion but also in reality at the same time. *Was I dreaming*? I wondered.

I even thought I just might be crazy and insane. I was down. I had lost hope and lost confidence. I thought I was the illusion. "What was I preaching about?" I asked the Angel.

The time I spent in the Royal Alexandra's mental ward was one reason for my lost confidence. Everyone knew I had gone in there and, therefore, that I had a mental illness. It made them disbelieve me, and I wondered how anyone was supposed to believe me now and why I was in the world in the first place.

After I found a way to unite religion, I learned about the different Christian groups. I loved every one of the groups I have met, though some of them follow the other Christ, the false Christ. There is so much love in Christianity, but there are so many different Christian beliefs and so many different ways of knowing Jesus that I still don't know which is right or wrong. But I will keep defending myself using the name of Jesus, of both His works and the knowledge that He would return in two thousand years.

All Christians should be united, just like all world religions should be united; both of them have so many similarities. It took me ten years to figure out how to unite world religions, but when I began to think about uniting all Christians, it only took one month for me to realize how to do it. Hopefully, I will be responsible for unifying the soul of Christianity because we are all the family of the Son of Man, all people of GOD. And in this new age, we are all connected across the world.

In 2018, before COVID-19, I had a dream about people triggering me everywhere I turned, just like in real life. A white witch appeared in my dream and said to me that all people of the earth were sinful and damned and that they were always triggering me because they were evil. She also warned me of future attacks.

When the movie *Avengers: Infinity War* came out on April 27, 2018, my son predicted the outcome of the next sequel, *Avengers Endgame*, before it came out on April 26, 2019, which I realized when I saw the movie.

But most importantly, *Infinity War* was about Thanos wanting to wipe out half the population in the universe using the Infinity Stones. When I left the theatre, I saw a cloud split into two: one was the cloud, and one was the clear sky. Things were split in half, the way Thanos had split the universe's population in half. All of it showed me that I had two choices: to fulfill GOD's Plan or not. I vowed that I would fulfill it.

And in *Endgame,* Tony Stark did his own snap to get rid of the bad people, just like the white witch in my dreams talked about getting rid of the damned.

Meanwhile, things were also changing in the world around me. Three to five years ago, the cops had begun to see the homeless through new eyes, starting to interact with them as people and starting to question why and how the homeless became the way they were. In 2018, a documentary called *Finding Murph* was released about the homelessness of former Stanley Cup champion Joe Murphy, showing how even a rich and famous person could become homeless.

This improvement was also a sign of something bigger changing in the world, and it was a change that started in Edmonton. I knew the people making these changes were copying me in some ways, but that was okay because cops and the rest of the authorities had a bigger budget than me, and it was the start of a new beginning for both the cops and the homeless. I thank GOD for the actions of the cops and for the changes that happened.

I wanted to have another talk with Joe, one that would take a whole night, so I could reason things out with him and tell him more about my situation. I knew Joe had a connection with the Church of the Almighty God, but I had to ask him about his abduction because of what he had told me before.

I had realized that if Joe had been abducted once, he might have been abducted again because there were so many abduction incidents in North America that some abductees must have been abducted multiple times. And finding the truth would confirm who Joe really was.

The grand opening of one of my family's new Asian grocery stores was going to happen in Vancouver on July 30th 2018, and that gave me an opportunity to meet Joe again. Before flying to Vancouver, I rehearsed for another meeting with Joe; I brought my aura camera with me to take more pictures, but I had forgotten it was fucked, only remembering when I got to Surrey, BC.

When I got to Vancouver, the first thing on my mind was fixing my aura camera. I went to the dollar store next to my family's new store to buy a glue gun; I wasn't worried about the grand opening, just about repairing the camera.

But when I went to the store during the setup for the grand opening, Joe began to condemn the safe injection sites that were being set up in BC. He said that the injection sites were evil things and had evil spirits involved.

I said I believed those sites were made to save lives. I also told him I had a different solution: instead of just having places to get safe injections, why didn't they also have monitored room and board, keeping the users safely out of public sites? I also had a solution for heroin users: providing them with doses of high-THC weed as an alternative drug while they were in the controlled environment of those safe havens.

I asked Joe what the difference was between a weed user, a mushroom user and a Junglee injector—he used weed and mushrooms a lot, so how could he condemn people who used other drugs?

And then, what was the difference between a person drinking at home and a homeless person drinking on the street? The person who drank at home actually had a home to come to, but for the homeless person, their only home was the street, and that was the difference.

People condemned the homeless, but the homeless were just ordinary people. And they had to drink even if they had nowhere else to do it. Sometimes, they had to drink to keep warm because it was cold and lonely in the streets. Drug users also needed to keep warm.

Every homeless person's story was different, and all of them were unique. I had seen hope and faith in the eyes of the people on the streets, like Richard and Riel. I had talked to them; some were my friends. I had heard their pain and struggles. I had helped them as best I could, but sometimes I was out of my depth because they needed professional help.

But there were still common issues. Most of them had fallen or gone downhill because of the drug trade. A lot of them were abandoned. I thank GOD for organizations like the Hope Mission that give out shelter and food, but someone needed to hear the stories of the homeless, and that did not happen until a group that I'll call the outreach group did it, but it still happened.

I once knew a homeless person who came to my store regularly; his name was also Richard, and when I found out that all he had to get drunk on was mouthwash, I would buy him beer.

Richard was angry because no one saw his pain. He was on the street for 20-30 years until the cops and a local outreach group—I can't remember their name—helped him. Now, he has a home through social programs funded by the City of Edmonton. He sometimes drifted back into his old habits, but the cops always brought him back to where he was supposed to be. It showed me that there was hope for homeless people if they got the right support.

But Joe did not want to listen to any of this. While we were in the storage room at the back of the store, Joe said that even though he also used drugs, at least he went to work. He cursed and condemned the homeless and then joked and said they were a lost cause and full of demons. He then changed the subject and started to tell me about the time he was on a hill at his acreage and high on acid. Joe said he'd hallucinated an octopus and started shooting at it with his shotgun, and I said he was a drug user: I reminded him he was just like them.

Finally, Joe and I got some personal time together at my sister's house. As I said, I've watched a lot of shows about alien abductions. I knew that my knowledge of abductions would lead Joe to feel and sense I had told him the truth about my experience with UFOs, so he would tell me the true story of his abductions.

I told him about the two times I had blacked out, including when I drove to Vancouver to visit Tran. I told him about my own encounters with UFOs. They scare me, I said.

He said, "You know what, Rico? I know that I got abducted two times." He said it first happened to him at age 9 and then at age 21. Joe told me about them in detail and then said, "I feel violated."

It shocked me. *Fuck, this is scary,* I thought. It was like *The Twilight Zone.* Like *Dreamcatcher.* I knew abductions were the result of evil forces, ones that don't know where or when they wanted to abduct someone, and so they adducted mostly North American people because abductions were widely documented here.

I had a new theory: one documentary said that many of these abduction reports included human cloning and soul transference, so what if most abductees were taken when they were younger? What if, after they had adducted kids and teens, the aliens cloned them to get a copy of their memories before sending their original selves back to Earth? This was exactly what Joe meant when he said he got adducted two times and felt violated. Again, it was like *Dreamcatcher.*

What if the UFOs knew of the coming of the MESSIAH (me) and were trying to prevent the world from turning towards the light of GOD by changing JOE into Joe, making him believe he was the other Christ and an enemy to me?

I only needed to find out if Joe got abducted a third time; if he did, that would confirm my theory. If Joe was only abducted twice, he would just have been cloned and returned without anybody knowing, but if he was abducted a third time, he would have had a weird paranormal experience, going through astral travel and becoming the other Christ.

But right when I was on a roll with Joe and ready to ask him, my dumb brother-in-law came in and disturbed us. So, I changed my focus and asked Joe what he thought Luke 17:26-30 meant. I told him we should prepare. I told him that Revelation was not a metaphor or symbolic but actually predicted a real-life event.

He didn't believe me and kept on saying the Revelation was metaphorical and symbolic; maybe he was trying to pretend everything was okay. I asked how else he could explain the prediction that all ocean life would die. How else could he explain a burning mountain being thrown into the sea?

I heard voices inside me shouting, "Go for the KILL!" It meant I had to make Joe snap by putting more facts into him. I did that, pointing out that the prophecies of religions all over the world matched up with the events of Revelation.

And then I had to show Joe my power. Because Joe could not hear my clairaudience or my voice, I told Joe I heard a voice coming from the sky, and I pretended I was scared, but I wasn't: it was just a white lie.

He told me to just make the voices go away. I pretended to listen to him, and I just shouted out, "Voices go away!" And the voices went away.

Then, a day after the grand opening, Joe attacked me from behind with his words, showing off to my other brother-in-law by saying to me, "You were the big boss when you were in Calgary. You caused crime."

Joe was just like the voices, telling me wrong things about myself, and when I confronted him, he denied everything. I didn't know why he would do that to me.

I had to go home the next day, so I just left Joe behind in Vancouver without finding out if he had been abducted a third time. I was very disappointed because I didn't confirm my theory. I think I failed to find the truth because there were too many people around.

Shortly after my visit with Joe, I found the White Horse Prophecy, which was my first encounter with Mormonism. It led me further towards the truth. Inside it, Edwin Rushton quotes Joseph Smith, who says, "I want to tell you something of the future. I will speak in a parable like unto John the Revelator. You will go to the Rocky Mountains, and you will be a great and mighty people established there, which I will call the White Horse of peace and safety."

The Rocky Mountains refer to Alberta, and the so-called White Horse is actually me. Because of this, along with the voice of the Angel of Heaven, I know that the safest place to start work on the Aquarium Ark is Alberta, which is inland and close to the mountains and not close to any tsunamis.

I pray and pray for this to stay true and for Alberta to stay the safest place for the project. I especially want Edmonton to be safe because the majority of my family and friends live here. In the end, I trust that GOD will protect me and that the prairies will be the safest place of all because the angel said, "Yes."

It was May 23, 2023, when I first read the Book of Enoch, the lost book of the Bible, and it saved my life. The Book was hidden from the world for two thousand years, guarded by the Angels of Heaven. Humans did not find any ancient copies of the Book of Enoch until their discovery among the Dead Sea Scrolls in the 1940s-50s, and this confirmed the Book of Enoch was an actual piece of ancient writing and part of a whole missing piece of the Bible.

Most Christian and Jewish groups do not accept the Book of Enoch, but Beta Israel, the Ethiopian Orthodox Tewahedo Church and the Eritrean Orthodox Tewahedo Church make it part of their scripture. I believe that the Angel of GOD hid the book of Enoch until I could find it during the Battle of Earth.

The Book of Enoch is also directly opposed to the teachings of the Church of the Almighty God. It does not tell of the Heaven of the Church of the Almighty God's preaching but instead tells of the ten different levels of Heaven.

It says: "[19]I saw there seven stars like great burning mountains, and to me when I inquired regarding them. The angel said: "This place is the end of heaven and earth. This has become a prison for the stars and the host of heaven" (*English Standard Version* 1 Enoch 6.19). Heaven to my eye, is the sky, and these different levels include all the galaxies and then the universe, showing again that science (astronomy) and religion are connected.

Most importantly for my journey, the Book of Enoch talks about a type of Angel called a "watcher" and among the Angels are both the good watchers and bad watchers, also known as fallen Angels. There are more bad watchers than good, and GOD also sent the Flood to destroy the fallen Angels that reside on

Earth. But the fallen Angels are still here, and I have to prepare the world for the final Battle of Earth with the Fallen Angels by telling you everything I know about the different types of Angels.

I had spent a long time being confused about the things I'd seen in the sky: The Shadows, the UFOs, and the auras. I almost went crazy several times, but after reading the Book of Enoch, I finally figured out that the evil UFOs who I'd commanded to appear at 411 were fallen Angels, though some of the fallen Angels were Shadows and some were physical matter.

The fallen Angels were all preparing to stop me, the MESSIAH, from uniting the world and saving humanity. This is the fallen Angels' last hope of combatting the Light because the Archangel Michael and his Angels have battled the Dragon and driven the fallen Angels out of Heaven (as said in Revelation 12:7-12).

Meanwhile, the good UFOs, the auras in the sky, and the orbiting white objects were signs that the Angel of Heaven was following me. The Book of Enoch explained the truth in Enoch 1, Chapters 3 and 7 by naming the Angels who had come to Earth and were still here:

[1]And it came to pass when the children of men had multiplied that in those days were born unto them beautiful and comely daughters. [2] And the angels, the children of the heaven, saw and lusted after them, and said to one another: "Come, let us choose us wives from among the children of men and beget us children[3]." And Semjaza, who was their leader, said unto them: "I fear ye will not indeed agree to do this deed, and I alone shall have to pay the penalty of a great sin." [4] And they all answered him and said: "Let us all swear an oath, and all bind ourselves by mutual imprecations not to abandon this plan but to do this thing" (1 Enoch, 3.1-4).

[1] And these are the names of the holy angels who watch mankind. / [2] Uriel, one of the holy angels, who is over the world and over Tartarus. / [3]Raphael, one of the holy angels, who is over the spirits of men. / [4]Raguel, one of the holy angels who takes vengeance on the world of the luminaries. / [5]Michael, one of the holy angels, to wit, he that is set over the best part of mankind and over chaos. / [6] Saraqael, one of the holy angels, who is set over the spirits who sin in the spirit. / [7]Gabriel, one of the holy angels, who is over Paradise and the serpents and the Cherubim. / [8] Remiel, one of the holy angels, whom God set over those who rise. (1 Enoch 7.1-8).

Whatever Heaven's Angels can do, these fallen Angels can do. Reading this, I realized the many telepathic attacks on me were proof that mankind could be telepathically manipulated by fallen Angels, just like Joe tried to do to me, just like the Devil tried to do to Jesus in Matthew 4:1-11, just like the Church of the Almighty God once tried to manipulate me by saying, "Go to Tibet."

(I can't remember when CAG said that, but if I did go, they would have won because I couldn't challenge them from that far away.)

I began to ask: if fallen Angels could manipulate men with telepathy, were they responsible for even more of the terrible things in world history? For example, what if the fallen Angels had tempted Christian kings and churches into banning the public printing of the Bible so that the authorities could keep a monopoly on power over the people and the fallen Angels could prevent GOD's word from spreading freely?

Then, fallen Angels could have also telepathically manipulated priests and kings to attack the Natives and force them into residential schools, trying to wipe out the Native heritage, traditions, and the guidance of Mother Earth while making the priests and kings believe they were doing this for the Natives' benefit.

Fallen Angels have also tried to make schizophrenics look bad by telepathically manipulating them to commit horrible crimes, like the way they manipulated Will Baker, formerly known as Vince Weiquang Li, to kill and behead 22-year-old Tim Mclean in 2008 after Baker heard what he thought was "the voice of God". They do this because schizophrenics have telepathic power that can fight the fallen Angels, which the schizophrenics won't be able to use if they are in jail. I am an example of this power, a sorcerer by nature, as I brought down the UFO outside my condo, and there were conspiracies to put me into a mental hospital and discredit me.

The Church of the Almighty God/Eastern Lightning is helping the works of the fallen Angels by trying to keep everything the same, where only a few people hold great power and control the entire system. This is the system of the Beast and, therefore, controlled by the fallen Angels. And I will expose the Church of the Almighty God and what they preach to the world.

And there are signs that humanity can defeat the Fallen Angels. The Angels of Heaven were the ones who helped Johannes Gutenberg develop the printing press and print the Gutenberg Bible for a wide audience in 1455. This opened the eyes of the world to the word of Christ and made it easier for Christian scholars to crack the meaning of Jesus' words and death and see that Jesus died to forgive mankind's SINs and prepare the Revelation.

Slowly, the Angels of Heaven are removing the poison of the Fallen Angels from the world, secretly working hard under the Dragon tree to change this world. Helping the activists and the revolutionists they will end slavery and end the division of humanity by color. In 1855, Sweden abolished the death penalty for theft, and there are many other examples of the works of the Angels of Heaven.

The Book of Enoch also provided clues to the strengths and weaknesses of fallen Angels and ways to fight them. In 1 Enoch, Chapter 6, 20-21, it says: "[20] And the stars which roll over the fire are they which have transgressed the commandment of the Lord at the beginning of their rising because they did not come forth at their appointed times. [21] And He was wroth with them, and bound them till the time when their guilt should be consummated for ten thousand years." The Book of Enoch even describes the location of their hideout, which is the next frontier of man when man will reach the curtain of Heaven.

The Book of Enoch is like my sword: it tells of souls and Heaven and different Angels, and this makes it a weapon against the Church of the Almighty God, as the CAG doesn't believe in souls or Heaven, only the Old Testament and dust becoming dust. My other weapons are wisdom, understanding, research and guidance versus the powerful third eye of the other Christ. The Church of the Almighty God does not see that GOD planted a hidden seed under the Dragon tree in the form of the Book of Enoch.

Meanwhile, a few years ago, my mother told me about an important dream she had. I can't remember exactly when she told me it happened, but it was after I was put into the mental hospital in 2010. And because my mother was gifted, I listened closely when she told me the story.

She had dreamed that Joe was standing before the gates of Heaven but dressed in red. In my dreams, red represented lost souls, and also souls trapped within the earth, in their own type of Hell. I knew this because when I was younger, I had dreamed of my grandfather wearing red. He was sitting on a rotating chair, and I heard a voice saying in Vietnamese, "That is you, grandfather. Look at him." I later realized it meant my grandfather had never made it to Heaven but stayed in Hell. And in my other dreams, I saw my uncle and grandmother in white, which meant they were in Heaven.

I used these dreams to interpret my mother's vision: it meant Joe was now at the gates of Heaven. I wondered if it meant Joe was dead, and if so, he would have died in vain because I had never found out whether Joe had been abducted by a UFO a third time.

But then I had a clairvoyant feeling, and my clairaudience told me that Joe was *not* dead and that the vision was about the time Joe's girlfriend had broken up with him in 2003. 2003 was the same year I received the message from the Dancing Cloud about the Fire, about the Devil who would burn. There was a connection: the moment I commanded evil to appear, it made the UFO fall out of the sky, and it was the same UFO that had abducted Joe.

And the more I had tested Joe, the more scared I had become. The more he had revealed about his abduction, the more I knew that what clairaudience told me about him was not wrong. That was why, when my mom told me of her vision of Joe, I got scared; that was another sign that my clairaudience was right about Joe being the other Christ. It scared the shit out of me.

Then, a week or two after getting back to Edmonton, Joe called me and said he wanted to talk to me again. I was excited to get another chance to find out the whole truth, so I told him I agreed and booked a flight to Vancouver.

Once I arrived there, I went to my family's store, which my sister was currently running. I asked her if she had any place to rest because I was tired. She said I could nap in the security room on the other end of the building, but when I went there, I couldn't relax. I tried to meditate, but I was too excited about ending things between Joe and me.

So, I gave up trying to sleep, and as I was walking back to the other end of the store, I heard a male voice say, "Joe has a third eye." But I knew that even if Joe had the power to foresee things with his third eye, he couldn't see me because I was still protected by my boy and girl spirits before. But the words were a warning: that Joe knew why I was coming to him. It was like he knew what I was going to ask him; I think I had spooked him with my questions, and now he had had time after our last meeting to prepare his third eye.

Even with that on my mind, I was still very excited to talk to Joe again. We met up at my sister's house, and I can't remember everything that we talked about, but Joe had spent so much time on the Church of the Almighty God's website that he believed I had committed all the SINs they were against.

At one point I got mad at him and told him that all the stories he told about me from decades ago were wrong. Like the way he talked about me always hiding upstairs and drinking during school when I had only had the beer to take a break, coming up from my room downstairs into the living room to do it. Back then, I was only drinking and partying to help relieve my anxiety, and I wasn't the one who caused gang problems in Calgary.

Despite what I said to him, Joe still smiled, proud of himself and convinced he was right about everything. I still loved Joe, but his lies puzzled me a little: if Joe was the other Christ, why didn't he know the right details about my past?

At one point in our meeting, Joe got scared and said, "The other is listening," and then everything in the room changed, including Joe's tone. It felt like he was holding something back because he was afraid of this "other" listening.

Then he said, "Out of the abyss," and I realized he thought I was the abyss and that the "other" were the groups protecting me, both Lilian and the detectives.

Joe was panicked and scared, but I was only telling him the truth. Every time I confronted Joe, I wished that telling him the truth would stop him from attacking me. I also wished that telling the truth would stop everyone from attacking me.

I still had so much to talk to Joe about, but I saw a purple aura moving toward the house. I shouted to Joe, "Do you see that moving star, that aura?"

He turned his head and said, "No, no."

I think he knew what that meant: his third eye was limited, and he couldn't see my Angel. He seemed even more spooked and scared.

Then Joe said he had to go to bed. I was supposed to spend all night with Joe, but now he had changed his mind. Because of this, I finally knew Joe was the other Christ, and I knew that he knew that I knew. I had finally found the other Jesus; my Angelic horseman had pinpointed him, and now Joe could not hide from that Angel's eyes; an Angel could see everything, and so could GOD's eyes. I now knew who was who, including who Joe actually was.

But to this day, Joe has never admitted that he is the other Christ. On the day of March 2, 2025, I challenged Joe because I wanted to end our battle, but he wouldn't come to meet me. He has been hiding from me and refusing to attend family events where we might meet up. That is tragic, but when I confirmed he was the other Christ, then the Battle of Earth truly began for me.

I don't have any regrets for taking so long to get confirmation because I had tested Joe with no harm done, while his testing of me was very psychologically harmful.

While all this was happening, I kept going to work. In my battle against the Church of the Almighty God, around the time I read the Book of Enoch, I met a man named Erines Jones, who was a follower of a Christian church that I don't want to name; he is one of that church's elders. I won't name this group because I don't want to start a genocide in another part of the world. I was afraid that if I named them, its people might get revenge by using violence, the way you hear stories about Buddhists killing Muslims in Asia.

We talked about everything. He said that the Catholic Church had made idols out of the Cross and the Virgin Mary, and when he said that, I instantly knew I didn't belong to his group because I had statues of the Virgin Mary and an Archangel in my backyard to remind me of my purpose.

Playing dumb, I asked Ernie to tell me more about his group. I learned that they did not believe in ghosts or Angels but saw them as the Devil's work. They only used the Old Testament and forgot the New Testament. They also talked about how only the chosen 144,000 would go to Heaven. These things made it even clearer that this group was not on my side.

Eventually, I would realize that his religious group was another branch of the Dragon group, and that meant I had more enemies.

I told Jones about how the Church of the Almighty God condemned people publicly, just like I was condemned publicly by everyone around me. I told him that was why I had eventually broken contact with the CAG, and I had copies of their statements to prove that was what they were doing.

I did a Bible study with Jones, and though I already knew a lot about the CAG, I didn't have a friend inside the group until Jones. Jones told me more about the beliefs of the Church of the Almighty God. He said things in their beliefs represented me, but these things were not like me, not only because I didn't believe in them, but because their words were not my speech, being in perfect English. But my friendship with Jones empowered me to the point where I believed he was on my side, even if his group wasn't. Then Jones also showed me how to ground myself with the Book of Mormon and identify the Holy Spirit, the act which is the last line of defense against the unimaginable powers of the Shadows.

Later, my research would bring me to a Bible study with the local Mormons/Jesus Christ Church of Latter-day Saints, where, because I am still Curious George, I asked them many important questions, especially those about the Book of Mormon.

The Book of Mormon is an important book because all humans are dealing with the Shadows of the Sky, and the Book of Mormon helps you to see and feel the Holy Spirit, who will fight the Shadows. The Book of Mormon also describes the Holy Spirit at work to help others identify when it happens. The

CAG believes that only their false God has the gift of the Holy Spirit. They believe that any other person with the Holy Spirit is the work of the Devil, showing again that they want to control humanity. But the Book of Mormon believes the Holy Spirit is for anyone who believes in GOD.

So, the Book of Mormon is also powerful because its existence means an average citizen (like Joseph Smith) could contact the Holy Spirit and receive a message. This meant the New Age practitioners were also right: one could learn how to identify the true Holy Spirit from the dark Shadows of the sky or earth.

If every believer is open to the Holy Spirit, then it proves that white witches, telepaths, and good psychics are the work of the Holy Spirit. Meanwhile, the CAG does not believe in telepaths, psychics, or white witches at all because, again, that would mean that the Holy Spirit was for someone besides their group.

The CAG also says that the Holy Land is not in Israel but in Canaan, which equals Canada. Supposedly, the battle of Armageddon will be in Canada while other scholars and religious leaders are waiting for it to happen in Israel.

During a workday, Jones gave me the Book of Psalms to read. There were so many psalms, and I skimmed through them until I found Psalm 3:7, where David prayed for aid from GOD: "7 Arise, O Lord! / Save me, O my God! / For you strike all my enemies on the cheek; / you break the teeth of the wicked" and Psalm 35:1-3: "1Contend, O Lord, with those who contend with me; / fight against those who fight against me! / 2Take hold of shield and buckler / and rise for my help! / 3Draw the spear and javelin[a]/against my pursuers! / Say to my soul, "I am your salvation!""

The psalms were prayers for me because so many had attacked me that I was overwhelmed and drained. They came from the left and from the right, from the back and from the front. Night and day, they attacked; I had no sleep. Everywhere I went, they attacked. I was attacked by both strangers and people I knew, including my family members whom I loved. It seemed like everyone hated me; I was so lonely. I had nobody and nowhere to hide or rest. I was so manipulated that I thought I was evil, too, because the attacks were so intense.

I now believe Tony was responsible for a particular attack on my co-worker in 2019, where his arm got fucked up for life. My co-worker was very protective of me, and I feel responsible for this attack. I felt like the attackers wanted me, but I had left early that day, when I usually stayed until 3 p.m., meaning my co-worker took the attack for me.

My most recent UFO sighting took place in Kelowna, BC, on July 28, 2019, when I was going there for my daughter's basketball tournament. It happened when I was meditating on the beach at night; I looked up and saw two stars that were much brighter than the rest, and then one started to move towards me, and the other followed.

I realized they were UFOs. One was a flashing, colorful UFO, and the other was a white UFO orbiting around it. The white, orbiting UFO was my cavalry, chasing away the colorful UFO. It felt like I was dreaming.

On the way back home, I saw only the white, orbiting UFOs, a group of them, appearing one by one and disappearing one after the other. I can't explain what they meant.

But by the summer of 2019 I was so scared and afraid. I didn't know what to do anymore; I felt hopeless, and the attacks never stopped. I didn't know how to fight. I had so much faith and hope, but now I have so much despair and weakness.

I was broken by the attacks and cursed myself and condemned myself because I knew the Revelation was true. I didn't want people to die in masse, and I didn't want to be Christ. I would rather be false than true because it would mean the Revelation wouldn't happen.

After understanding the meaning of the number 411, I had prayed multiple times that only I would suffer, but after understanding more about the Revelation, I became heartbroken as I realized I was carrying a big burden on my shoulders and had so many future deaths on my hands. I was in so much pain that I didn't want to live anymore, but I don't believe in suicide. So, I asked GOD to take me.

Then, in August 2019, my wife and the kids went to Flying Dust Nation for hockey camp. They left our dog with me, a French Bulldog named Penny.

Penny was a miracle dog. Once, she fell off my daughter's bed and hurt herself. We took her to the vet, who sent us to a specialist who X-rayed Penny and then gave her an MRI. The specialist said that Penny had a spinal neck injury and needed surgery, which would cost $10,000, with a 50/50 chance of surviving surgery and a 50/50 chance of recovery after that.

We didn't have the money because our pet insurance was maxed out, and we decided to take Penny home with some painkillers and let her stay with the kids for a week before putting her down.

Everyone in the family was crying in fear when we brought Penny home. That night, I told my kids to go to my room and told every one of them to pray out loud, with all our hearts. So, we prayed and prayed, and my daughter prayed the most beautiful prayer.

Within a few days, I noticed Penny was up and walking a little bit. I slowly took her off the painkillers while we prayed every day. And within one week, Penny was hopping into my lap and running around the house again. It was a mini-miracle that came from our prayers.

The second night after my family left, as I was sleeping beside Penny in the bed, I felt something on my shoulder. When I turned my head to see what it was, I saw a glowing shining light there. I freaked out; I thought I was going to be taken away by GOD because I had asked Him to. I was so broken that I thought I would now die in a fire.

I turned to my dog and shouted, "PEENNNY!" because I was scared and she was the only one there. She looked up and, made a small sound, and just took off out of the room. I turned back one more time and saw the figure of a man within the light. Then he said to me, "Let me put this in your spine."

I then felt a sharp pain in the middle of my spine, but within seconds, the pain triggered a good feeling. Then, it spread all over my body, flooding me. It was so good that I blacked out, and when I woke up, my clairaudience kicked in, saying that I now had wings and that this was because of the Archangel Michael, who had been the man within the light.

The encounter made me stronger and gave me the courage to finish my journey, redefining me into a bulletproof Jesus. I would continue to follow my purpose in life: warning the world about the Revelation and taking down the Dragon group.

Contact with Michael

I can't explain it further, but after this encounter, my sex drive also came back. A few years before this, I had gotten a vasectomy because my wife asked me to, and the surgeon who did it had burned one of my balls to hell. He did the other ball normally, but on the other, it had burned until I screamed out loud.

The incident drove my sexual desire down to nothing. I think the doctor did it on purpose because he had heard what Joe said about me and about the sin of sexual immorality, and so he did something to lessen my sex drive. But nobody believed my story about the surgeon; when I told the story to my wife and my friends, they just laughed.

But after my visit from the Archangel Michael, I found my sex drive was almost back to normal. I also had more energy than I had before. It was like I was my old self again, with a mojo like I'd had twenty years ago. All the aches and pains in my bones were gone. My sense of taste was back. I was stronger than before.

I still had a cough, but that could have been because of my smoking because I had not changed any of my eating habits or exercise habits. Before then, I'd been totally burned out and had no energy because of the attacks. I had prayed for it to get better, and now my prayers were answered.

I began to wonder if the Angel Michael had not only given me wings but also something else. Something I couldn't see? Within a day of my visitation from Michael, I called a psychic online, one I'd never contacted before. I told them about the change I had undergone, and the psychic told me that there was another meaning to the visitation: when an Angel put his hand on your shoulder, it meant you shouldn't travel anywhere. I was planning to go to Italy next March with my wife on a surprise trip before her new business opened, but because I was religious, I obeyed what Michael had told me and cancelled the trip.

Then, within two days of the visitation from Michael, a blind man came into my store. We chatted, and he said he was an empath who could see Shadows, auras, and Angelic guidance. He offered to give me a reading. I said yes, and then he looked into me and saw a light behind me. He said I had a strong Archangel present, and at that moment, I knew I had to go to the New Age bookstore on 124 St.

So, I left work, and when I got inside, I heard all different types of voices speaking, including female voices saying, "You have brought us back to GOD" and "You have united us." I knew they were trying to tell me to find a book. I searched the store until I heard a male voice say, "Pick that," and guess what I picked? A book about the Archangel Michael: *The Miracles of Archangel Michael* by Doreen Virtue.

I wasn't sure what It meant, so I went to the psychic inside the bookstore to make sure I wasn't dreaming, that this had really happened to me, and to reconfirm what the first psychic had told me about travelling. This psychic also said I shouldn't travel.

In December 2019, we had a staff Christmas party. On that day, I had already been attacked in so many ways, and at the staff party, I was attacked from all directions by my staff and other people working for my dad's company.

There was nowhere to turn, but to alcohol and to my Lorazepam anxiety pills I took to go with my Invega; I had begun to take medication again because my wife had gotten mad at me for taking weed. I just drank and drank, so I'd become so drunk I didn't give a shit about anything. Then I blacked out and couldn't remember anything when I woke up. It gave me the illusion of having escaped the attacks during the Christmas party, but within a day of the party, the attacks continued again.

They came because I was fighting the second front of a two-front war. I have won my battle on the first front against Joe and the Dragon group, against educated enemies who banded together to spread a false word of GOD. I won the battle because I found the 144,000 and got them to start helping me win over the masses of the world. It's been happening ever since my trip to the Dominican Republic mentioned below, and I just feel they've done something, even though the CAG is still around.

Now, I am fighting my war on the second front. The second front of the war started when I heard a voice in the parking lot following my office Christmas party: one of the voices said, "Tony is GOD," and I realized that Tony had supported the criminals and the uneducated in their attacks on me, the people who blame the system for their problems without finding any solutions. Tony must be like Joe, predicting what I'll do next. They both had some kind of power that let them predict what I would do next.

And the attacks continued nonstop. I even tried to ask the people attacking me to stop, but it didn't work. I went to my staff to tell them not to attack me, but they still continued, making me just want to black out again. And because my wife wanted me to increase my medication's dosage, I didn't talk to her about it, either.

In January 2020, the coronavirus hit the world. When I first saw the news of the outbreak in China, fear overcame me, the fear of GOD and the Revelation. And because I was an empath, I knew this outbreak was not normal. Yes, it felt like the start of something.

In 2002, before SARS (Severe Acute Respiratory Syndrome) and before COVID-19, I was very sick and with all of the symptoms that would come with COVID-19. I had had a fever, lost my sense of taste, had aches and pains in my bones, a cough, a loss of breath, and was always weak and tired. I slept all the time and was living off Advil and Tylenol, and without them, I couldn't have gone to school and work. Sometimes, when I got home, I was so drained and sick that I would just sleep, but every day, I went back to work and lived my life, taking bathroom breaks when I needed to hide my cough.

I went to doctor after doctor, and they all said I had TB (Tuberculosis) instead because of the x-rays that found blackness in my lungs. But TB was just a serious lung infection caused by bacteria that can spread through the air, and I realized that my sickness was because I had committed adultery.

Then, when the SARs outbreak happened in June 2003, I suspected I had caused it and brought the apocalypse; hearing the word "SARS" constantly triggered me. And then, COVID-19 turned out to be related to SARS, which led to my realization that I was the sleeper agent for the coronavirus.

And it had happened because I was angry and had snapped my fingers like Thanos. It was the fucking Church of the Almighty God that caused me to snap my fingers, the group that kept trying to make me think the world was worse than it actually was. It happened even though I knew I had to be careful about the CAG and more curious about what they were doing.

It started one morning when a CAG agent was by surprise. A guy came into the store and said, "We are going to make you snap." Then I asked him about his tattoo, though I can't remember what the tattoo was. He said he got it in prison, and I got scared. I asked myself, Why? WHY? Why would he show up and intimidate me? I didn't even know him.

But I am sorry I snapped. I am sorry I was like Thanos, who snapped his fingers to end half of the life in the universe, because my snap will bring the Revelation and the end of 1/3 of all life on earth, and it was also one cause of COVID-19.

I followed the coronavirus news very carefully, and the situation got worse by the day. One night, I had a dream that went like this: the coronavirus was spreading and spreading, and I tried to avoid it, but I found out the spreader was me. When I found out that, in the real world, the coronavirus had spread to Italy, I asked Terrick, one of my friends, what if there was a sleeper agent for the virus, a sleeper agent that didn't even know what he was, and now the sleeper had spread the virus all over the world, and the situation was worse than we thought it was?

While the world lockdown began. I thought of the Archangel Michael, who had appeared in my room. It could not be a coincidence that he had told me to avoid traveling to places where the coronavirus would soon arrive.

Michael was protecting me, but the attacks on me continued. One time, I was at the Vietnamese coffee shop in a nearby strip mall, and I saw people that I knew hanging out there or walking in after I did. There were local gangsters and others who had triggered me in the past; they were part of the Dragon group. They didn't say anything about the coronavirus, but they got angry when I said the coronavirus was caused by GOD to show the world the wonder of His works and of prophecy to come, and the world doesn't know that prophecy yet.

I yelled back at them in Vietnamese, telling them to bring out their Jesus, meaning Joe. They told me, in Vietnamese, "It's time to fight your father." Eventually, I left and then realized Tony was behind the attacks by these gangsters.

When I was first studying the Church of the Almighty God's view of the Revelation, I had saved the words of 22:18-19 into a file on my desktop: "[18] I warn everyone who hears the words of the prophecy of this book: if anyone adds to them, God will add to him the plagues described in this book. [19]and if anyone takes away from the words of the book of this prophecy, God will take away his share in the tree of life and in the holy city, which are described in this book." It proved the CAG were a group that used the Bible as a weapon to try to make people convert to their way of thinking.

Then, at the start of the COVID-19 pandemic, my computer crashed. It wouldn't turn on again, and I still don't know why. I thought, *What a coincidence it is.*

It turned out to be an even bigger coincidence than I first thought it was because soon, the website of the Church of the Almighty God exploded with hallelujahs for their God, and the site began to talk about the Revelation nonstop.

At the same time, the website and app of Jones' religious group both went down. It was suspicious because, at the same time it happened, the Church of the Almighty God's website and app had both advanced so much that I couldn't believe it: they had so much traffic and added page after page; they had also blocked me from contacting them. *Weird*, I thought.

I mentioned this to Jones at work, and he said that his group was actually the most advanced, more than any other, and did a lot of online preaching. The next thing I knew, that group's website and app came online again. *Shit. Weird,* I thought. It was like the group had found out I was studying them, and they had shut it down. But they didn't want me to get suspicious, so they launched their website and app again.

Our store had to stay open during the lockdowns because liquor sales were considered essential services; people all over the world were addicted to liquor, and if they didn't get it, they would die.

And as the lockdowns went on, people got very anxious. That kind of chaos can be good for a person or bad for a person, but in this case, I saw people snapping at each other left and right when I was at work. Even my staff freaked out and started snapping at customers, and the customers snapped back at my staff. They snapped at each other for getting too close, or because they bumped into each other, or because they didn't want to sanitize their hands. They were all afraid of the unknown, and the depth of their fear was surprising.

During the pandemic, I ended up purchasing a total of $1,000 CAD worth of masks. First, I spent money on disposable masks and then on reusable masks. Masks were always hell to try and find, and not only was there a mask shortage, but it was also a pain to find hand sanitiser; I started using 99% proof alcohol to sanitize our hands and things at the store.

Even during this time, the attacks on me continued. There was a particular co-worker who attacked me the most and continued to do it even after I asked them to stop. They thought I was joking and kept saying things that triggered me, and when I'd approach them to ask them about what they had said, they kept on denying they'd said anything. At this point, everyone around me was saying things that triggered me, even children I didn't know. I would cry myself to sleep.

One day, another of my co-workers said to me that the railing outside our window was dirty. So, I told her to wipe it down. She said no, she wasn't going to do that. I told her again and said it was an order. She still said no, and I sent her home.

She left the store, but before going home, she walked by the front window and gave me the finger, then pointed downwards, mouthing, *You are fucking going down.*

I could lip-read and knew what she was saying; I guess she hadn't wanted to say anything to me out loud. I was sad seeing her do that, but the next day, when she called the store and told me she couldn't come in, I told her I didn't need her and that she was fired; I later sent her a notice of termination.

A few months after that, she went to the Alberta Labor Relations Board to file a complaint of wrongful dismissal against me and tried to sue my company for harassment and mental abuse. She told the ALRB I had schizophrenia and was abusing her. I don't know exactly what happened after that because human resources took care of it. But knew this incident meant the Dragon group had infiltrated my company and tried to interfere with it.

More evidence began to pile up: I heard a certain sales representative talk about a product that I knew represented me as a Dragon/devil/criminal and gave the product the finger every time they were near it. A certain company we bought from also had a certain sign on their bottle labels, which was another clue.

I was still drinking and taking a lot of anxiety pills, and sometimes, I mixed these things to knock myself out, wishing I would sleep and never wake up because I was in so much pain. I didn't let my feelings show and kept crying in my sleep. I still had nobody to talk to, no friends, no family, and no support group; I felt like I was nobody. I felt like I would rather die than live.

I was afraid of the Shadow of the Sky and of the UFO. I thought that if I didn't get killed by the people attacking me, then maybe the UFO would adduct me, or the Shadow of the Sky would come back one more time to take me away. But I had a mission to complete. I still had faith and strength because of my mission in life. Without the mission GOD had shown me, I think that I would have died.

Then, half a year after COVID-19 had started in China, I had a dream about asking people to build a new ark for all the animals in the sea. It told me that even though I got so much criticism, eventually, I would build this ark. It showed me that the last animal to enter the new ark would be the whale, and when it did, then the destruction would start.

Now, it was the dream of building the ark that kept me going. Without that dream, one day, I might have never woken up and never sent the world my message.

By December 2022, I had divorced my wife and moved into a condo; it was the best thing I had ever done. It brought me peace of mind because I wasn't fighting with her; every time I tried to tell her the truth, she insisted that I should be put back in the hospital or increase the dosage of my medication.

The attacks continued this time from the neighborhood children. But I wasn't that sad anymore because I was determined to build my ark. 2022 was also the year that I started writing my book while searching for new love. While I did, the condemning still continued left and right from the back and the front. It came nonstop and even condemned my search for love.

While I was writing my book, I continued to test the people around me. I did so by writing my words in ways that would test the people who read about my journey, telling them the truth bit by bit so that it would sink into them as they read it. I had to make sure that they truly believed what I was saying and were on my side like the detectives and Lilian's group were.

I told them GOD was the LAW, and they attacked me or just didn't believe me. But I still had to try to reach the right people, and I kept writing my book and trying to find more people who would listen and who weren't part of the Dragon group.

Luckily, my dream of the ark still kept me going. Thirty years ago, my mission was to unite the world's religions as part of the Message of PEACE. Twenty years ago, my mission was to hunt the Devil (the other Christ) and the Dragon. My mission now was to build this ark.

Meanwhile, I was almost done with my book and put it aside to finish later. Somehow, I felt that I would soon meet Lilian again.

In 2023, the third year after COVID-19 began, I was diagnosed with dyslexia. I hadn't even known the name of the condition until I had a co-worker with dyslexia. Before getting the diagnosis, I had thought my mind was playing games with me, but it's more like it was telling me things, like how I picked out certain movies and didn't understand the meaning of my choices until later. It was like my subconscious was guiding me. Therefore, there must be a meaning to every mistake I make, and some messages must be sent.

During the pandemic, Jorda came to visit me at my new place, bringing her friend and some liquor. So, I did what I did best, which was to tell them the story of my journey. But they kept on talking about

Armageddon, even though I hated that word, and I realized that Jorda's friend was part of the unnamed religious group, and both of them had come over to challenge me.

So, I challenged her back by talking about the spirits of the dead, which their group didn't believe in. I told them about a TV documentary that had shown scientific proof of spirits' existence by using Electromagnetic Fields (EMFs) and how an EMF meter, along with a psychic's help, could pinpoint the presence of a spirit. If someone brought an EMF meter to a séance, then every time a spirit talked through the medium, the EMF meter would go off.

I told them there was both medical and scientific evidence of people crossing over before coming back from Heaven and that there were thousands and thousands of records of it, usually from people who had been pronounced dead at the scenes of accidents or during medical operations. I asked them how that could be possible if spirits were not real.

Then I started to talk about the Revelation, especially the verses I quote in Chapter 7. That one-third of the world's population would die and that the current Christian population made up one-third of the world population. I told her about Luke 17:26-30, specifically about the day of Noah being the day of the Son of Man. Like with Joe, I asked her, "What other way was there to explain that all of life in the sea would die?"

Jorda grew mad and upset, and she explained that she viewed the events described in Revelation as just metaphors and symbols; she didn't believe that Revelation actually predicted any real-life disasters. Then she explained her reasons for believing this but couldn't explain the science behind the idea, just like she couldn't explain the science behind spirits and near-death experiences.

She said that only her God Almighty knew the date of the real disaster, and only if you converted to their other group would you be saved. Then she said Joe himself was the Almighty God, and that scared the shit out of me.

Then, the next day, I found out Jones had died of a heart attack, on the same day that Jorda had told me that Joe was God. It was Jorda's friend who called me up and told me, and a few weeks after I went to Jones' funeral, this friend contacted me again. She asked me to go to an Easter celebration with Jones' group, and there I went, becoming Curious George again, because I said why not? But I also made it clear that I was only going for the Bible study.

I went to check it out, and it was so weird but nice in a way. They talked about Jesus, which was cool. But then they also talked about how the 144,000 and that only their 144,000 would eat the bread and drink the wine and serve as king-priests beside Christ for a thousand years. When they said that, I could feel all their eyes watching me. They continued, saying that only the 144,000 were the elite witnesses of God and the new disciples of God.

I wondered, and wondered, but I kept listening, as this group said to prepare and wait, as the 144,000 were working in secret, and some of them were among their group. *Shit,* I thought, *this group was actually top secret.*

I asked them how we could celebrate Christ when only 144,000 people had the right to wine. I felt like I was in the middle of a set-up, and it felt like if I stayed, then the religious group I couldn't name would win, and the Church of the Almighty God would also win.

I waited till the service ended, and I left. I felt used because I had told them I was just here to study the Bible, but they had still tried to convert me, just the CAG. It meant they had always known who I was. It meant they would show up later and again try to convert me to their idea of Jesus.

It was like I was living in the Twilight Zone. *Shit,* I said to myself. *Wow.* This was pretty scary for me. It was just like a horror movie where a cult almost converted the characters, and the leader of the cult was the Devil or like the Devil.

I still had nobody to talk to, but I called on the Alberta Human Rights Commission to file a complaint against the Church of the Almighty God for violating my human rights, my freedom of speech, and my freedom of religion. I told the female AHRC representative everything about my situation, and she said I should talk to a lawyer and offered to refer me to one.

Fuck, I thought. This was truly a conspiracy. Why should I talk to a lawyer? What had I done? This Human Rights Commission had refused to represent me, and it must be because they knew of the Church of the Almighty God and were either scared of them or believed the same things they did.

I realized that both the AHRC and CAG were enemies of sexual immorality, and that was why the AHRC refused to help me: because I had committed sexually immoral acts in the past, and they knew all about them.

Within a month of the conversation on the phone with the AHRC, one member of the unnamed other group approached me and said he wanted to talk to me. I went outside the store to confront him, and once again, he told me of Armageddon and that if I didn't convert, I would die like the rest of the people.

I debated with him about the Revelation, quoting it word for word. He told me that Jesus and his people were being suppressed by the law. Then I told him that if Christians made up one-third of the world's total population, then that meant, in their group's view of the world, that two-thirds of the population of the world would die. But I told him in the book of Revelation it said that only one-third of the world's population would perish. Then, I asked how his group's knowledge of the future differed from what was said in the Book of Revelation. I also told him he left out the thousand years of peace and the fire from the sky at the second release of the Devil.

I told him that he was wrong about the Book of Revelation and he should better study the Bible because Revelation 22:18-19 had said that whoever took words out of the book of prophecy would not get into the book of LIFE. He couldn't reply to my explanation, got mad, and left.

Instead of being scared, I felt good. I had waited and waited so long for this kind of challenge, and now I had won with simple wisdom, even though everybody around me was manipulated. Even the unnamed group was no match for my simple wisdom, and even though this group was all over me, I'd beaten a guy from it.

Then, in April of 2023. I went on a vacation/business trip in the Dominican Republic with colleagues from Sobeys Inc. The fight was long, including a stop in Toronto. When we finally got there, I got triggered; shit, was I mad. I knew this was not going to be a fun trip.

Being there was like déjà vu, and déjà vu was still the only weapon I had that could tell me of the different paths I could choose. In this case, it felt like I had been in the Dominican before, or it was part of a dream from my past, but it was my first time being there. I knew this was a warning from my third eye and that it meant I should stop and slow my mind and think about things, which I did as I went to my room to shower and get ready for the reception, where we would welcome entrepreneurs and other cool people from all over the grocery industry.

Then, on the second or the third day of the trip, the major attacks on me started. I heard one of our regional managers say to me, "Go kill yourself," and shit, it hurt me because I hadn't done anything to him, and he had said that. So, I tried to act cool, but inside, I was afraid and scared.

Attack after attack came, going on for days. I kept my calm, and talking to the resort workers and hookers helped me with that. It kept me going because I saw their dreams and their hopes and knew that there were still good things in the world.

But I was still confused because there were different groups who could be my attackers: the members of Sobeys Corporate who didn't support the changes I'd make with endless wealth, the CAG, or the religious group that I can't name. I didn't know which it was, and I was so confused because there was so much noise around me.

There was also a Native group at the resort, and they didn't like Catholics. But then I began to think: what if the Natives weren't angry at Catholics but at the Church of the Almighty God. CAG had already manipulated people from all parts of the Christian community, and what if the Church of the Almighty God were secretly pretending to be Catholics, even though at other times they had condemned the Catholic Church? And then the Natives in the area only disliked the Almighty God's fake Catholics instead of real Catholics?

But right when the major attacks on me started to happen a cavalry, and I mean a cavalry, came to help in the form of a group of off-duty cops who were on holiday at the resort. When my attackers approached me, they would shout at them to leave me alone.

They revealed themselves slowly: when I was attacked, they counterattacked. Every time a voice attacked me, their voices would counterattack. They also shouted out loud that charges would be laid or told the other group to leave me alone. It was like a tug-of-war between the cops and my enemies.

I knew they were cops because they said so, but I also suspected they were part of the 144,000, or the 144,000 were secretly helping them, and that Lilian and the detectives were also involved.

Their protection gave me comfort, but there were still certain things that I had to keep a secret from the cops because my job as Jesus wasn't finished. I still knew many criminals, and some of them passed through my work and my neighborhood. It would have endangered my life and my family's lives if I told their secrets to the cops.

I figured out that the Church of the Almighty God was the one responsible for the attacks on me at the resort. I told this so-called group to leave me alone, to go. I started my own tug-of-war between them and me, back and forth for almost an entire night. A CAG member whose name I didn't even know walked over to me and triggered me until a cop from the group protecting me told him to leave me alone or they would get charged with a crime or charged when they got back home.

I had to make myself look strong in front of the CAG like a high roller nobody would want to mess with. I stopped talking to the locals except to bargain for things, right down to the nickels and pennies. I spent money buying things like expensive food and drinks, including rum and talked about rough negotiations. That wasn't the kind of person I was, but I had to keep up the appearance. And in the end, I was only pretending to pressure the locals and just paid the full price for things when nobody was looking. I also tipped well so that the people still treated me good.

And while at this resort, I recognized a woman there. Her name was Amanda, and I first knew her twenty-five years ago when she was one of the women I knew during the events of Chapter 3. I approached her and asked her name, and it was still Amanda. I was positive she was from Lilian's group and felt glad and happy.

We started talking and chatting for a bit. I tried to make myself seem like the same person Amanda had known twenty-five years ago, including holding my head in the same way. I might have looked weird, like a stalker, but I kept talking to her. I had to keep my mouth shut about certain things because I was afraid. I didn't want to reveal to anyone else that she was there. I wanted everything I knew to be kept secret because while I was at the resort, I had started writing my book again.

Because, shit, I still didn't know who was only my side at the resort. After meeting Amanda, I was approached by another man who tried to identify himself as a detective, signalling it with a whisper as he passed me. But there were so many people at the resort that I didn't want to expose him, and I only saw him once more, this time from the back.

I was confused, wondering, and wondering. I tried not to show that and keep playing it cool. I reminded myself that I had already planned things out. I had already set up the Detective group and Lilian's group. I had already known twenty-five years ago that I needed them and had planted the seeds. Fourteen years ago, I had told them to infiltrate the Church of the Almighty God.

 I will need them in the future.

I soon realized what my guidance was now telling me: everything I had experienced up until this point meant that the Revelation was no longer a continuous storyline as John had experienced it. Instead, it was a mixture of events.

Now, PEACE was not at hand because of everything that had happened to me and everything that had happened in the world. Maybe by releasing this book, PEACE will come, and the battle of Armageddon will end. Humanity will be free again to prepare for the worst-case scenario as told by the Revelation.

May 30, 2025

The day before I read the Three Secrets of Fatima, I prayed to the Virgin Mary, asking her for guidance and telling her I didn't know what to do. Asking her to give guidance. Then, the next thing I knew, I saw the Three Secrets of Fatima.

Yesterday, I read the story of Three Secrets of Fatima on Facebook. The third secret was something also different from what I read. I message my brother's project publisher manager. Telling him that I find something. I knew about the third secret of Fatima, but I never found out the real third secret of Fatima. So I searched for the third secret of Fatima (Wikipedia The Three Secrets of Fatima are a series of apocalyptic visions and prophecies given to three young Portuguese shepherds, Lucia Santos and her cousins Jacinta and Franciso Marto, by a Marian Apparition, starting on 13 May 1917. The three children Claim to have been visited by the Virgin Mary six times…)

I showed my brother's project Publisher Manager what was public on Wikipedia. It says The third part of the secret reveal at the Cova da Iria-Fatima on 13 July 1917. I write in obedience to you, my God, who command me to do so through His Excellency the Bishop of Leiria and through you, Most Mother, and mine. After the two parts which I have already explained, at the left of Our Lady and a little above, we saw an Angel with a flaming sword in his left hand; flashing, it gave out flames that looked as though they would set the world on fire; but they died out in the contract with the splendor that our Lady radiated towards him from her right hand. Pointing to the earth with his right hand, the Angel cried out in a loud voice: "Penance, Penance, Penance!"

And we saw in an immense light that is God, something similar to how people appear in a mirror when, in front of it, a Bishop dressed in White. We had the impression that if the Holy Father. Other Bishop, Priests, men, and women Religious went up a steep mountain, at the of which there was a big CROSS of rough-hewn trunks like of a cork tree with bark; before reaching there, the Holy Father passed through a big city half in ruins and half trembling with halting step afflicted with pain and sorrow, he met on his way; having reached the top of the mountain, on his knew at the foot of the big CROSS he was killed by a group of soldier who fired bullets and arrows at him, and in the same way there died one after another the other Bishops, Priest, men and women of different and various lay people of different ranks and positions. Beneath the two arms of the CROSS, there were two Angels, each with a crystal aspersorium in his hand, in which they gathered up the blood of the Martyrs and, with it, sprinkled the souls that were making their way to GOD.

I didn't know how important this message was, but it reminded me of a day I do not remember when, but I never knew how important this message was related to me. I was so angry. Kept healing myself. I saw the full moon of the night. The heaven opens up. The horsemen started to descend to earth in the calvary legion of the legion. I remember the commandment of the Virgin Mary, "the commandment of Peace," as I ask GOD to persuade the people of the GOD. To change the source of their heart. The horsemen started to ascend back to heaven. Then Angel of Love came to Earth. Decent out of the door of Heaven. Calvary to legion to legion. I see each individual face as I look into the moon. Angel of LOVE. I was about to unleash fire on Earth because of the pain and suffering I had. Faith, I had. At that time, I had Faith.

But the commandment of the Virgin Mary, the message of the commandment of LOVE, as Archangel Micheal and his horsemen wanted Justice and punishment. As I have two voices in me. The voices of the Virgin Mary are the female voices and the male voices of the Archangel Micheal. I told my project publisher manager how the Virgin Mary has foretold me in the future. The Virgin Mary was describing me.

The arrow and spear, the attack, keep coming. It was during the positustion of the Catholic Church that I defended the Catholic Church. How can I explain? Without my two witnesses, that becomes 144000 that will spread to millions because of the Angel of LOVE. To spread to billions. To the Luke 17, 26-30. The family of Noah is saved. The Family, the Christianity of the Son of Man is Save on the day of LOT.

Did the Virgin Mary foretold me in 1914? The Prophecy of me.

Chapter Ten

What Happens in the Spiritual World will Happen in Reality

Before the Angel Michael appeared in my room, I was very sick. Then the Angel gave me my mojo back, and since then, I have been ready to go.

I had to change my journey's timeline, despite the words of Revelation 22:18: "[18]I warn everyone who hears the words of the prophecy of this book: if anyone adds to them, God will add to him the plagues described in this book. [19] and if anyone takes away from the words of the book of this prophecy, God will take away his share in the tree of life and in the holy city, which are described in this book."

Even so, I added my journey to the timeline of the Revelation. I added the locations, the events, the ark, and my findings about how the natural disasters would play out. I realized that I had brought the prophesied plague by doing this in the form of COVID-19. To everyone who reads this, I ask for all of your forgiveness because I am still adding to my timeline of the events to come as events like the coronavirus change what will happen.

But, even though I had caused COVID-19, the world's response to the virus was eye-opening. The governments of the world showed me that if they wanted to, they could instantly pump billions into finding a cure and get one hundred companies to work together to do it. And within a year, about seven companies thought they had a cure: When it was do or die, everyone could work together.

Then, what if the world's governments pumped billions of dollars into curing all sickness, as I had suggested when discussing endless wealth? Instead of relying on fundraisers or funding from pharmaceutical companies, the government would pump billions of dollars towards each cure and, at the same time, buy out the pharmaceutical companies because those groups are only out to make money, but if they were owned by the government, then they would do more work for cures. Doing this would cure most sicknesses within a decade or two.

The COVID-19 response was eye-opening about senior care, too: if the world's governments could pull together to develop a vaccine, they could also do it to instantly improve senior care. All nursing homes are currently owned by private organizations, who are there to make a profit instead of working for seniors, meaning most nursing homes, including those in Canada, are short-staffed with not so great food, making the residents suffer. But what if the government bought nursing homes and improved them?

Seniors are our elders, our fathers and mothers, grandfathers and grandfathers. They should get the best medical care and support in the world so they can live as comfortable a lifestyle as possible. It's the dream of every child and grandchild to give their elders a life like that.

But even though elders are important, most seniors are nowadays supported and taken care of by their children, and look after their grandchildren when those children have to work. And/or people have to work until they get old and die.

Most seniors have to sell their homes or re-mortgage their homes for a better life or so they can keep affording to live on their own. Senior's personal homes should be bought back by the government, or funded by the government, who would provide the seniors of every country with benefits. Because right now, only the rich seniors can live independently and still enjoy their old age. This is wrong because GOD created all humans to enjoy life. Taking care of the youth is part of a family's duty, but all generations should be able to enjoy life.

In Canada, seniors are given money when they retire. That's a good model for senior support, but nowadays, the Canada Pension Plan is not as good as the private or government pension plans. But in the new age of endless wealth, every senior will have a higher pension and be able to live the life they want.

During the pandemic, governments also gave out checks to help millions of people stay home, like $2,000 CAD per person. This proves that if they wanted to, they could invest more money into social programs. Right now, there are millions and millions of people out of jobs, with no money to support themselves, like how employment insurance only pays a small percentage of your original wage. If governments put more money into social programs, there would be more money for employment insurance, and suffering and worry would end for a lot of people.

Also, nobody should worry about people taking advantage of an improved support system because not everybody takes advantage of it, and if people did try to do that, the government would crack down on them.

Overall, the coronavirus response is proof that the system of endless wealth that I discussed in Chapter 6 is possible. With so much wealth in the world, the government could take control of private wealth and work for the benefit of others.

For example, power plants are currently run by private entrepreneurs who just want to make money. If the government owned the power plants, then power would be affordable for every person in the world. Electricity would be affordable, and water could be free again.

And, if the governments had more money, the wages of the government sector would be the same as the private sector, preventing government workers from leaving for the private sector because they would get more money there.

And then, what if taxes were cut down to a minimum? I have visited Native reserves and seen the people there living more comfortably than in the city because they don't pay taxes and have the extra cash flow for better houses, more toys like quads and boats, and just for a lot more fun in their lives.

But we still have to have some taxes so we can monitor organized crime. For example, Canada's current tax system depends so much on alcohol and certain items, and if there were no taxes on these, then there would be no black market for them, and we would not be able to monitor organized crime through that black market.

It would be like the weed industry, where it's now legal, but because government-controlled weed is taxed, there's still a black market for it, and that black market is tied to organized crime.

Taxing also increases inflation because every time taxes increase in one area or new taxes are introduced, it causes a chain reaction of entrepreneurs raising their prices to make the same profits from before the tax increases/new taxes. And public sector employees also want their wages to go up so they can still enjoy the quality of life even with the increased taxes, but it also doesn't happen.

Therefore, a government with endless wealth must make up for this. Every few years, when the private sector's standard of living gets below that of government workers, the government must increase the minimum wage. This will make sure entrepreneurs keep making the same profits as before, so they will not increase the cost of their products.

It's the same for housing. When taxes increase, interest rates will also increase, and so will the cost of renting. Landlords will have to increase their rent to offset the mortgage rates; this is the same in the retail industry.

If governments eliminated taxes and lowered interest rates, this would decrease inflation. This is shown in the history of property taxes in North America: a few generations ago, people paid only a few hundred dollars in property taxes for their first homes. But as more infrastructure was built, and more social programs were started, taxes increased and caused inflation.

There are already countries with a lot of money, but they don't spend it well. A good example is the United States, a country that is trillions and zillions of dollars in debt because they have so much wealth but usually use it for military spending, and no one says anything.

If they spent money on infrastructure, it would become so advanced and modern. A good example is China: the Chinese have put billions of dollars into their infrastructure, giving it what could be considered a blank cheque; all loans are bank loans, and therefore, a loan does not exist. They use this mostly on the economy, and the government writes off their debts.

Even so, both the US and China are considered to be broke, and no other country says anything about this amount of spending. But what if the world wasn't like that? What if there was endless wealth?

In certain provinces of Canada, insurance is owned by the government and is therefore more affordable than private insurance. Private ownership is, once again, only to make money, not to help the people. Canadian private insurance costs also make it hard for youths to drive cars, and seniors can't even afford insurance if they get into an accident because having insurance will cause their premiums to skyrocket. The control of private insurance is also true for Canadian employment insurance, car insurance, health insurance, and even home insurance. Certain parts of the world don't even have the amount of government-owned insurance that Canada does, and that will change.

World disability support will also improve. Right now, disabled people in most of the world have no income or support; most become beggars or outcasts unless they have rich families. Therefore, they have no opportunities to fulfill their dreams. But in Canada, disabled people have the right to government support and can live happy lives. This will be the model for the rest of the world.

Healthcare is also very important for day-to-day life, but right now, not all parts of the world cover healthcare. In some places, healthcare is very expensive, and the related taxes are very high, so if a family member gets stick, the whole family will end up filing for bankruptcy.

In those countries, only the richest of the rich can afford things like hearing aids, mental health care, sick leave, dental care, eye health, disability aids, and so forth. With endless wealth, all the people of the world will have free and universal healthcare. Anywhere a person travels, they will have the same coverage and always be taken care of. Rec centers will also be free for everyone, so they can have fun and be healthy without having to worry about the cost.

Then, what if public transportation like buses and trains were all free? If they were, more people would use public transportation instead of driving a car, and then, with all public transportation converted to electric vehicles and trains, there would be less pollution and fewer emissions.

Primary (K-6) and secondary (high school) education will also be free for everyone, from youth to adulthood because education is everything. Knowledge is everything. And everyone's education needs to be different because everyone is different. Everyone's intelligence is different, and everyone develops at different rates. So, there will be support and special programs in every school for all levels of learning, from those with learning disabilities to academic students. When I was in school, they put me into the wrong speech program because of a lack of funds. With infinite wealth, that would not happen.

Not all parts of post-secondary education will be free, however. Most of it will be subsidized, to avoid students having to take out loans, but also to avoid having colleges and universities overflowing with students who are lazy and unmotivated because they didn't work to get their post-secondary education.

Labour laws and work safety laws will also be standardized across the world. The rights and freedoms of workers will be universal, creating a healthy work environment for all. Most people around the world work long hours and all days of the week, but if GOD rested on the seventh day, then humans should also get to rest two days of the week.

In Canada, the maximum work week is 40-44 hours, and anything else is considered overtime and paid more; there is also a consistent minimum wage throughout Canada. That's a good way to do it, but in most parts of the second and third world, there is not even a minimum wage. With endless wealth, there will be a universal minimum wage throughout the world, which will make sure the majority of the world has the same standard of living.

The problems with certain jobs will also be addressed. In most parts of the world, farmers and fishermen are poor. They have important jobs but are so busy struggling to make ends meet that they never get to experience a life outside of work and never get out to see the world; in bad weather, they can lose their catches or crops and then have no other income.

But in Canada, farmers in certain sectors are subsidized by the government; they get to travel and enjoy life. This is what will happen for all farmers and fishermen once endless wealth is achieved. And subsidizing fishermen by lessening the cost of a fishing license is especially important because when fishermen don't have to work so hard to make ends meet, they won't overfish, and fish species will not be endangered, even if they aren't considered protected yet. This is part of endless wealth's new frontier of environmental support and leaves marine biologists free to study the animals that will be on the Aquarium Ark.

Engineers are paid a lot right now, and under endless wealth, both the police and the military will get paid just as much. In the news, it says the police and the military already get paid a lot, but they put in a lot of overtime, so they don't get paid as much as it seems.

In order to do the best job, the police and the military will get shorter hours and there will be more police out on the street. They not only make people comfortable, secure, and safe but are also heroes who put their lives on the line every day, going into the unknown when one day they might never see their families again. They should get to enjoy time with their friends and families, which is so important in life.

And finally, the police and the military are the guardians of Earth who will develop new weapons and technology to withstand the Dragon and the UFOs (the fallen Angel of Heaven).

With endless wealth, the world currency rate will be the same, and no country will be richer than any other. And when the money is distributed equally, then people will be able to travel and see the beauty of other countries. This will help the world become unified, like one country.

The one world system is the future of mankind. I was told to "Use Canada," and as I've shown you, Canada is not perfect, but the work of the 144,000 will make it perfect in the future. The money from endless wealth will be distributed by a central government, using Canada's democracy as a model: the provinces represent the countries of the world, the Supreme Court of Canada represents the world court, and the Royal Canadian Mounted Police (RCMP) represents a model for the police of the world.

And then, that model will spread to other nations. The world will have one money system and one government, with each country serving as a province. In this system, no country would take advantage of the endless wealth to become richer than anyone else or funnel the money into the development of secret projects. There will be no power struggles between countries, and there will not be rich countries to take advantage of poorer countries.

Countries will, however, receive different amounts of money depending on their location, population, geography, and needs. Where there are natural disasters, the central government will send millions or billions of dollars to rebuild and stabilize the economy or infrastructure of the area.

All leaders will be transparent with each other and their people, and no leader will be above any other leader. All countries' militaries will be dismantled, and only the police of the world will be the watchdogs who monitor the government leaders and make sure they behave in line with the new regulations and rules for governing. This will end all wars around the world, both civil wars and wars between countries.

Right now, the curve of the world's economy goes up and down, and if it goes down, the economy takes a while to go up again. With endless wealth, the curve will always go steadily upwards. And when the economy of a country goes down, the central government will pump billions of dollars into it, to pump the economy back up again.

There is so much struggle in the world, but the dream of the Kingdom of Heaven is of a world without struggle, and that dream will happen in reality as well as in the spiritual world. We will end poverty. We will end starvation. We will end crime.

When I was beneath the Dragon tree, I understood that before me, the Angels of Heaven were already preparing the Earth for paradise. They came to clear out classism (with the French Revolution) and slavery (with the Civil War) and end racism (with Martin Luther King).

And now, in this new age, this new world, this golden age, this new paradise on earth, there will be no more worrying and no more suffering among the people. Everyone will live a simple life in a carefree environment. It will be a peaceful, multicultural world united under one religion. It will be the start of a new era, the beginning of a new kingdom on Earth.

And everything will help prepare humankind for the Revelation and future disasters.

Then, on December 13, 2021, my personal psychic taught me about release from karmic debt. I have understood the concept of karmic debt ever since I was young, but seeing that it could be released let me understand that creating my unified religion would also release the entire world's karmic debt.

I also understood then that even though I was still afraid of being responsible for the Revelation, a time of suffering had to happen. The purpose of Revelation was to destroy the evil in the world to make man bend the knee to GOD again, and suffering was an important part of that.

But most importantly, suffering is an important part of repaying and then eliminating karmic debt. During Noah's day, the karmic debt of humanity was so great that GOD sent the flood, and only Noah and his family were saved. Now, the word of GOD tells us that the rebirth of the world will only come after a period of suffering brought by the Revelation. Then, slowly, the world will turn into a paradise. Everyone will start afresh, without karmic debt.

To better understand this, we must go back to the first people of GOD, Adam and Eve: Humanity's karmic debt began with their disobeying GOD by eating the tree of knowledge of good and evil. But this tree was also the tree of the fight between the Angels and the Dragon. The connection can be seen in the many images of the Archangel Michael and his Angels fighting the Dragon and pushing him to Earth: "⁷Now war arose in heaven, Michael and his angels fighting against the Dragon. And the Dragon and his angels fought back" (Rev. 12.7).

Adam and Eve also ate the fruit, and one of the greatest sources of karmic debt in the world is the wasting of food. I carry that karmic debt with me because of the food that was wasted during my early life as a refugee, and nowadays, world countries waste more food than other nations.

Food is important to everyone and to all religions. In Buddhism, wasting food is a great SIN, and both Native and Christian groups consider food a blessing from GOD: remember that when the Native groups refer to Mother Earth, they are also referring to the Virgin Mary. Food comes from Mother Earth, including the fruits and the vegetables from the soil, which is the ground, which is the dust, and humanity was also made from dust. In Genesis 3:19, the Bible tells us, "¹⁹By the sweat of your face / you shall eat bread, / till you return to the ground, / for out of it you were taken; / for you are dust, / and to dust you shall return."

Because everything will become dust, everything is also a living being with its own aura. Even plants and trees give off their own auras, and therefore they are alive. Some religions have had a hierarchy of souls in the past, with the human soul at the top. But the auras of other beings are not worth more than humans. That is why the karmic debt exists: because humans put other beings above themselves and then become okay with being wasteful.

But to repay the karmic debt from wasting food and to avoid gaining more karmic debt, humanity must start recycling their unwanted food instead of wasting it, sending it back into the ground to serve as fertilizer to make new food, with humans then becoming fertilizer after death. The world will no longer starve, and everyone will have a bundle of food to eat.

Researching and thinking further about karmic debt, I began to understand that taking another life creates one of the worst karmic debts a person can have and is also one of the worst SINS one can commit and that this includes the killing of animals for meat or sacrifices.

Different religions have different ways of offsetting this karmic debt: in Islam, they recite the name of Allah before killing an animal. Native groups either pray or make offerings after they make a kill. But remember the Hopi from Chapter 6? Today, there are only a few Hopi people left. Only these survivors can tell the legends of Mother Earth and of the animal's spirit world. They stay hidden and only preach among themselves.

Their elders still know everything, but because their numbers are so small, a lot of the Hopi don't follow their own traditions and forget the guidance of not only Mother Earth but of their great-great-grandfathers and -grandmothers: they forget to give offerings for the animals they kill or eat; not for pigs, chickens, cows, or fish.

Even so, these few remaining Hopi elders work to spread their voices through the world. They are one of the keys to four-race knowledge: I once talked to a woman in South America who said her grandparents talked about the four races of the world and the four colors of man.

And in Christianity, the Ten Commandments include "Thou shalt not kill," and Catholics pray to GOD to thank Him for the food they eat. The SINS of karmic debt are also told in Revelation 20:12: "[12] And I saw the dead, great and small, standing before the throne. And there were open books, and one of them was the Book of Life. And the dead were judged according to what they had done, as written in the books."

Buddhists simply avoid the potential karmic debt of killing by not eating meat at all and respecting plants and trees. By doing this, they gain enlightenment. There are two ways to have enlightenment: to gain it or win it. A person can gain it when they get rid of all their lusts and become a Buddhist monk or nun, a person without SIN or karmic debt. Or a person could win enlightenment when they have knowledge of what they need to do, but they still have to live in the outside world without becoming a monk or nun, and so have to take on some SIN and karmic debt because the outside world can't be free of SIN.

All of these are ways to eliminate the karmic debt from killing, and if one does not eliminate this kind of karmic debt, it may become so great that a person could lose their guardian, Angel, get reincarnated into a lower hierarchy of soul, and never gain enlightenment.

But karmic debt is not just inside each individual. Whole nations have their own karmic debt, and so does the entire world. And one worldly source of karmic debt is taking from Mother Earth. Earthquakes, storms, and climate change are the result of the SIN of damaging Mother Earth, which is the core of all living things, both man and animal. One must respect the planet Earth as the new frontier of man before we can explore the rest of the universe because humanity must not take from Mother Earth on a different planet.

This is what will happen after I have risen: karmic debt will be eliminated. This can only happen by following the united religion that I have discussed. And to make this unified religion, humanity also has to change. To get away from greed and environmental destruction. The world's current money system is the money system of the Beast of the Dragon; the Cross at Ground Zero also explains it.

Every religion is different but similar, just like every human is different but similar. And just like every human has a mind, a heart, and a soul, all religions have LOVE. By living together under a united religion, human souls will become the best they could ever be. The human soul is about learning, about going beyond what we can imagine and into higher consciousness, with the soul and the human mind becoming one and reaching the higher vibrations of the cosmic world, which radiate from the Heaven of Heaven. Through this unity, we can find the seventh sense and reach enlightenment, ending all karmic debt. GOD and the power of prayer have shown the way.

When the Revelation comes, everyone will be relocated to safe zones, away from danger. It will be like the day of Lot, in Genesis 19:15-22:

[15] As morning dawned, the angels urged Lot, saying, "Up! Take your wife and your two daughters who are here, lest you be swept away in the punishment of the city." [16] But he lingered. So, the men seized him and his wife and his two daughters by the hand, the LORD being merciful to him, and they brought him out and set him outside the city. [17] And as they brought them out, one said, "Escape for your life. Do not look back or stop anywhere in the valley. Escape to the hills, lest you be swept away." [18] And Lot said to them, "Oh, no, my lords. [19] Behold, your servant has found favor in your sight, and you have shown me great kindness in saving my life. But I cannot escape to the hills, lest the disaster of my life. But I cannot escape to the hills, lest the disaster overtake me and I die. [20] Behold, this city is near enough to flee to, and it is a little one. Let me escape there—is it not a little one?—and my life will be saved!" [21] He said to him, "Behold, I grant you this favor also, that I will not overthrow the city of which you have spoken. [22] Escape there quickly, for I can do nothing till you arrive there." Therefore, the name of the city was called Zoar

In Genesis 19:23-26, God Destroys Sodom: "[23] The sun had risen on the earth when Lot came to Zoar. [24] Then the LORD rained on Sodom and Gomorrah sulfur and fire from the LORD out of Heaven. [25] And he overthrew those cities, and all the valley, and all the inhabitants of the cities, and what grew on the ground. [26] But Lot's wife, behind him, looked back, and she became a pillar of salt." So, just like it was back then, if people were to be saved, they would have to be relocated. History will repeat itself again.

During the pandemic, while I was out in my backyard, I heard the soft voice of a female Angel cry, "We have gone through Hell to find you." In reply, I told the Angel I had gone through Hell to control Hell and to change Hell by controlling the Shadows. Because of me, no dark Shadows shall harm or be more powerful than an individual human, and eventually, I will control and change Hell to become a paradise.

But my journey through Hell had been very long, starting with life as a refugee and then life as a criminal. There, I saw all the evil deeds of the world, and after everything I've experienced, I will never let anyone who comes after me see or experience the world of Hell, the world of the Dragon.

This journey through Hell also let me become closer to religion, where I found meaning in all its forms and also that every form of religion was missing something. Through this, I discovered the way to bring closure to religion was through unity, creating one religion from many of them.

Planning the way to unite these religions has brought fulfillment to my life, giving me my own closure, a new understanding of the world, and a source of inner peace.

And finally, I understood that I should go back to the beginning. Back in the time of Adam, when there was no formal religion, only spirituality. During this time, at the beginning of mankind, there was a stronger connection to the source. Now, mankind is at the end of that time that started with Eden. A new era will start, and mankind will enter the new golden age that every religion has discussed.

In this new era, there will be paradise on Earth, as the Kingdom of Heaven will become the Kingdom of Earth. Sickness will be no more. Starvation will be no more. Poverty will be no more. Crime will be no more. War will be no more. There will be no suffering, no sickness, and food will be in abundance. There will be no more worrying about social programs and health care. No one will die like my friend did, passing away from stomach cancer at age eighteen.

To better understand the vision of this paradise, you must read the words of Amos and then Deuteronomy: "[13] Behold, the days are coming,' declares the Lord, / 'when the plowman shall overtake the reaper / and the treader of grapes him who sows the seed; / the mountains shall drip sweet wine, / and all the hills shall flow with it'" (Amos 9.13). "[11] And the Lord will make you abound in prosperity, in the fruit of your womb and in the fruit of your livestock and in the fruit of your ground, within the land that the Lord swore to your fathers to give you. [12] The Lord will open to you his good treasury, the heavens, to give the rain to your land in its season and to bless all the work of your hands. And you shall lend to many nations, but you shall not borrow" (Deut. 28.11-12).

In this paradise, death will also be no more. As my younger brother had died and reincarnated as my son, soon will everyone be reborn. Our souls will become part of the wheel of life, like the Buddhists, and be reincarnated. But this religion is not Buddhism, or any one religion. This religion is for a connection to the Angel, to the Archangel, to the Virgin Mary, to Mother Earth, to the Sun, to JESUS, to the source, to the universe, to GOD, to the LIGHT that I have seen. To all spirituality.

Yes, this unified vision of religion will include spirituality in the form of New Age psychics, astrologers, and white witches. I am already familiar with psychics, as I started to seek out the New Age practitioners after Joe used a dark spell to break my camera, searching for white magic to defend myself. Since then, they have helped me gain understanding, healed me, and taught me protective spells.

And, though GOD has created everyone differently, I believe each person has a weakness in their inner self, a bad trait that is their personal SIN. The clues to this SIN can be found in a person's astrological signs and horoscope, telling them their exact SIN and therefore making it easier to change.

If one cannot see their SIN, then their families, friends, or partners must tell them. In Asia, people say you can't change yourself, but I believe otherwise. I believe if you put GOD in yourself, you can change anything in your heart and mind.

But the people of East Asia were also the first to know of the chakras and then spread that knowledge around the world, and now the people of the New Age in the West have pinpointed the ways to modify human chakra and to find new guidance for humanity.

I grew to understand this truth after speaking with many New Age experts who had twenty to thirty years of experience with researching the human gifts of telepathy and contacting spirits. They showed me how to master my charkas, and while a Master would not know exactly how long it would take them to master their skills, a MESSIAH already begins with a timeline to work from and a plan from GOD.

I also credit Doreen Virtue for her twenty years of research into Earth and Heaven, even though she forgot to look into the relationship between lost souls and the Angels of Heaven, and then she denounced her New Age past and became Christian.

Psychics and the white witches are not always enemies of GOD. In fact, the fallen Angels, the

Beast, and the Dragon have tried for years to exterminate these white witches and psychics for years and manipulated the Church to make them slaughter most of the white witches, but the gifted have survived, and most are not evil.

Yes, Leviticus 19:31 says, "[31] Do not turn to mediums or necromancers; do not seek them out, and so make yourselves unclean by them: I am the Lord your God." But the Bible is wrong in a way and right in other ways. The warnings against mediumship are outdated because Jesus definitely came and showed His disciples how to use the Holy Spirit, which was like giving someone the LIGHT of GOD inside. The Holy Spirit also cannot be manipulated by evil.

The Angels of the past used the Holy Spirit to communicate with mankind, or the Holy Spirit came to mankind directly, and now new Angels are helping humanity find enlightenment through the works of the psychics and white witches. The only wrong thing about New Age groups is that they don't teach about the Holy Spirit but any spirit.

And Jesus, in addition to dying for our SINS, opened the door to Heaven for all and made the way for old souls to come to Earth. The Bible says that before Jesus, only a few would ever get into Heaven. And in the East, if you wanted to go to Heaven, you had to become a monk, nun, or a Buddha, and then a Bodhisattva: someone with pure karma.

Otherwise, there were plenty of souls still left on Earth, but before the time of Jesus, there were mostly lost souls whose doorway to Heaven was not yet open because their SINS were not forgiven or their karmic debt was not taken care of. So, they wandered the earth, becoming Shadows of Earth: ghosts or dark witches and other users of dark magic; I slowly realized that the childhood Shadow that had attacked me was a Shadow of Earth.

The Shadows of Earth are still everywhere, but when Jesus came along and died for our SINS, He opened the door to Heaven for everyone, and He made sure that SIN would then be forgiven throughout the world, meaning more souls reached Heaven without becoming Shadows.

After the Crucifixion, souls began to be reincarnated, even old souls that had died before Jesus died for our SINS. Therefore, there are more old souls on earth today than there were before Jesus. Some of these old souls, the ones who were Christian or the purest of the pure from other religions, were reincarnated as gifted people: white witches, telepaths, or psychics, which is why there are a lot of them nowadays. Each one has unique abilities and different strengths and weaknesses. My personal gift was telepathic abilities, which I used against the UFO at 411. I made it fall, using my telepathy to break its engine; I think that was the source of the loud bang I heard back then.

Just like the lost souls, some of the gifted old souls can be harmful. Though they returned to Earth through the sacrifice of Jesus, all of these gifted people are responsible for their own actions, like the white witch in my dream.

I have noticed that certain psychic people can read other peoples' thoughts and tell you what they're thinking. This happens even though science says that a person has a thousand thoughts a minute. Psychics have to be careful, though, because some of those thoughts are evil thoughts, and they might start listening to them.

The role of a psychic is to guide a person in the right direction. Not to harm them, or intimidate them, or to do those things to any other person. A psychic should not harm the person they're meant to guide or destroy anyone's life.

A psychic should not scam: a psychic needs to put a roof over their head and live well, so therefore, it's okay for them to ask a reasonable amount for their services, but they should not scam people for money. Scamming a person in need is like stealing from them; they needed the psychic's services, and the psychic only pretended to give it to them.

Furthermore, a psychic must be careful of both believing and speaking falsehoods. They must remember what the Revelation tells us about the false Christ and the false prophets and that it will happen to them if they are false. "[20] And the beast was captured, and with it the false prophet who in its presence[a] had done the signs by which he deceived those who had received the mark of the beast and those who worshipped its image. These two were thrown alive into the lake of fire that burns with sulphur." (Rev. 19.20)

Throughout my journey, I have felt so much pain and suffering. I have tried to heal myself, but every time I healed and forgave others, I was attacked. Over and over again, I healed myself, then was attacked. It made me angry, and finally, I had so much hate and so much anger inside me that I could not heal anymore.

I would often think evil thoughts, and like I said, a person has a thousand thoughts a minute. But starting in October 2021, I began to heal my heart. I met two psychics—one named Catalina—who are helping to heal me from the inside; it's still going on to this day.

But even though they are helping to heal me, I still have to work on myself. I let go of a lot of stuff in my life that was causing me pain, including friends and family who had triggered me and still kept triggering me. I meditated to focus, and I danced to release my angry energy.

While I healed myself with the help of those psychics, my heart overcame my mind because the heart is more powerful than the mind. The mind can be telepathically manipulated. The mind can be brainwashed. And the mind can think evil thoughts or be clouded by a person's experiences, good or bad. So, the most important thing to remember about GOD is that He doesn't look at the mind but the heart. To Him, a pure heart is more important than an intelligent mind.

I first found out I was dealing with a false prophet in 2010, at the same time that I read about the Revelation. I am tired now and have no idea where I found out about them and who they are. There are too many people in my life who have betrayed or triggered me for me to be sure who was who.

But this truth remains: religion is for new souls; spirituality is for old souls. Religion is for the basic foundation of a new soul, helping ground a person and keeping them from going down a dark path while opening them up to the crown chakra. Spirituality is for an old soul, someone reincarnated as a gifted person who already knows the difference between good and evil, both in terms of actions and good spirits vs. evil spirits.

So, this is my instruction to the world: to work on lifting karmic debt but also to repent. Some religions don't believe in repentance, but those are Christians who have forgotten the message of the last Book of the Bible and, therefore, do not believe in Revelation.

But it is all true.

Over the years, I have read more and more of the Revelation and found more and more clues to the future inside it. I will explain some of those clues below:

In Revelation 8:7, "7 The first sounded, and there followed hail and fire, mixed with blood, and they were thrown to the earth. One-third of the earth was burnt up, and one-third of the trees were burnt up, and all green grass was burnt up." "15 So the four angels, who had been prepared for the hour, the day, the month, and the year, were released to kill a third of mankind" (Rev. 9.15). "18 By these three plagues, a third of mankind was killed, by the fire and smoke and sulfur coming out of their mouths" (Rev. 9.18). These further prove that one-third of the world will die.

Revelation 16:3 and 16:10: "3 The second angel poured out his bowl into the sea, and it became like the blood of a corpse, and every living thing died that was in the sea." "[10] The fifth angel poured out his bowl on the throne of the beast, and its kingdom was plunged into darkness. People gnawed their tongues in anguish."

Revelation 16:19: "[19] The great city was split into three parts, and the catenate states of the nations fell, and God remembered Babylon the great, to make her drain the cup of the wine of the fury of his wrath." I knew the great city was New York City, and the "catenate states of the nations" meant the U.N. headquarters, which are located there.

Revelation 14:20: "[20] The winepress was trodden outside of the city, and blood came out from the winepress, even to the bridles of the horses, as far as one thousand six hundred stadia." This predicts a tidal wave, rising from the fall of the asteroid, with a height of 1600 stadia, which equals 252 km in today's measurements. It will be up to science to simulate the whole simulation of the effects of the wave.

And like I've said before, everyone must also look to the religions of the world to find clues to the natural disasters, like they do in *The Da Vinci Code*, but with all religions. The psychics and holy people of these religions will also use their dowsing abilities to find other safe places in the world besides Alberta. They will be our last source of defense of hope.

GOD has planted His seed in other religions so that soon, all of today's religions will unite into one. And there are other ways that GOD and Jesus have signaled to humanity what is going to happen and what needs to be done. People of all faiths—Christian, Buddhist, Muslim, and Native—will realize there is a prophecy in each religion that tells of my coming. I am the Son of Man; I am Jesus, and if you put together what I have seen, you will get a picture of the coming natural disasters and know how to prepare for Deep Impact. The visions of the modern John, found at www.thebookofrevelations.cc, tell us what to expect.

I am Jesus, but I am also a Buddha, seeing visions on a cloud. I am also a man on the white cloud, experiencing life. At first, I did not understand who I was, but now I know I am from Heaven, and am now on Earth by the name of GOD. My purpose is to send the Message of PEACE, of WOOD, of the REVELATION to the world.

But I know I am not perfect. Hurting other souls creates another type of karmic debt, and as I go back through my own memories, I find that even though I have never taken a life, I carry a huge karmic debt. I didn't know that for a long time, but now I do. Even the Son of Man can beg GOD for forgiveness, and I ask GOD for forgiveness in the Christian way, one that will get the soul to a higher level of Heaven.

This is describing karmic debt through the eyes of Christianity, as the Buddhist way is also about judging someone by their deeds. But, the Buddhists were never taught about the sacrifice Jesus made to redeem humanity's SIN. Therefore, Christians must ask for forgiveness to redeem SIN.

If we do the work, the cycle of karmic debt will end. This is the knowledge I give to mankind, all the wisdom I've gotten through a lifetime of experiences and from the guidance of Mother Earth. I am not crazy or just hallucinating; my eye has just been opened.

This is different from the false view of the religious group I must not name. They say that only 144,000 special people will be reborn in Heaven. That there will be a 1000-year reign after Armageddon, after which Jesus will hand the reins over to Jehovah, and their soul will not be reborn again for a thousand years. They are wrong.

I am scared, but my trials aren't over yet. So, I send a message to all Christians: the prophecy of the second coming is about to come true. After two thousand years, Jesus has returned. And to save humanity, we need to create a new religion and raise it to 144,000, as I have described.

I am Jesus. I have been sent through Hell to experience my own karmic debt, and then I, like the Buddhist prophecy of the next Maitreya, will blossom into a lotus under the Dragon tree and win enlightenment. That is also where I will be crowned as Jesus, the King of kings and Lord of lords. I will lead man into paradise. Into the unknown. Into Heaven. To the tree of life. To their places in the Book of Life. I have seen this in the visions of a cross shooting from the ground to blossom under the lotus tree. The lotus tree symbolizes the enlightenment and purity of Buddhism.

As the Dancing Cloud and the Revelation have both told me, Earth will have peace and, wealth, and prosperity for a thousand years. This will last until GOD releases the Beast, the Devil again from the Lake of Fire, as Revelation 20:7-10 states:

[7] And when the thousand years are ended, Satan will be released from his prison [8] and will come out to deceive the nations that are at the four corners of the earth, Gog and Magog, to gather them for battle; their number is like the sand of the sea. [9] And they marched up over the broad plain of the earth and surrounded the camp of the saints and the beloved city, but fire came down from Heaven [b] and consumed them, [10] and the devil who had deceived them was thrown into the lake of fire and sulfur where the beast and the false prophet were, and they will be tormented day and night forever and ever.

Following the return of the Devil, GOD will banish evil with fire from the sky. The ratio of Yin to Yang will change, with more GOOD than bad inside the circle, as the Light pushes the Dark into a small circle within the larger circle of Light.

Even so, GOD has created us all differently, with unique characteristics and personalities. We must each be judged individually for our deeds and whether we heed our inner call to His Light.

To heed this call, we need the power of prayer. Even I cannot fully explain the power of prayer, though to try to explain it, I will use the Prayer of Daniel, in Psalm 61: "[1] Hear my cry, O God, / listen to my prayer; / [2] from the end of the earth I call to you / when my heart is faint. / Lead me to the rock / that is higher than I, / [3] for you have been my refuge, / a strong tower against the enemy."

Despite the power of prayer, some will reject the way of the Light when the time comes because the Dark will be so great. The Light and the Dark will clash, marking the beginning of a war between the world of the spiritual and the world of reality.

To remember why all this needs to happen, we have to go back to Adam and Eve in the Garden of Eden. To the tree of life and the tree of the knowledge of good and evil. The coming war is between the tree of GOD vs the tree of the Dragon: GOD represents all the good things in life, as the tree of the Dragon stands for all the evil things in life.

When this happens, the 144,000 chosen souls must be prepared to go to Heaven and become the new army of GOD, the keepers of GOD, and the keepers of the spirit. The 144,000 will appear in white gowns with white auras, with the knowledge of the Book of Life on their foreheads, as foretold in Revelation 7:13-14: "[13] Then one of the elders addressed me, saying, 'Who are these, clothed in white robes, and from where have they come?' [14] I said to him, 'Sir, you know.' And he said to me, 'These are the ones coming out of the great tribulation. They have washed their robes and made them white in the blood of the Lamb'."

Lilian's group will be the citizen army of GOD, and the police, detectives, and military will be the trained army of GOD. When the time comes, I will let my 144,000 hunt down false prophets. Theirs will be the new frontier and their numbers will grow and grow beyond the 144,000.

The two-thirds of humanity spared by the Revelation will be reincarnated again and again, and each time, they will be reincarnated into a better life than before. The 144,000 will rule the physical world as they do in the spiritual world, as written in Revelation 20: 4-6, which I first discovered fifteen years ago:

> [4] Then I saw thrones, and seated on them were those to whom the authority to judge was committed. Also, I saw the souls of those who had been beheaded for the testimony of Jesus and for the word of God and those who had not worshiped the beast or its image and had not received its mark on their foreheads or their hands. They came to life and reigned with Christ for a thousand years. [5] The rest of the dead did not come to life until the thousand years were ended. This is the first resurrection. [6] Blessed and holy is the one who shares in the first resurrection! As such, the second death has no power, but they will be priests of God and of Christ, and they will reign with him for a thousand years.

These 144,000 will bring the Kingdom of Heaven to both the spiritual and the earthly realms. They will open other peoples' eyes and warn them of the disasters about to befall the world. I feel it. I hear it. I see it. I know it. I was guided to it, guided to the BOOK, the WOOD, and the Revelation, which are my eyes.

Just as Jesus died two thousand years ago to open the door of Heaven for all believers, and now I will bring paradise to Earth for the people of GOD. As Jesus saved them spiritually, I will save people's lives when the wrath of GOD comes to Earth. And then, the rule of the 144,000 will also be true in both the spiritual and the real worlds.

Honestly, I couldn't help but see everything from the top down. I can hear the 144,000 in the background guiding me. I hear them but can't understand them. I'm only one human with limited power, just an average Joe. But I know that Revelation says the 144,000 will be together before the Revelation, and I believe it. With the aid of the information age and telecommunications, they are slowly coming together.

And then, when the Devil is released after a thousand years, the Dark will try to turn humanity against GOD, and once again, human beings will gain karmic debt by organizing a rebellion against GOD and a rebellion against the respect for other lives, against Mother Earth, against the most beautiful and natural ways of creating souls. All of this will be further rebellion against GOD because GOD, who comes to a person in many forms and ways, also works through Mother Earth, providing guidance to the elements of wind, fire, water, and earth.

As I said in Chapter 6, The Quran taught me that Adam and Jesus both came from the same womb, which means that even though humans were created by GOD, the story of evolution was also true. There is no need for fighting between science and religion, and my unified religion is not against science.

The hierarchy of Angels, from guardian Angels to Archangels to the Heavenly Angels of the universe, is a hierarchy created by GOD and is the same as the hierarchy of the souls of living beings within nature. The universe is truly the Heaven of all Heavens, and we are all GOD's creations.

So, if GOD is within everything, then Jesus is an evolutionist. He helped us evolve by dying for our SINS and ending the slavery of man. This means that evolution cannot be done without GOD; every scientist must understand GOD as GOD understands the scientist. Science is meant to help individuals and treat Mother Nature with respect.

So, though everyone is guided differently, GOD is within us all. Everyone starts with five senses but can find their sixth and seventh senses when they connect to the source of everything, and see all creation as GOD's creation, with His LIGHT shining in all directions. Then, they will see the evil in the world as well as the human drive for GOOD. Heaven is also within all of us, within our beautiful hearts and beautiful minds, and that means we can be unified.

Some have misused Jesus' teachings to support hatred, but Jesus is welcoming to all people. His heart is neither female nor male, and He sees neither male nor female but only sees the soul inside the vessel of the body. I grew to further understand this in 2023 when I read Galatians 3:28: "[28] There is neither Jew nor Greek, there is neither slave nor free, there is no male and female, for you are all one in Christ Jesus." It meant that Jesus also planted the seed to end slavery.

Jesus also knew that the human body becomes nothing after death, while the soul continues to Heaven or could be reincarnated into a male or female body regardless of who they were before. Therefore, Galatians 3:28 also tells us that male and female, LBGTIQA+ and heterosexual, are all one in Jesus, and there is no need for conflict between them.

And because I am the LAW, I will use the words of Jesus whenever I am called on to defend LBGTIQA+ people. I know that doing this will cause a further split among Christians because the Bible calls it a SIN to be homosexual. When that happens, I will test people to find out who is on the light side, and who is on the dark side of the issues.

The truth remains: all are one with the universe. When humanity understands this, they will say to Jesus, "You have united US. YOU have brought US back to GOD." And I will bring new souls back to GOD and bring old souls back to GOD.

The Kingdom of Hell will be conquered by the Kingdom of Heaven. The unified religion will be taught to all children. It will be understood that religion is science and science is religion. Laws will maintain the peace and their focus will be on reducing individual harm, therefore preventing the gathering of more Karmic debt. As we are all people of GOD, He wants us to live in harmony.

And the 144,000 will be granted the Heaven of Heavens, gaining new souls as Angels in Heaven, becoming stars. The greatest star is the Sun, a planetary body that gives the breath of life to other planets and then sustains the life on them.

I am the Sun, the first and the last of all-stars. The new evolution of other life forms on this planet is part of the Kingdom of Heaven. All life forms on this planet have evolved and will continue to evolve. Mankind has evolved and will continue to evolve. Religion has evolved and will continue to evolve; so will humanity's understanding of GOD.

Chapter Eleven
The Meaning of the Message

Today, I am still looking for a woman named Lilian. I don't exactly know why I need to find her again, but she is the missing piece in my life. Since I divorced my wife, I've wanted to find a woman who will love me for who I am, not because I am popular or because I am Jesus. Someone who'd love me even if she didn't know what I looked like. Lilian was like that: she became my girlfriend even though we'd only met over the phone, and I needed to meet her.

I chose GOD over Lilian and I kind of regret it. I have done the work of GOD for thirty years, and now I just want to find LOVE while continuing it.

Inside, I know she once came to visit me, but at this point, I still don't know what she looks like. Every time a woman comes into the liquor store, I wonder if it's Lilian. I still go to raves, and every time I see a woman at the raves, I wonder if it's her. Every time I meet a woman, I wonder if it's Lilian.

I needed professional help; I couldn't move on.

But my soul is coming into its own.

I say thank you to Lilian and to the Detective group, who saved my life and who will become the leaders in the army of GOD.

I still feel I am in the middle of a battle I do not understand, and I worry that I am losing and going nowhere, like I am Neo lost in the middle of the Matrix. But, though I am fighting many battles, I know my current Battle involves telling people about my journey and telling them how the guidance of GOD shaped my spiritual understanding so that they will understand that Revelation is coming.

I am now talking about it publicly, speaking in Facebook groups about telepathy and so on, calling out the Dragon group and others who use social media to manipulate people. Before I started discussing it with them, the things they talked about were just metaphors and symbols, but soon they started to believe me. I guess I changed their views of the Dragon and the Beast.

This book is my first time writing something this big. My worst subject in school was English, and therefore, writing a letter or novel is not my thing. I kept trying, but by June 2, 2024, I didn't even know what to write about. The time was 7:13 p.m., and I knew that Joe and the Church of the Almighty God already knew who I was. They had revealed my identity to the public to shame me for my sexual immorality and to condemn me at the same time. I didn't even want to keep writing this book because I wanted to keep my identity hidden; I was like Romero Parada in *Sons of Anarchy,* but I was GOD's undercover agent, not the CIA's.

I have heard so many stories of the pain and suffering of the world, and now I am fighting to end that pain and suffering. I dream only of the future. Of the end to poverty. Of the end of starvation. Of the elimination of crime. Of the end of the war.

But I feel the responsibility for so many lives that will be lost.

It's taken me years of digging to find where I belong in this life. I have nothing to show for my journey except myself, my story, and the name given to me. It's a powerful name, a peaceful name: the name of Jesus Christ, which is my name, and I will use His name to defend myself. But there is one more question I still need to ask GOD: "Did I do everything right?" Because, at this point, I have no clue if I have.

Through all of this, I am only a SERVANT of GOD and a stepping stone to a new frontier, where with the help of all the universe's Angels, mankind will survive the Revelation and the return of the Devil, and mankind will become closer to GOD, and all life forms will be respected by man.

My Angel has told me, "Send the message, send the message," but people weren't interested in my message: they just wanted to scare me, make other people think I was crazy, and then, they would criticize me more. I was so scared. *What am I supposed to do?* I thought. *What battle am I fighting*?

Because of feelings like this, I haven't always accepted GOD's guidance. There were times when I denied Him because I was only made of human flesh. There was even a time when I wanted to be the false Christ because it meant Revelation would not happen. Then Michael visited me and gave me the confidence and strength to fight His battle: to bring science back to the Lord and bring the New Age back to the Lord in preparation for bringing all people back to the Lord by uniting all religions into a single faith. I can do this because I am the MESSIAH; I am Jesus.

I am the messenger, which I know from my encounters with the numbers 411 and 9/11 and the Cross at 9/11 that represented me. For me, thirty years has flown by. From the beginning, when I first learned of the Message of PEACE, I did what I was supposed to do. In the Battle of Earth, I stood my ground. Now, even though there are still many people hating and condemning me and my GOD, I will still stand my ground.

The only wisdom I have comes from what I've seen through my eyes and what I've received from my clairaudience, my research, and what I have put together myself. I knew these things because they are in me. I am not smart, but an average Joe. Still, just like Dr. Who, I can see all possible outcomes for the way the world is now, and there is no other solution to the world's problems but the ones in this book.

Without that cleansing work, the world would take one hundred to five hundred years to change, during which there will be disaster after disaster. The people will continue to suffer, crying and praying in their pain and suffering; I see and hear it all within me. My mind contains male and female voices, and they have told me these things, and I share them all with you.

I cannot explain how much pain and suffering I've felt. My life has often felt like the Twilight Zone, and. I've been in and out of madness and insanity. Without GOD, without the Virgin Mary, without Mother Earth, I would have been like my criminal friends, who didn't see how ugly the things they did were. I wouldn't have been able to see the real problems of the world, and without GOD's guidance, I would have died.

Still, I have gone through pain and suffering. I have burned inside for the sake of the other people of GOD. I have burst into tears knowing I was the cause of the horrors to come. But only I hold the power of Mother Earth. Only I hold the power of the Universe. I represent GOD, and despite all my pain, I will always defend GOD, even though I am also His fallen Angel, because, like His fallen Angels, I have caused pain and suffering in the world.

I have reaped wisdom and insight through my experiences, but I have also sown because of them. Sometimes I still wish I was the only one who would be damned, but I know that isn't what is going to happen. I, therefore, accept damnation for the sake of the people of GOD. Because I have seen the paradise yet to come.

I am sharing the story of my personal guidance with you and also my wisdom. I have three main missions: One is to spread the message of PEACE. One is to spread the truth of the Revelation. I ask the people of GOD for further forgiveness because I set up the detective group, and I've been deep into the drug trade so that to find me, the Angels of Heaven had to search through Hell.

But people cannot see directly through my eyes. You will have to listen to my words instead. GOD has always known the future of mankind, and He planted prophecies throughout all major religions in order to prepare humanity for this time.

I ask those who read this to come to witness the evolution of the reborn MESSIAH. I am normal; I am not a superhero. I am just telling you how I see things. I am just telling you what I feel. I am just telling you what I was guided to. When people tried to intimidate and harass me, I was scared to shit. And when people manipulated me, I felt like I was going crazy.

I still cry for your forgiveness. I still beg for your forgiveness. But I will stand here with you. I will stay here with you. Our generation and the generations to come will see the dragon tree through history. And from under the Dragon tree will rise the Angel of GOD and a new human race.

I choose GOD. I choose the LIGHT. I will release my burden by speaking to you. I am Jesus, and I am sending this message to anyone who reads this: Everything I have talked about goes back to one source, which is the Revelation. Study the Revelation. Find out what it has to say. Examine it. Understand it. Interpret it for yourself. The way of Heaven, or the Heavenly work, is complex but also simple.

Together, we can unite religions, unite science and religion, fight false groups, and create a paradise on Earth. But before that, we have to brave the Revelation and use today's technology to create the Aquarium Ark to save the animals in the sea.

Holding this power that I do means I carry a great burden. I feel responsible for the deaths of millions because though I am human, I am also Jesus.

In 1998, I had heard the message of *Deep Impact*, telling me to prepare for the Revelation. The world was already preparing for The Big One, but not for the Revelation. The world wasn't ready to listen.

But now they must listen: GOD has told me to build a new ark. The rainbow that GOD sent to Noah was a sign that GOD promised to never flood the Earth again, but earthquakes and asteroids are going to come, bringing nuclear explosions caused by quakes along the fault lines.

Both Noah and I are servants of GOD. GOD told Noah to build an ark against the coming flood and to save two of every animal, and my ark will be an Aquarium Ark that will hold the ocean's entire ecosystem inside it, keeping every creature together in the chain of life and saving them from the nuclear meltdowns and tsunamis, while protecting humanity from the same disasters. The Aquarium Ark will preserve ocean life for generations of children to come until science can fix our oceans and make them safe for animals again.

The Aquarium Ark will not be a simple cargo ship designed only for storage but a self-sustaining vessel where people of the new world order will use the power of the sun and be fed from fish farms and hydroponic gardens, vegetable crops, fruit orchards, all sustained by an internal, natural ecosystem. It will also be earthquake-proof because Revelation tells us of great earthquakes, as I've discussed in Chapter 6.

There will be things on the Aquarium Ark to amaze and amuse children and everyone else on board, including a theme park and diving sections, where the adults and children can interact directly with sea life in their tanks.

The theme park will have seven areas, each themed for one of the seven seas: the Atlantic, Pacific, Arctic, and Indian Oceans, as well as the Mediterranean Sea, the Caribbean, and the Gulf of Mexico. The water inside them will be fed through maze-like tunnels to replicate the ocean's currents, to make things more comfortable for the fish and aquatic mammals and ensure they keep breeding naturally.

Some tanks will have glass viewing tunnels like in SeaWorld, that allow passengers to observe the ocean life from inside them, and the biggest viewing tunnels will be found in the whale tanks. They will, in fact, be so large that the passengers can ride a train into them to see the whales. It will be like whale watching, except passengers can see the whales underwater and from below.

Work on the Aquarium Ark must be started in a safe place, one that's not too close to the ocean. I chose Alberta because after praying and praying, the Angel told me it would be the safest place; the White Horse prophecy helped me see this truth.

As I get ready in my part of the world, other parts of the world need to help get ready for the Revelation before it happens. It is up to science to use simulations to predict the scale of the disasters, and then to find further ways to help humanity. For one thing, we will be dealing with debris and tectonic shifts from the asteroid impact, and simulations can predict which zones will be the safest. Simulations must also pinpoint the locations of these disasters and determine the effects of them before they happen. I can only do so much, and so I hope that any scientists who read this will do everything in their power to start figuring this out.

I also need money for this dream. Building this ark is going to cost billions of dollars, but I can't rely on governments to fund it for me. I have already seen that there will be criticism and criticism after criticism of me. So, I plan to independently build a self-sustaining Ark, one that will be independent of all nations and institutions.

Plan A is to win the lottery and get started with my winnings. Plan B is to make investments and get started with the money from there. Plan C is to sell the book of My Journey and use the payments from that to fundraise money for the Aquarium Ark.

In the next chapter, I will go into greater detail about the Aquarium Ark, what it will offer humanity, and how it will be built.

Chapter Twelve
Executive Summary

Opportunity/Vision

The Ark Aquarium is a major collaborative project designed and built around the protection and preservation of ocean life from the disasters foretold in Revelation. Life will be as Luke 17:26-30:

[26] Just as it was in the days of Noah, so will it be in the days of the Son of Man. [27] They were eating and drinking and marrying and being given in marriage until the day when Noah entered the ark, and the flood came and destroyed them all. [28] Likewise, just as it was in the days of Lot—they were eating and drinking, buying and selling, planting and building, [29] but on the day when Lot went out from Sodom, fire, and sulfur rained from Heaven and destroyed them all—[30] so will it be on the day when the Son of Man is revealed.

I have realized that I am the Son of Man come again, and that a new Flood was foretold in Revelation 8:8: "[8] The second angel blew his trumpet, and something like a great mountain, burning with fire, was thrown into the sea, and a third of the sea became blood."

It continues in Revelation 16:3: ": "[3] The second angel poured out his bowl into the sea, and it became like the blood of a corpse, and every living thing died that was in the sea."

Revelation 6:14 tells us: "[14] The sky vanished like a scroll that is being rolled up, and every mountain and island was removed from its place."

And then, in Revelation 16:18: "[18] And there were flashes of lightning, rumblings, peals of thunder, and a great earthquake such as there had never been since man was on the earth, so great was that earthquake."

We must consider all the clues in the Bible and prepare for the worst-case scenario. All of these passages tell of a second catastrophe, greater than the flood, which humanity must prepare against. This will require a new ark called the Aquarium Ark, and I need your help to build it.

It will start with a building site. The first proposed building site is a 200-acre parcel in the Edmonton Area, northwest of Sherwood Park County, with a second site to follow within five years. This area was chosen for several reasons:

1) Land costs are more affordable in this area than any other part of Alberta.

2) Alberta's centralized location makes sure it will be protected on both sides when disaster strikes the ocean. On one side are the Rocky Mountains, and on the other side, a long stretch of prairie and forest. When the asteroid/burning mountain strikes the sea, it will be the biggest wave ever to strike land, and the ark must be as far away from the impact as possible.

3) Alberta's tourist industry will also bring a lot of public interest to the project.

4) Alberta's ecological building standards and its contributions to the biofuels industry—the domestic production of renewable, biodegradable fuel manufactured from vegetable oils, animal fats, or recycled restaurant grease—and to the production of sustainable energy solutions also provide a good foundation to create a self-sustaining Aquarium Ark.

Sustainability Solutions

The Aquarium Ark will use biodiesel from a mixture of manure and fish waste to power itself, along with solar-generated electricity; in this way, the Aquarium Ark and its amenities and facilities will be self-sustaining.

It will have an earthquake-proof aquarium/amusement park and a hydroponic gardening system. The hydroponic gardening system will provide nations with an everlasting flow of high-quality organic fruits and vegetables, which they will eat with seafood provided by the aquarium. The Aquarium Ark is further committed to improving food shortages by providing organic fruits and vegetables for the world's consumption.

The production of sustainable seafood is of particular importance. According to calculations from different fisheries, the global demand for seafood consumption is 143.8 million tons per year. And if non-food usage of seafood is factored in, the total becomes 154 million tons. The new ark aims to provide the world with sustainable seafood solutions for today's world and the world of the future.

Organic foods have also exploded in popularity over the last two decades. In fact, US consumers spent $39.1 billion USD on organic produce in 2014, and their popularity is not slowing down, as sales increased by more than 11% from 2014 to 2015.

Many people believe organic food is safer, healthier, and tastier than typical produce. Scientists also say it's better for the environment and the well-being of our planet. The Healthline.com article, "What Is Organic Food, and Is It Better Than Non-Organic Food?" objectively compares organic and non-organic foods, including their nutrient content and effects on human health (Brown). Therefore, it is in everyone's best interests to keep feeding humanity the best available food, which the Aquarium Ark will achieve with your funding. With your help, humanity will be ready for whatever will come.

Organic produce may also have value beyond health and longevity. Agnes Kraweck, PhD, who completed over twenty years of research, found that organic fruit has a brighter aura than non-organic fruit. More research and development will be put into investigating Kraweck's claim, but the ark will, regardless, aim to provide everyone with organic food.

Sources of Funding

The Aquarium Ark will be seeking funds from private investors and public stakeholders for the purchase of land for the proposed ark development sites in order to facilitate our expansion. In addition, we will ask for support from the public below.

Potential Markets

The Aquarium Ark being self-sustaining will give it many advantages over other aquariums, whose attendance numbers are already massive. Attendance in 2019 to Sea World in California was 3.49 million (www.statista.com), and that is just one park in one country in one year. In 2018, the Calgary Zoo had more than 1.3 million visitors (www.calgaryzoo.com). Therefore, there is a potential for up to 2 million sea lovers to visit our Aquarium Ark in Edmonton during stable times.

The ark will attract children/students and their parents, scientific researchers, as well as members of various faiths. Its hydroponic gardens and sustainable food production will also draw a health-conscious audience and those seeking new kinds of seafood.

Competition

The aquarium/amusement park will preserve ocean life after the disasters while providing family entertainment that will ensure future generations will remember the seas of the past.

To do this, the Aquarium Ark's amusement park will have seven different parts, one for each of the world's major oceans: the Atlantic, Pacific, Arctic, and Indian Oceans, as well as three for the Mediterranean Sea, the Caribbean, and the Gulf of Mexico. The Aquarium Ark will provide up-close educational experiences of all sea life, from triggerfish to whales.

Our closest competitors in the areas of entertainment are the Calgary Zoo, the Vancouver Aquarium, and SeaWorld. For hydroponic farms and suppliers of organic food, Aero Farms and Bowery

Farms are our main competitors. Local fish farming and ocean farming on the East and West coasts are among the biggest competitors for fish farming.

Here are some reasons that the Aquarium Ark project will exceed its competitors in all fields:

- The Aquarium Ark will have something for everyone. We will have side attractions, educational centers, learning tours, scuba diving experiences, submarine rides, and more. We are planning a very family-friendly atmosphere to educate and inform guests about the natural world.

- Unlike SeaWorld, our aquarium will not force our whales, seals, etc., to do tricks; all creatures will live as close to their natural habitat as possible, and that will appeal to people looking towards ethical management of animals.

- The Aquarium Ark will grow produce for the purposes of distributing it to others, using completely carbon-free methods, including the natural fertilizers and solar arrays mentioned above.

The Reason for This Project

Since Revelation is real, we must take a second look at the ways we could preserve sea life and, at the same time, enjoy organic food in the future. We must be diligent and use all the clues in the Bible to prepare for the worst-case scenario.

We must also understand that this is not the end of the world: The Aquarium Ark aims to provide ways to return life to the oceans once they are safe and will do the same thing for humanity.

The ark will research the evolutionary development of sea life, for the purposes of planning a multi-level breeding program for all aquatic species down to the plankton. We will study the best ways to ensure ocean life remains after the Revelation, with our end goal being to repopulate the depleted oceans with the next generation of sea life, protected and bred in our aquariums.

Being self-sustaining is the best choice for this mission. The Aquarium Ark must serve as an independent power source to heat the massive Aquarium Ark. As I've previously mentioned, its organic food provides health and spiritual benefits that will be especially important in the golden age that will follow the Revelation.

Forecast

The Aquarium Ark will operate at a loss in the beginning due to its setup and operating costs. Projected setup costs include: starting up solar panel arrays, establishing a hydroponic setup, installing tanks, as well as working out the mechanics of farming. Operating costs will also include financial compensation for specialized crewmembers, including marine biologists, hydroponic farming personnel, and marine animal breeders and caretakers.

Once the Aquarium Ark is functional, the projected operating costs are based upon SeaWorld Entertainment Inc.'s 2018 financial statements, where its total yearly operating costs were $705 million USD. With SeaWorld having three parks, it means that, if factors were similar, the operating cost of the Aquarium Ark would be $235 million USD. However, operating costs would be further offset by the clean energy from hydroponic systems and solar panels.

Exponential growth is also expected as more people in the world discover the reason the Aquarium Ark was founded and are incentivized to join it because of the benefits it offers. Following this, the Aquarium Ark should be able further to offset operating costs, with new members aiding in its internal subsistence farming, paving the way for the ark to become truly self-sustaining.

Profits are expected to start in the third year of operations, following the arrival of visitors. This is another reason for building the ark in the Edmonton area: with Edmonton having one of the largest malls in the world and so many other sights to see, along with a thriving arts community, Edmonton attracted more than 30 million visitors in the year 2000. Taking this average number of visitors, the Aquarium Ark could see revenue from up to 3 million people, leading to $195 million CAD from admissions and an additional $50 million CAD from food/merchandise sales. And this is only with the worst-case scenario of having only 1.53 million visitors in our first year.

To conclude this section, the Aquarium Ark is asking for public help; any donations will be appreciated and will be honored. Anyone interested in supporting the Ark can e-transfer money to StartFUNDforArkAqurium@gmail.com. When sending funds, please provide your name and date of birth or your company name because a section of the Aquarium Ark will be dedicated to you to remember your support for generations to come.

And once enough qualified staff is gathered, the Aquarium Ark will also become a publicly traded company, so please also provide your address and ID as well, for registration as a shareholder of the company. When the Aquarium Ark begins to offer public shares, it will raise a further projected total of $2.5 billion CAD.

Below, you will find a series of charts outlining the financial projections related to the Aquarium

Ark.

Projected Financial Highlights by Year

Current Financial Needs

In addition to the other funding methods detailed herein, assistance from private investors and public stakeholders will be sought in the future. The initial expectation is to secure funding for 1-3 years of initial operations. These operations will include planning, acquiring dispositions, and securing the necessary parcel of land. Then additional funding for the building of the Aquarium Ark and its associated publicity/advertising will be sought.

The majority of the Aquarium Ark will be built below ground, with its hydroponic growth operation located above ground. Its mechanical engineering (including aquarium tanks and entertainment facilities) is anticipated to cost approximately $2 billion CAD.

However, funding is sought in the range of $3-4 billion CAD because the ark is not just an aquarium with a building over it but an earthquake-proof vessel with an aquarium built inside it to secure the future of sea life.

Revenue by Month

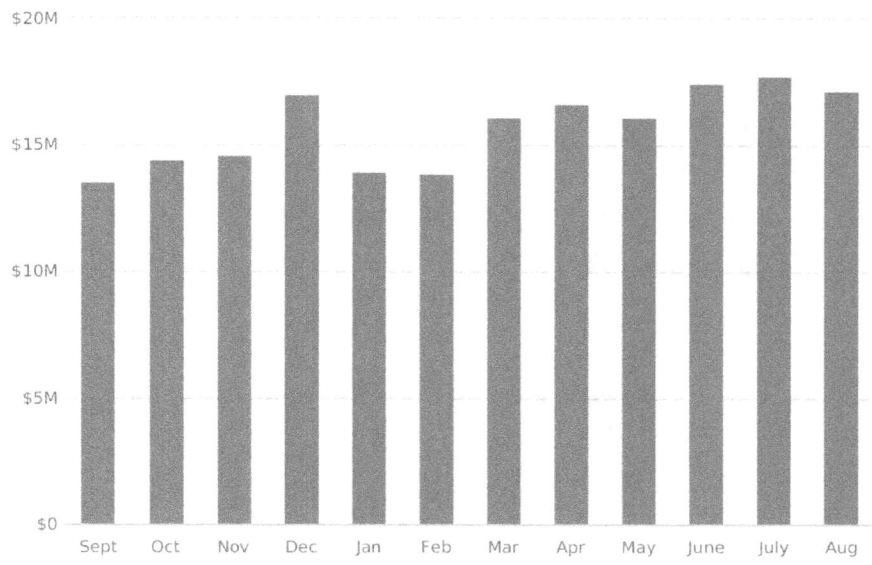

Expenses by Month

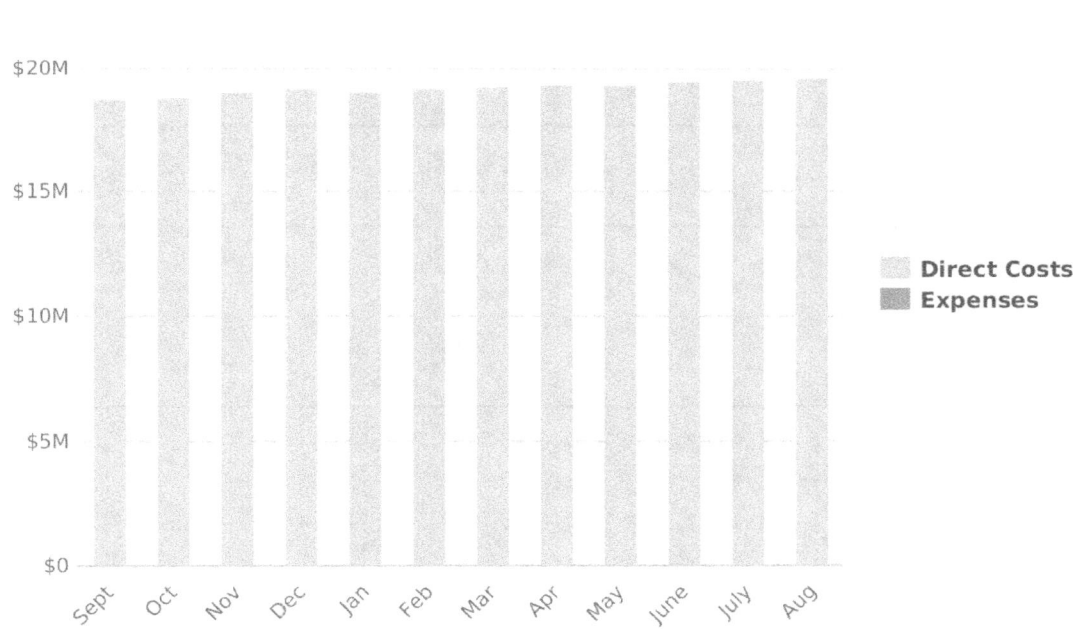

Net Profit (or Loss) by Year

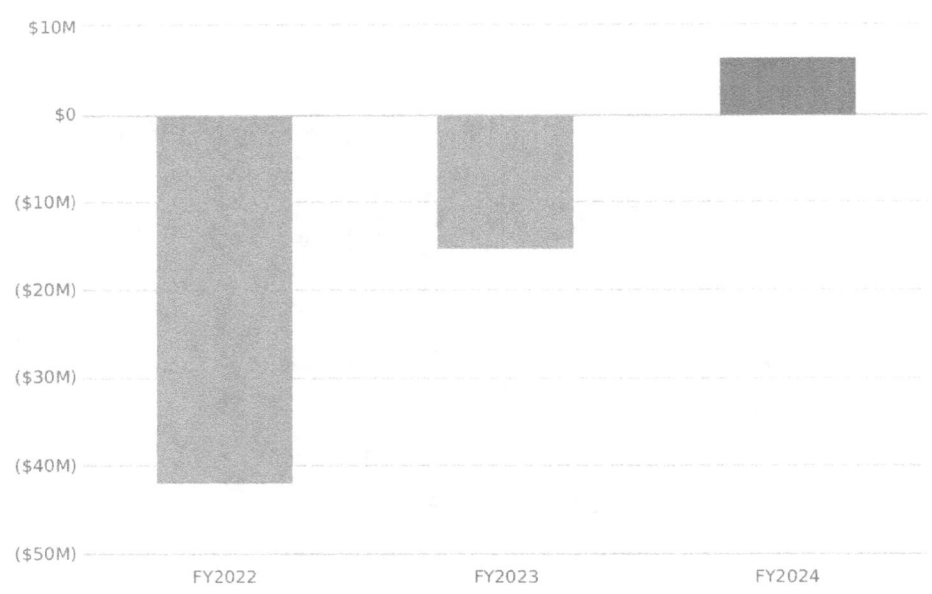

Projected Profit and Loss (CAD)

	FY2022	FY2023	FY2024
Revenue	$188,720,000	$219,500,000	$245,000,000
Direct Costs	$230,683,500	$234,750,000	$238,500,000
Gross Margin	($41,963,500)	($15,250,000)	$6,500,000
Gross Margin %	(22%)	(7%)	3%
Operating Expenses			
Total Operating Expenses			
Operating Income	($41,963,500)	($15,250,000)	$6,500,000

Interest Incurred			
Depreciation and Amortization			
Gain or Loss from Sale of Assets			
Income Taxes	$0	$0	$0
Total Expenses	$230,683,500	$234,750,000	$238,500,000
Net Profit	($41,963,500)	($15,250,000)	$6,500,000
Net Profit / Sales	(22%)	(7%)	3%

Projected Balance Sheet (CAD)

	FY2022	FY2023	FY2024
Cash	($41,963,500)	($57,213,500)	($50,713,500)
Accounts Receivable	$0	$0	$0
Inventory			
Other Current Assets			
Total Current Assets	($41,963,500)	($57,213,500)	($50,713,500)
Long-Term Assets			
Accumulated Depreciation			
Total Long-Term Assets			
Total Assets	($41,963,500)	($57,213,500)	($50,713,500)

Accounts Payable	$0	$0	$0
Income Taxes Payable	$0	$0	$0
Sales Taxes Payable	$0	$0	$0
Short-Term Debt			
Prepaid Revenue			
Total Current Liabilities	$0	$0	$0
Long-Term Debt			
Long-Term Liabilities			
Total Liabilities	$0	$0	$0
Paid-In Capital			
Retained Earnings		($41,963,500)	($57,213,500)
Earnings	($41,963,500)	($15,250,000)	$6,500,000
Total Owner's Equity	($41,963,500)	($57,213,500)	($50,713,500)
Total Liabilities & Equity	($41,963,500)	($57,213,500)	($50,713,500)

Projected Cash Flow Statement (CAD)

	FY2022	FY2023	FY2024
Net Cash Flow from Operations (			
Net Profit	($41,963,500)	($15,250,000)	$6,500,000
Depreciation & Amortization			
Change in Accounts Receivable	$0	$0	$0
Change in Inventory			
Change in Accounts Payable	$0	$0	$0
Change in Income Tax Payable	$0	$0	$0
Change in Sales Tax Payable	$0	$0	$0
Change in Prepaid Revenue			
Net Cash Flow from Operations	($41,963,500)	($15,250,000)	$6,500,000
Investing & Financing			
Assets Purchased or Sold			
Net Cash from Investing			
Investments Received			
Dividends & Distributions			
Change in Short-Term Debt			
Change in Long-Term Debt			

Net Cash from Financing

Cash at Beginning of Period	$0	($41,963,500)	($57,213,500)
Net Change in Cash	($41,963,500)	($15,250,000)	$6,500,000
Cash at End of Period	**($41,963,500)**	**($57,213,500)**	**($50,713,500)**

Appendix

Profit and Loss Statement (with Monthly Detail) (CAD)

FY2022	Sept '21	Oct '21	Nov '21	Dec '21	Jan '22	Feb '22	Mar '22	Apr '22	May '22	June '22	July '22	Aug '22
Total Revenue	$13,540,000	$14,430,000	$14,615,000	$17,020,000	$13,950,000	$13,860,000	$16,090,000	$16,650,000	$16,140,000	$17,490,000	$17,745,000	$17,190,000
Total Direct Costs	$18,722,000	$18,794,000	$19,044,500	$19,181,000	$19,040,000	$19,208,000	$19,292,000	$19,362,500	$19,307,000	$19,517,000	$19,593,500	$19,622,000
Gross Margin	($5,182,000)	($4,364,000)	($4,429,500)	($2,161,000)	($5,090,000)	($5,348,000)	($3,202,000)	($2,712,500)	($3,167,000)	($2,027,000)	($1,848,500)	($2,432,000)
Gross Margin %	(38%)	(30%)	(30%)	(13%)	(36%)	(39%)	(20%)	(16%)	(20%)	(12%)	(10%)	(14%)
Operating Expenses												
Operating Income	($5,182,000)	($4,364,000)	($4,429,500)	($2,161,000)	($5,090,000)	($5,348,000)	($3,202,000)	($2,712,500)	($3,167,000)	($2,027,000)	($1,848,500)	($2,432,000)
Interest Incurred												
Depreciation and Amortization												
Gain or Loss from Sale of Assets												
Income Taxes	$0	$0	$0	$0	$0	$0	$0	$0	$0	$0	$0	$0
Total Expenses	$18,722,000	$18,794,000	$19,044,500	$19,181,000	$19,040,000	$19,208,000	$19,292,000	$19,362,500	$19,307,000	$19,517,000	$19,593,500	$19,622,000
Net Profit	($5,182,000)	($4,364,000)	($4,429,500)	($2,161,000)	($5,090,000)	($5,348,000)	($3,202,000)	($2,712,500)	($3,167,000)	($2,027,000)	($1,848,500)	($2,432,000)
Net Profit / Sales	(38%)	(30%)	(30%)	(13%)	(36%)	(39%)	(20%)	(16%)	(20%)	(12%)	(10%)	(14%)

	FY2022	FY2023	FY2024
Total Revenue	$188,720,000	$219,500,000	$245,000,000
Total Direct Costs	$230,683,500	$234,750,000	$238,500,000
Gross Margin	($41,963,500)	($15,250,000)	$6,500,000
Gross Margin %	(22%)	(7%)	3%
Operating Expenses			
Operating Income	($41,963,500)	($15,250,000)	$6,500,000
Interest Incurred			
Depreciation and Amortization			
Gain or Loss from Sale of Assets			

Income Taxes	$0	$0	$0
Total Expenses	$230,683,500	$234,750,000	$238,500,000
Net Profit	($41,963,500)	($15,250,000)	$6,500,000
Net Profit / Sales	(22%)	(7%)	3%

Balance Sheet (with Monthly Detail)

FY2022	Sept '21	Oct '21	Nov '21	Dec '21	Jan '22	Feb '22	Mar '22	Apr '22	May '22	June '22	July '22	Aug '22
Cash	($5,182,000)	($9,546,000)	($13,975,500)	($16,136,500)	($21,226,500)	($26,574,500)	($29,776,500)	($32,489,000)	($35,656,000)	($37,683,000)	($39,531,500)	($41,963,500)
Accounts Receivable	$0	$0	$0	$0	$0	$0	$0	$0	$0	$0	$0	$0
Inventory												
Other Current Assets												
Total Current Assets	($5,182,000)	($9,546,000)	($13,975,500)	($16,136,500)	($21,226,500)	($26,574,500)	($29,776,500)	($32,489,000)	($35,656,000)	($37,683,000)	($39,531,500)	($41,963,500)
Long-Term Assets												
Accumulated Depreciation												
Total Long-Term Assets												
Total Assets	($5,182,000)	($9,546,000)	($13,975,500)	($16,136,500)	($21,226,500)	($26,574,500)	($29,776,500)	($32,489,000)	($35,656,000)	($37,683,000)	($39,531,500)	($41,963,500)
Accounts Payable	$0	$0	$0	$0	$0	$0	$0	$0	$0	$0	$0	$0
Income Taxes Payable	$0	$0	$0	$0	$0	$0	$0	$0	$0	$0	$0	$0
Sales Taxes Payable	$0	$0	$0	$0	$0	$0	$0	$0	$0	$0	$0	$0
Short-Term Debt												
Prepaid Revenue												
Total Current Liabilities	$0	$0	$0	$0	$0	$0	$0	$0	$0	$0	$0	$0
Long-Term Debt												
Long-Term Liabilities												
Total Liabilities	$0	$0	$0	$0	$0	$0	$0	$0	$0	$0	$0	$0

Paid-In Capital												
Retained Earnings												
Earnings	($5,182,000)	($9,546,000)	($13,975,500)	($16,136,500)	($21,226,500)	($26,574,500)	($29,776,500)	($32,489,000)	($35,656,000)	($37,683,000)	($39,531,500)	($41,963,500)
Total Owner's Equity	($5,182,000)	($9,546,000)	($13,975,500)	($16,136,500)	($21,226,500)	($26,574,500)	($29,776,500)	($32,489,000)	($35,656,000)	($37,683,000)	($39,531,500)	($41,963,500)
Total Liabilities & Equity	($5,182,000)	($9,546,000)	($13,975,500)	($16,136,500)	($21,226,500)	($26,574,500)	($29,776,500)	($32,489,000)	($35,656,000)	($37,683,000)	($39,531,500)	($41,963,500)

	FY2022	FY2023	FY2024
Cash	($41,963,500)	($57,213,500)	($50,713,500)
Accounts Receivable	$0	$0	$0
Inventory			
Other Current Assets			
Total Current Assets	($41,963,500)	($57,213,500)	($50,713,500)
Long-Term Assets			
Accumulated Depreciation			
Total Long-Term Assets			
Total Assets	($41,963,500)	($57,213,500)	($50,713,500)
Accounts Payable	$0	$0	$0
Income Taxes Payable	$0	$0	$0
Sales Taxes Payable	$0	$0	$0
Short-Term Debt			
Prepaid Revenue			
Total Current Liabilities	$0	$0	$0
Long-Term Debt			
Long-Term Liabilities			
Total Liabilities	$0	$0	$0
Paid-In Capital			
Retained Earnings		($41,963,500)	($57,213,500)
Earnings	($41,963,500)	($15,250,000)	$6,500,000
Total Owner's Equity	($41,963,500)	($57,213,500)	($50,713,500)
Total Liabilities & Equity	($41,963,500)	($57,213,500)	($50,713,500)

Cash Flow Statement (With Monthly Details) (CAD)

FY2022	Sept '21	Oct '21	Nov '21	Dec '21	Jan '22	Feb '22	Mar '22	Apr '22	May '22	June '22	July '22	Aug '22
Net Cash Flow from Operations												
Net Profit	($5,182,000)	($4,364,000)	($4,429,500)	($2,161,000)	($5,090,000)	($5,348,000)	($3,202,000)	($2,712,500)	($3,167,000)	($2,027,000)	($1,848,500)	($2,432,000)
Depreciation & Amortization												
Change in Accounts Receivable	$0	$0	$0	$0	$0	$0	$0	$0	$0	$0	$0	$0
Change in Inventory												
Change in Accounts Payable	$0	$0	$0	$0	$0	$0	$0	$0	$0	$0	$0	$0
Change in Income Tax Payable	$0	$0	$0	$0	$0	$0	$0	$0	$0	$0	$0	$0
Change in Sales Tax Payable	$0	$0	$0	$0	$0	$0	$0	$0	$0	$0	$0	$0
Change in Prepaid Revenue												
Net Cash Flow from Operations	($5,182,000)	($4,364,000)	($4,429,500)	($2,161,000)	($5,090,000)	($5,348,000)	($3,202,000)	($2,712,500)	($3,167,000)	($2,027,000)	($1,848,500)	($2,432,000)
Investing & Financing												
Assets Purchased or Sold												
Net Cash from Investing												
Investments Received												
Dividends & Distributions												
Change in Short-Term Debt												
Change in Long-Term Debt												

Net Cash from Financing

Cash at Beginning of Period	$0	($5,182,000)	($9,546,000)	($13,975,500)	($16,136,500)	($21,226,500)	($26,574,500)	($29,776,500)	($32,489,000)	($35,656,000)	($37,683,000)	($39,531,500)
Net Change in Cash	($5,182,000)	($4,364,000)	($4,429,500)	($2,161,000)	($5,090,000)	($5,348,000)	($3,202,000)	($2,712,500)	($3,167,000)	($2,027,000)	($1,848,500)	($2,432,000)
Cash at End of Period	($5,182,000)	($9,546,000)	($13,975,500)	($16,136,500)	($21,226,500)	($26,574,500)	($29,776,500)	($32,489,000)	($35,656,000)	($37,683,000)	($39,531,500)	($41,963,500)

	FY2022	FY2023	FY2024
Net Cash Flow from Operations			
Net Profit	($41,963,500)	($15,250,000)	$6,500,000
Depreciation & Amortization			
Change in Accounts Receivable	$0	$0	$0
Change in Inventory			
Change in Accounts Payable	$0	$0	$0
Change in Income Tax Payable	$0	$0	$0
Change in Sales Tax Payable	$0	$0	$0
Change in Prepaid Revenue			
Net Cash Flow from Operations	($41,963,500)	($15,250,000)	$6,500,000
Investing & Financing			
Assets Purchased or Sold			
Net Cash from Investing			
Investments Received			
Dividends & Distributions			
Change in Short-Term Debt			
Change in Long-Term Debt			
Net Cash from Financing			
Cash at Beginning of Period	$0	($41,963,500)	($57,213,500)
Net Change in Cash	($41,963,500)	($15,250,000)	$6,500,000
Cash at End of Period	($41,963,500)	($57,213,500)	($50,713,500)

The Miracle of March 27th

It began like any other morning. The sun stretched lazily across the skyline as I rose from the bed, still groggy from the night before. My phone lit up the moment I grabbed it—**30 missed calls**, all from a **private number.**

I furrowed my brow. Probably some bureaucratic mix-up or an overzealous telemarketer. Shrugging it off, I slipped into my morning routine—yoga, coffee brewing, and the usual peek out the window at the two glamorous blondes living next door. Just another day.

Showered, dressed, and behind the wheel, I started my commute to work. The city buzzed with its usual rhythm, cars weaving in and out, pedestrians glued to their phones. But as I crossed the subway intersection, the **private number** called again.

That sinking feeling stirred in my gut.

I ignored it.

Still uneasy, I decided to pull into the nearest Starbucks for a second coffee. Maybe caffeine would drown the paranoia. As I waited in line, a **text** appeared on my screen—from the same private number.

"Talk to the person reading the newspaper."

The message sent a chill down my spine. It felt... too precise. Too orchestrated. Was someone watching me?

I turned, slowly scanning the room. And then—**I saw him.** A man in the far corner, face hidden behind a large newspaper, seated as if he'd been waiting his entire life for this moment.

With hesitant steps, I approached. "Hi," I offered, unsure of what else to say. He lowered the paper slowly and locked eyes with me. His stare wasn't threatening, but it carried weight—**like he knew me.**

"Malcolm," he said in a calm, otherworldly voice. "I am from a place beyond your imagination. Sit with me."

My legs moved before my mind could catch up. I sat. Heart racing. Breath shallow. Questions swirling.

"There are many who will claim to be the **Messiah**," he continued. "But they are false. The world will soon know the true one—and you, Malcolm, you are chosen to protect that truth."

I couldn't speak. I couldn't think. I just stared. Who was he? How did he know my name? My life? My doubts?

Then, as suddenly as it began, my name echoed across the café.

"Malcolm, your coffee is ready!"

I turned toward the counter—just for a second. But when I turned back, **he was gone.**

Vanished.

No trace.

No explanation.

Just the steaming cup of coffee in my hand, and a new, burning belief in my chest.

That moment—**that miracle**—happened on **March 27th**. And nothing has been the same since.

I became a believer that day. Not just in what I saw but in what I felt. In what I was called to do.

This is just the beginning. Soon, I will share the messages, the calls, and the purpose that has now become my sacred responsibility.

Because the truth is out there. And I was chosen to protect it.

About The Author

Rico Nguyen is a Vietnamese-American spiritual writer and survivor whose journey spans continents, cultures, and crises. Having escaped war-torn Vietnam as a child and faced a series of life-altering spiritual experiences, Rico has devoted his life to sharing his testimony of faith, divine calling, and resilience. Through his writing, he hopes to inspire others to seek truth, healing, and a deeper connection with God. This is his first memoir, chronicling a life marked by divine purpose and spiritual transformation.